MW01173595

Seven Short Plays

from

Theatre Ontario

Seven Short Plays from Theatre Ontario

selected by Theatre Ontario
and introduced by
Marian Doucette and Skip Shand

Playwrights Canada Press
Toronto • Canada

Seven Short Plays from Theatre Ontario © Copyright 2002 Theatre Ontario

Playwrights Canada Press
54 Wolseley Street, 2nd Floor
Toronto, Ontario CANADA M5T 1A5
416-703-0013 fax 416-703-0059 info@puc.ca http://www.puc.ca

CAUTION: These plays are fully protected under the copyright laws of Canada and all other countries of The Copyright Union, and are subject to royalty. Changes to the script are expressly forbidden without the prior written permission of the author. Rights to produce, film, or record, in whole or in part, in any medium or any language, by any group, amateur or professional, are retained by the author. For amateur or professional production rights, please contact: Playwrights Canada Press

No part of this book, covered by the copyright hereon, may be reproduced or used in any form or by any means—graphic, electronic or mechanical—without the prior written permission of the publisher except for excerpts in a review. Any request for photocopying, recording, taping or information storage and retrieval systems of any part of this book shall be directed in writing to The Canadian Copyright Licensing Agency, 1 Yonge St., Suite 1900, Toronto, Ontario CANADA M5E 1E5 416-868-1620.

Playwrights Canada Press acknowledges the support of the taxpayers of Canada through The Canada Council for the Arts and the Ontario Arts Council.

Cover photo of *(l to r)* Rena Polley, David Fraser, Blair Williams, and Catherine Hayos by Rob Gray.

Production Editor: Jodi Armstrong

National Library of Canada Cataloguing in Publication

Main entry under title:
Seven short plays from Theatre Ontario / selected by Theatre Ontario and introduced by Skip Shand and Marian Doucette

ISBN 0-88754-642-0

1. Canadian drama (English)—Ontario. 2. Canadian drama (English)—21st century. I. Shand, Skip II. Doucette, Marian III. Theatre Ontario.

PS8315.S49 2002 C812'.608'09713 C2002-901949-4
PR9196.6.S48 2002

First edition: May 2002.
Printed and bound by AGMV Marquis at Quebec, Canada.

Copyright resides with each playwright. The authors assert moral rights.
Rights information for each play may be obtained through
Playwrights Canada Press.

Introductions © Marian Doucette and Skip Shand 2002

bittergirl © Annabel Griffiths, Alison Lawrence & Mary Francis Moore 1999

Mail Order Annie © Carl C. Cashin 1999

Derailed © Emil Sher 1995

Bellies, Knees and Ankles © W.A. Hamilton 1997

Suffering Fools © Herman Goodden 1988

Buttonholes in Silk © Gail Fricker 1997

The Terrible False Deception © Rafe Macpherson 1988

TABLE OF CONTENTS

ACKNOWLEDGEMENTS

Special thanks to Katrina Baran, Coordinator of the script selection process and Theatre Ontario's play selection panel: Maureen Dorey-Lukie, Marian Doucette, Andrea Emmerton, Jane Gardner, Skip Shand and Vinetta Strombergs. This special 30th anniversary publication is a joint project of Theatre Ontario and Playwrights Canada Press – thanks to the Executive Directors, Jane Gardner and Angela Rebeiro for making the idea a reality.

Theatre Ontario brings people and theatre together all over Ontario. Our members come from every corner of the province and encompass every aspect of theatre – actors, directors, musical theatre performers, designers, technicians, theatre managers, teachers, students, playwrights, producers, enthusiastic audience members, studios and more.

Theatre Ontario provides a central source of information on training, career opportunities, awards, publications, productions and resources focused on theatre in Ontario. For more information about Theatre Ontario's services to individuals and groups active in professional, community and educational theatres, contact directly at:

416-408-4556
www.theatreontario.org

GENERAL INTRODUCTION

This volume aims to address a need, expressed by school and community theatre groups in Ontario, for short home-grown scripts which will challenge and stretch developing directors, actors, and designers, and which are worth showing to their audiences. There are a number of reasons for the shortage of such scripts, but perhaps the most concrete of them is simply that it is less easy to get a short script into print (it takes several of them to fill a volume, after all) than it is to publish a full-length play. As if to confirm this point, we note that a number of the finest scripts considered for this volume had languished in their authors' desk drawers for a decade or more, despairing of ever seeing the light of print.

So Theatre Ontario approached Playwrights Canada Press proposing a mutual thirtieth-anniversary project: a collection of one-act plays written in Ontario and suited to school and/or community groups. A call went out for such scripts in the summer of 2001. Plays submitted were required to have had production, and the submissions were divided into those that had been professionally mounted, and those that had appeared in amateur venues. Some 150 plays answered the call, and two panels, one for the professional scripts and one for the amateur, read them all, and met separately in December 2001 to select four and three plays respectively. The amount of choice available to us was both exhilarating and daunting – we have had to pass over any number of wonderful scripts to arrive at the present collection. The number of excellent plays we received speaks volumes for the energy and excellence of playwriting in this province.

We expected that our process would produce an eclectic volume, and it has done so. Among these seven scripts, directors and actors will find the abstract and the realistic, the soft and the edgy, the earnest and the wacky, the polite and the rude. There is demandingly physical theatre and there is highly meditative text-centred theatre. There are characters with fully-psychologised interiority, and characters who are pure theatrical gestures. Some of these plays depend on a strong fourth wall, and some of them have no walls at all. We tried to avoid the potential blandness of a volume filled with plays suitable for all audiences – some of the plays collected here will be most appropriate for school groups, others seem to bridge the gap between school and community production, and some may be suited only to the most theatrically-astute adult companies and audiences.

Beyond being engaging and skillfully created, what our panels asked of the chosen scripts was that they provide significant developmental opportunities for emerging directors, actors, and designers. We tried to ensure that time devoted to mounting these scripts, and time devoted to seeing them in the theatre, would be time well spent. So we sought entertaining plays with seriousness of purpose and with flair – plays that respect the intelligence of the audience and that celebrate the value and pleasure of making theatre. In addition, although this was not one of our initial goals, we find that our selections address the often-voiced complaint about the scarcity of substantial roles for women in the community theatre repertoire. This collection has a total of 19 roles for women, and 12 for men. Two of the scripts are all-female.

The reason for making an anthology is the same as the reason for writing or directing a play: that is, these scripts are printed here because we want to see them on stage. We hope that they will appeal, and we look forward to your productions.

Marian Doucette and Skip Shand
Co-chairs, Theatre Ontario Selection Panel

BITTERGIRL

by
Annabel Griffiths,
Alison Lawrence
& Mary Francis Moore

As an actor **Annabel Griffiths** has performed extensively both in the UK and Canada. As a writer/director, she has created a variety of collaborative pieces, and has written and directed numerous plays for young adults. Together with Mary Francis Moore, she wrote, produced and starred in *Synchronecessity* for the 1998 Summerworks festival.

Alison Lawrence has worked extensively throughout Ontario as an actor and has directed plays for The Upper Canada Playhouse, the Toronto Fringe, the Gathering and Rhubarb! festivals. She was part of the writing team that created the Shaw festival's acclaimed street production of *1984*, and has written the solo show *Biff*.

Mary Francis Moore has written, and performed at theatres throughout Ontario and Quebec. She is the former Associate Director at Magnus Theatre and co-founder of Primary Colours Theatre. She has directed numerous collective-based creations at theatres such as Buddies in Bad Times Rhubarb! festival, Tarragon Theatre's Spring Arts Fair and Toronto's Fringe and Summerworks festivals.

Together the three wrote and have performed in *bittergirl* since its inception at the 1999 Rhubarb! festival at Buddies in Bad Times theatre; at the Tristan Bates Theatre at London, England's Actor's Centre; at the Tim Sims Playhouse, Second City, Toronto (two sold-out runs); at The Bluewater Summer Playhouse in Kincardine; and as part of Harbourfront Centre's Fresh! festival in Toronto. The trio has also written *Flush* which premiered at the 2001 Toronto Fringe Festival.

INTRODUCTION TO *BITTERGIRL*

bittergirl is an irrepressibly upbeat comic exploration of abandonment and resiliency. It introduces three women, A, B, and C, whose somewhat generic man, D, sets the piece in motion by announcing in the first scene that the relationship is over and he is leaving. In a sense, this moment is the play's action, the rest all reaction. But what exhilarating reaction it is! The three women run the gamut of response, from shock to grief to anger to relief to vengeance. Individually, they blame him, they blame themselves, they blame the other woman, they blame the longstanding dispute over how to hang a toilet roll. Collectively, they go forward and they grow: "We laugh and move on."

The women's voices are often choric, their shared sections creating a strong image of sisterhood (and a nice technical challenge for actors). And the play is frequently wildly funny – excerpts have found their way into numerous comedy venues. The playwrights have a generous sense of laughter as the crucial strategy both for containing the hurt of the breakup, and for enabling personal growth so that the women can live with, and live beyond, their individual stories. Fantastic scenes of acting out enable them to put pain into a comic frame, to achieve moments filled with release and heartbreak in equal measure. At one point, for instance, C plays out her own betrayal with Ken and Barbie dolls, ending up with Barbie smashing Ken again and again and again until C loses control and bites off Ken's head. There is a beat. "*(A clears her throat. C exits guiltily.)* Sorry."

Along with its choric moments, the script's avoidance of names might suggest that the women are interchangeable, representative types rather than real people, but in fact they are strongly individualized by the authors, and what the tactic really does is to suggest that together they incorporate their individualities into a community of suffering and survival. So, though the gender politics are clear, an audience comes out of the theatre knowing each woman as the sum of her own experiences, and not as a mere cog in a polemical machine.

D's role, on the other hand, is a kaleidoscopic skewering of self-indulgent weak-willed masculinity. As A's partner, "Coward," he defends his departure by citing his need to "quit my job, start listening, take that trip to India… work on my golf swing, maybe get the band back together." The only need he acts on, apparently, is getting into bed with "the Office Bitch." "Magic Man," telling B why he is going, "can't explain, it's just a feeling I have." But before long he is putting that feeling into pathetic words, labelling their relationship "a made-for-TV movie," pinning the breakup on his lost creativity, and blaming that in turn on her use of a fabric softener, her sloppy tea-pouring, her disposable razors, her bad choice of bath soaps. And C's version of manhood, the "gun-hating pacifist professor" whom she put through graduate school, abandons wife, child, and career for the fantasy goal of finding some personal space by joining the RCMP. We get to know him as "Mountie Boy."

In its 26 short scenes, the play charts the women's journeys. At first, C plunges into the mind-numbing routines of mother and working woman, while B wallows in pizza and classic love songs, and A cleans house obsessively, stays obsessively positive, rationalizes equally obsessively. Scrubbing the floor, she tells us, "He needs his time. I'm okay. There's just so much to get done. I'm so busy, feeding the homeless, reading to the blind, working out, eating well." After the wonderful release of a scene in which they sneak out together at night to take a little satisfying revenge on A's behalf by keying Coward's car, we see them at last growing away from victim psychology, and toward selves that may bear the scars of the past, but are newly well, newly wise, selves that are laughing and moving on. In the words of the Bittergirl Manifesto which closes the play, "Everyone has their war story." Indeed, the play suggests, everyone needs to transform bitterness and hurt into story, and comic story at that: "It's what we do. It's how we get through."

Skip Shand

l to r: Annabel Griffiths, Mary Francis Moore, Alison Lawrence.
Photo by Delight Rogers.

bittergirl was first produced at Buddies in Bad Times Rhubarb! Festival, 1999 with the following cast:

A Mary Francis Moore
B Annabel Griffiths
C Alison Lawrence
D Stephen Reich

Directed by Michael Waller

CHARACTERS

A A woman
B A woman
C A woman
D A man

The bittergirls are dressed in dark evening gowns and heels throughout the show.

BITTERGIRL
by Annabel Griffiths, Alison Lawrence & Mary Francis Moore

<u>FRANCO'S</u>

Three women enter through the house, greeting the audience, as they take their places onstage at a small café table.

D, a man, enters, carrying three bouquets of roses. The women gasp in unison, smell them and begin to speak.

A, B, C We are sitting in our favourite

B Saturday night

C restaurant

A he and I

B him and me

C us

A, B, C having some

A wine

B caber

C net sauvignon

A out of our usual price range

B Franco brings us our

C appetizers

A, B, C hi Franco *(they wave)*

C we share

A oysters on the half

B shell and artichoke

C hearts. He plays with the stem of his glass,

A sexy,

B his watch reflects off the

C knife – he's wearing the blue

A sweater, the one I made him!

B he's so handsome – I

C look up and he's got that

A little boy

C half

B smile

A what?

B I say

A you've been acting strange all day, he's

C got that faraway look

A what are you thinking

B about – this morning?

D No

A do you

C have something

B to ask me? He clears his throat *(D clears his throat)*

D I don't know how to do this

B oh

C come

A on

B just

C do

A it!

D you know how much you mean to me

A, B, C and… *(and repeat ad lib: and, and, and)*

D but…

A, B, C but… *(and repeat ad lib: but, but, but)*

D we need to talk, it's too soon it's too much I feel trapped…

The women speak simultaneously with D as he speaks.

A …I'm instantly nauseous…

C …I can't see…

B …everything is in slow motion…

D …I need to be alone I'm a mess I'm a really shitty person…

A …I'm sweating…

C …everything sounds muffled…

B …I have an oyster stuck in my throat…

D …this hurts me so much I wish I wasn't the one leaving you're too good for me…

A …my mind is racing…

C …I'm going to throw up…

B …was it the sex?…

D …it isn't the sex I can't give you what you need I love you I'm just not in love with you.

C …this isn't happening…

B …does everyone else know?…

A …is there another woman?…

D *(alone, after A's final line)* …you will always be my best friend.

A Franco arrives with our main course

A, B, C hi Franco

B linguini

A arabietta with

C shaved parmesan

A, B, C yum

A no words

B just wine

C sobs

D are you alright?

A, B, C I'm fine *(big smiles)*

A the restaurant is very quiet

B people are staring

C I'm convulsing *(The women start to shake with sobs.)*

D maybe I should go

The women lunge at him with outstretched arms.

A NO DON'T **C** GO DON'T **B** LEAVE ME!

He leaves.

C Franco turns the music up

D I'll call you.

A, B, C Franco brings me the cheque

Beat, they burst into three sobs.

I Have to Go

C So I'm touching him, y'know, just touching him? and he's been away and now he's back and we haven't, well, done anything for how long? and suddenly he stiffens, just stiffens and says

D I have to go.

C Go where? To the bathroom? To the kitchen? To the theatre? To his mum's? France? Go eat? Go pee? Go do something? Go build a house, fly a kite, write a play, eat a meal? GO WHERE?

D I have to go.

C Yeah, well, I have to go too. I have to go DO some things, some big things, some important things… I have to go finish my law degree, produce a movie, no, that'd be a film, I have to write that novel, paint that painting, run that corporation I have to sit on the Supreme court I have to BE someone really important in the cultural life of our country…. No, I have to go, go pick up our child at daycare, go cook our dinner, go do our laundry, go organize your life, pay the mortgage, do my taxes, cut her toenails, clean the lint out of the dryer…. Where?

D What do you mean where?

C What do I mean, I mean where do you have to go?

D *(simultaneously with C below, ending on the same beat)*
Somewhere. I have to go
Somewhere. Somewhere, where
I can get some space. Where I
can be alone. This is killing me.
This life is crushing me. I'm
losing myself. As an artist. As
myself. I don't know who I am
anymore. I think I need to be
alone. Just alone. Just myself.

C *(simultaneously with D above, ending on the same beat)*
Somewhere. He has to go
Somewhere, anywhere but here.
Somewhere where he can be
alone. We are killing him. This
child and I are crushing him.
Squeezing the lifeblood way the
hell out of him

D *(simultaneous)* The more I love you and the child the less I have of myself.

C *(simultaneous)* The more I love you and the child the more I have of myself.

D *(simultaneous)* The more I take on the more paralyzed I become.

C *(simultaneous)* The more I take on the more I am capable of.

C *(pause)* So I guess sex is out of the question?

D That's not funny.

C I know.

IN HIS CAR

B We sit in his car – for hours and hours. There's a lot of silence, a lot of staring. Out of the window, into his eyes. "I don't understand."

D "I can't explain, it's just a feeling I have."

B "Explain the feeling."

D "I don't know. I've just lost my drive, my passion. I need to feel inspired again. I can't love my work and you too. It's draining me."

B "No. Tell me you don't love me anymore, that you don't find me attractive, that I'm nothing like the person you want to be with. Something I can grasp onto." Instead…

D "But you're the most amazing person I know, this isn't about us, it's about me. I admire you so much, you're just so special…"

B "I don't understand, I don't understand, I don't understand…"

D "There's nothing more I can say."

B I can't say anything. Just, "why?" *(They kiss.)* "why?" *(They kiss.)* "why?" *(They kiss.)* And then his car door opens and he comes around to my door, opens it, takes my hand leads me into my apartment to my bed, undresses me. "Take me, just take me please away anywhere take me."

D "I love you."

B And that is his final peace offering to me. He leaves before morning with a drawer full of stuff and my heart in his hand. I won't get out of bed for days.

Director of the Breakup

A Lights!

A enters, hands B and D their scripts and B a wig the colour of A's hair, and sets them up in their positions. She gestures at B to start the scene.

A Sound! Act!

B What will you do?

A *(to audience)* I ask him.

D Quit my job, start listening, take that trip to India–

A *(to audience)* India?!?

D ...work on my golf swing, maybe get the band back together. Find out what's missing.

A *(to audience)* I thought we couldn't afford India. I thought he was too busy for us to go to India. Get the band back together? Who is he, the fucking Eagles? *(snaps fingers at actors)* Act!

B *(repeats)* But I...

D I'd rather we didn't rehash this.

B Rehash this?

A *(to audience)* For months I have asked if anything's wrong, for months I have tried to talk, for months I have clung on for dear life to preserve this, to preserve us while he's withdrawn yet reassured me nothing's wrong. Months.

D Let's not have a scene okay?

B Um, okay.

D Let's do this as professionals.

A *(to audience)* Professional what? Professional breaker-uppers?

B *(nods)* Sure.

D Good. I've drawn up an alphabetized list of what's mine and what's yours, so maybe we should start from there.

Silence. B is not reacting.

D I've covered all the bills for the month so you should be okay. This is, well this is hard for me you know. You've got to understand that.

A I'm sorry, I should've made this easier on you by being the one who's so confused, who's fucked up over nothing, who has everything he's ever wanted and now doesn't know what to do with it! I'm sorry, I hadn't realized we'd assigned roles in the drama of you leaving me. I should've asked which role you'd prefer. *(to audience)* I didn't say that of course. I just sat there. He said...

D I'm going to be the bad guy in this. Nobody will understand. God, I'd much rather be the one who gets left than the one who leaves. I wish I could be the one staying...

A How about wishing this wasn't happening, how about using that wish to get over your fucking self? You stupid fucking coward! *(to audience)* I didn't say that either. *(to B)* I muttered something about searching for your happiness...

B Happiness...

A And the strength...

B Strength...

A it takes to find it.

B What will I tell everyone?

A *(to audience)* Because I knew it would be me who was the spokesperson in all of this.

D Tell them that I'm an idiot, that I'm making the biggest mistake of my life.... You're so strong.

A *(to audience)* I stand there smiling my strong but vulnerable smile, watching him go.

A, B Hey. It was nice living with you.

D Yeah.

REACTIONS

C 7:30AM – Time to get up!
8:00AM – Making lunch for school bag, breakfast for the child, coffee for me.
8:30AM – Take the child to school
9:00AM – Rush to the gym
11AM – Run out of the Y, leap into car and race to
11:15 meeting with the woman you need to get that contract from.

B *(on the phone in her housecoat, eating popcorn, watching TV)* Hi. I'm sorry I can't make it in to work today – I think I have food poisoning or something. Yeah, oysters.

A *(on hands and knees in full cleaning garb, scrubbing the floor)* Yeah, I'm fine. It's for the best. No, honestly, I saw it coming, I was prepared. He needs his time. I'm okay. There's just so much to get done. I'm so busy, feeding the homeless, reading to the blind, working out, eating well.

C *(continues with her list of things to do as A & B speak – she finishes this section as A says "I'm so busy".)*
12 noon – Drive back to the school – it's volunteer-in-the-library day!
2PM – Home! Check messages, get dinner ready for the child and the sitter.
3PM – Dress for work, rush out the door with a peanut butter bagel in hand.
3:30PM – Work till
9PM – Done.

B Hi, I'd like to order a large pizza with mushrooms, pineapple, pepperoni and green olives. Oh, and extra cheese!

A *(pulls self-help books out of cleaning bucket)* I'm reading a lot about relationships, you know, so if at some point, he ever needs to talk… I'm doing a lot of work on me…

B Hi. I just ordered a pizza. I'm sorry I'm going to have to cancel that order.

C 9:30PM – Home, pay off sitter, call her a cab.
10PM – Pick up house, do dinner dishes, check on the girl.

10:30PM – Answer phone messages, do paperwork for tomorrow, check schedule, set up the child's knapsack for school, check her homework, set table for breakfast.
11PM – Tuck the blue sweater you made him into the fireplace, pour a little lighter fluid on it, set a match to it.

A It's not like it was a surprise or anything. Oh yeah, I'm as much to blame as he is.

C 11:45PM – Pour a stiff Scotch.

B Hi. I'd like to order the 100 Classic love songs double disc.

C 12midnight – Shower, cry.
12:30AM – Soap has melted in your hand. Knock on the bathroom door, "Mummy, I need a drink of water."
12:35AM – Tuck her in, dripping wet, with towel falling off.
12:45AM – Collapse on own bed.

B Hi. I'm a Sagittarius. Are there any new planetary developments?

C 7:30AM – Wake up, stiff. Wet hair has dried in tangles. Drool crusted in corners of mouth.

A He wants to be friends.

C "Mummy, why are you sleeping in a towel? What's for breakfast?"

WISHING AND HOPING

As a breakup song begins, the three women simultaneously open identical compacts, apply lipstick, powder nose, fluff hair, put on brave, facing-the-world faces and begin to speak.

A, B, C Hey you, where's the boy?

C Oh, he's not,

A Well…

B We're not…

A, B What?

A, B, C Together.

A, C Wow, you look great considering…

B Oh, I'm fine. He'll be back.

A, B I can't believe it.

C He left… he left…

A, B Oooooh babe.

C, B How are you? I heard, I'm sooooooooo sorry. You guys were so perfect together.

A You think so?

A, C So, what's his deal?

B He just needs to work some stuff out.

B, C I mean I thought you guys were, like it, you know?

A Well, you know.

B, C He-has-no-idea-what-he's-losing – NOW-tell-me-everything.

A Maybe if we'd gone on vacation.

B Maybe if I'd let him alphabetize my CD's.

C Maybe if I'd worn more makeup.

A, B Look at you.

C Yeah.

A, B Yeah, so are you, you know, are you?

C What?

A, B Pregnant.

C No, not pregnant, no.

A, B Well, I didn't mean.

C Maybe if I'd had skinnier legs.

B Maybe if I'd tried to understand football.

A Maybe if I'd stayed up late.

B, C You guys were so great, what a couple! How tragic for you, what are you now 30?

A 29.

B, C Ugh. I mean, if you two couldn't make it work, who can?

C He lee-ee-eeft… he leeeeeft…

A, B Oh my god.

A Look, it's going to be okay.

B He's just got a lot of stuff going on.

A Maybe if I'd worn plum eye shadow instead of beige.

B Maybe if I'd said I didn't want children.

C Maybe if I'd watched more hockey

A, B So what are you going to do?

B He just needs some more time.

A Maybe if I'd had better underwear.

B Maybe if I'd walked on the North side of the street.

C Maybe if I'd worked out more.

B, C Well I am devastated, just devastated. This throws my dream of happily ever after right out the window.

A I'm sorry, we tried, we really did. I'm sorry. I know I let you down, I know.

B, C Just remember, everything happens for a reason.

A Maybe if I'd let him read at the table.

B Maybe if I hadn't talked to my mother so much.

C Maybe if I'd let him pick the movies.

A, B Say it.

C What?

A, B Say, he left me.

C *(little voice)* He left me.

A, B Again.

C He left me.

A, B Again.

C He left me.

A, B Again!

C *(shrieks)* He left me!

A, B There now, doesn't that feel good?

A Maybe if I'd been better.

B Maybe if my face was oval.

C Maybe if I'd let him become a Mountie.

The Mountie Scene

D I want to join the RCMP.

C What?

D I want to join the RCMP.

C You want to be a Mountie? You want to be a cop?

D Yes.

C But…

D But what?

C You hate guns. You can't shoot guns. You hate guns.

D You never support me. I can never count, y'know, on you, for support.

C But…

D Because you won't support me. I come to you, y'know, just needing a little, a little, all I want from you is…

C But you can't shoot a gun.

D …support – not all policemen shoot guns.

C Yes they do. Policemen have guns.

D I could sit behind a desk. I could solve crimes. Do desk work. Answer phones. Help people.

C You'd have to do basic training! You'd have to train! They'd have to send you to police school and you'd have to shoot a gun! You hate guns! You're a gun-hating pacifist professor!

D You think I couldn't do it, don't you? You think I couldn't… do you think I'm not capable – is that what you think?

C No, I – yes. Yes! I think you couldn't. You couldn't because you don't want to. You're not a gun-shooter you're – where did this come from?

D It came from me, from what I want, from you not supporting me, supporting me in my choices, in my – what do you think of me, anyway? Do you think I just dreamed this up? I just woke up this morning and thought, " Hey, maybe I'll be a Mountie?"

C No, I, I don't – you're a thirty-five year old asthmatic professor who hates guns – it's an assumption I've – I don't know – no – look, honey, I do want to support you if that's what you want, I'll help you, we'll do this, I'll support you through basic training of whatever it is they do.

D You've never believed in me, have you? Never trusted me, never – god. Never mind. God!

Answering Machine

B Hi, no-one's here to take your call right now. *(she looks around)* No-one's here. Shit. *(She erases the message and is re-recording.)*

Hello, I am unable to take your telephone call at the moment, because he… because he… because he-ee-ee-ee-ee *(sobbing uncontrollably)* Shit. *(erases and re-records)*

Hi, sorry I'm not here to take your call. If you're looking for Magic Man, he's no longer practically living here, using up all my hot water, eating my groceries and checking my messages. If you'd like to contact him, he can be reached at 1-800-I-NEED-SOME-FUCKING-INSPIRATION!

Ken and Barbie

C is cleaning up toys and picks up a Barbie doll, a Ken doll, and a baby doll and creates Barbie, Ken and baby voices for the rest of the scene.

C *(as Barbie)* Hello, my name's Barbie. What's yours? I have a fabulous figure, a great career, an amazing apartment and a sensational single life.

(as Ken) Hi, I'm Ken. Wanna get married?

(as Barbie) Okay!

Ken and Barbie are kissing each other.

(Ken) Love you!

(Barbie) Love you too!

(Ken) No, love you.

(Barbie) I love you more. I love you so much I'm going to work you through grad school.

(Ken) Okay!

(Barbie) la la la la la la la – work, work, work, work – Study, study, study, study. Work! Study! Work! Study! Work work work!

(Ken) Barbie, I'm home – and guess what? I got a big fat tenure position today!

(Barbie) Oh goodie, Ken! Now you're making money, we can pay off your student loan, buy that new car, I can resume my career…

(Ken) Barbie, I want to be a Mountie.

(Barbie) What?

(Ken) A Mountie, Barbie, a Mountie.

(Barbie) But Ken–

(Ken) You don't support me, Barbie – I don't love you and I never did.

(Barbie) Yes you did. You did. We had the motorcycle, and the Barbie camper and the kissy kissy.

(Ken) Nope, never loved you. Want to be a Mountie.

(Barbie) But what about Barbie Baby Kelly?

(as Baby Kelly) Waah, waah!

(Ken) Leave Kelly out of this.

(Baby Kelly) Waah!

(Ken) I love her, it's you I can't live with.

(Barbie) But Ken…

(Baby Kelly) Waah waah!

(Ken) Sorry Barbie, but a man's gotta do what a man's gotta do.

Ken gets on the motorcycle.

(as C) Vroom vroom!

(Baby Kelly) Waah waah!

(C) Listen Barbie. Are you just going to take this lying down!?!

(Barbie) No! *(starts hitting Ken with Barbie)* This I give you Ken and that I give you Ken and take that and that and that and…

Barbie beats up Ken and C, as a final coup de grace, bites his head off.

(C) Sorry.

Box Poetry

A is sitting on a box of moving stuff, surrounded by cleaning supplies, a journal, a bottle of wine and a wine glass.

A Things you should know. THINGS YOU SHOULD KNOW!
I'm just fine. My uncle Fred died.
I got a promotion.
Groceries are cheaper without you.
Everyone says I look fabulous.
My father never liked you.
Your sister's a bitch.
If you really quit the firm, how will you get rich?
How's the band, the band, the band, the band, the band?

Air guitars and mimics "Boys in the Bright White Sports Car".

I lied, you really can see your bald spot.
Fortune 500, I don't see your name on the list.
You're never going to make the NHL.
India, India, why was I so INTO YA?
It's not like I thought we would last. I barely even miss you.

Splenectomy

B and C are working out on a cross-trainer.

C Oh, did I tell you? I'm having a splenectomy.

B What?

C A splenectomy. I think I'm developing a thing on my spleen right now.

B When did this happen?

C It happened two days ago, when Mountie Boy invited me to his big party. I'm telling him I can't come because it's the day I've been scheduled for the spleenoplasty.

B Are you insane? What happens if he asks you about how it went?
C Oh he will, even he can't be so completely unfeeling. He asks and I tell him… tell him that they took some more X-rays and now they're not sure.

B You know what? I don't think it works that way.

C What the hell do you know about spleens? What do you know about spleencoscopies? I could have my spleen removed and be walking around today. That's it. I tell him I did have it removed. "Oh, poor me, I've got no spleen."

B What the hell does a spleen do anyway?

C I don't know. I could read up on it. Read up on my spleen. I should have this all figured out before I have to RSVP.

B You are certifiably insane. You have really and truly lost it.

C No, no, this could be really great. He calls me up, all contrite, to ask me how I am and I tell him I'm fine, a little weak.... He might offer to go with me to the hospital. No, I want to go with my friends, my true friends, my women friends, my support through this terrible time. And when I do see him again I'll be wrapped in blankets, looking pale and wan—thank god for makeup, eh?— and I'll have trouble getting up to greet him... I have to remember to do this in the daytime while the kid's at school and can't blow my cover – oh this could really guilt him up but good. Oh it is so, what's that movie you like? With the Empire State Building?

B Yeah, but didn't Cary Grant really love her? Wasn't he being noble?

C Yeah, noble schnoble. I want him to feel bad, really bad, nasty bad.

GARLIC PRESS

D Hi

A Hi

D Are you okay?

A What do you mean?

D Well, you sounded a little weird on the phone.

A Oh no I'm fine I couldn't sleep so I re-grouted the bathroom tile, then I ended up tackling the closet in the hall and some of the kitchen drawers and I found some things of yours and I just thought you might need them, setting up house and everything, and oh yeah, I was cleaning the medicine cabinet when it hit me! It's November! I know your allergies are crazy this time of year and I know what you're like not taking your medication, so I thought you could take some of this new stuff I'm using of course my allergies bug me in August but God allergies are allergies aren't they? You seem wheezy are you wheezy?

D I'm fine. The place looks great. You've been busy.

A Yeah. Busy busy.

D Sorry about this, forgetting this stuff…

A Mustn't have been on your list.

D I thought I took everything.

A Well you must've forgot.

D Yeah, must've what with everything.

A Yeah, with everything. So, you're good?

D Mmmm, yeah, great, I was at Derek and Wendy's wedding over the weekend.

A Really? Wow, how long have they been together?

D A year. I guess they just knew.

A Hmmm, imagine that. Oh, you know what? You forgot the garlic press.

D Right. No, no you take it.

A No, I couldn't, you use that garlic press.

D I know but so do you. You always use it to cook, my god you love garlic. You are eating aren't you? You look thin.

A No, yeah, I'm fine, I'm eating, it's just, I mean I can buy a new garlic press.

D But why buy one when it's already–

Scene freezes and A comes out of the scene to explode at D.

A Take your goddamn garlic press you piece of shit coward. And all your cookbooks for the meals you never made, while you're at it, take the wine rack, drink yourself silly and choke on your own vomit!

A re-enters the scene and breaks the freeze.

A No, really, you take it.

D You take care of you, okay? I should go, I've got band practice.

MY RELATIONSHIP VS. YOUR RELATIONSHIP

D knocks, then enters in a hurry.

D Hi. Sorry I'm late.

B It's okay. I'm glad you called. It's good to see you. You must be busy.

D Yeah, I am. Look, I'm sorry to bother you.

B No, not at all.

D I can't stay or anything.

B …Of course, no, and I have a lot of stuff to do…

D Thanks for coming… I just came to give you your keys back.

B Oh… right, my keys.

D Yeah. So, here they are. *(He puts them on the table.)*

B Yep, there they are.

B stares at them and doesn't move to take them.

D I forgot to give you them the other night.

B Yeah, the other night.

B takes the keys.

D Well, I'll talk to you.

B Thanks. For bringing the keys.

D No problem. It's the least I could do.

B You know, I still don't understand.

D Look, I've tried to explain.

B It was the fairy tale relationship.

D The Frog Prince.

B Cinderella – you just got chicken. *(no response)* It was like poetry.

D A made-for-TV movie.

B An "Affair to Remember".

D "When Worlds Collide".

B But, we never fought.

D Exactly! That's not normal.

B But you were so happy.

D I know.

B And we were so good together and so comfortable.

D That's it. Comfortable. But, I stopped writing late at night.

B Because you said you wrote better in the morning.

D Only because when you were up doing your Buns of Steel, I had peace and quiet.

B But that was our ritual though.

D Your ritual.

B Okay, then. You started the rituals.

D Name one.

B Tuesday night – sandwich night. Whoever's is better doesn't clean up.

D To make up for boys night the night before.

B What about quiet night then, date night?

D I lost my magic!

B That's not good enough.

D Fine. You wanna know? You really wanna know? I hate the smell of Downy.

B It was to drown out your smelly socks.

D You're a sloppy tea pourer!

B At least I don't leave teabags in the sink.

They clasp hands and begin an arm wrestle.

D I love coffee!

B You should have told me!

D I hate your disposable razors!

B I hate your liquid soap.

D Dove sucks.

B Toilet paper has to be put in roll down, not roll up!

D Unbearable.

B I stole one black sock from your laundry every week just to drive you mad!

D But…

B I secretly plotted to destroy all of your friendships – because that's who I really am. I watched you type in your password so I could check your messages while you were in the shower.

D …you…

B And all this time you were thinking that it was just the little things that were getting to you, you couldn't even see the major plan to take over your life!

B wins the arm wrestle, throwing D to the floor. D crawls offstage.

D Get over it.

HONOUR

The three women are at a table.

B I think he still loves me.

C How?

B By the way he looks at me, the things he, if things weren't so, well just stuff.

C Really? What stuff? What looks? Name one.

A Easy, I think she's just saying that she–

C No! She can't think like that. She has to get on with it, she has to realize–

A What she needs to do is–

B Hey! She's in the room! Look, maybe he loves me, maybe he, anyway, if I want to believe in us, I will. It's my fairy tale.

C *(mocking)* It's my fairy tale…

B Hey!

A Sometimes I think our fairy tale was too much to live up to.

C What do you mean?

A Our story, our tale. Everyone thought we were so perfect, the mythology of us was so fabulous even we couldn't live up to it.

C leaves the table.

B But it's not like it wasn't true, remember the sonnets he wrote you, the breakfasts in bed, that time in France, carrying you through that field of–

A Yeah, yeah, yeah, but at some point did he do it just to keep up with expectations? I did. I didn't want to wait for him at the subway every night, but it became one of those things that made us "us".

C re-enters with a tray of tequila shooters.

Everyone else loved the romance of it, but stand outside the subway station when it's 30 below and see how romantic you feel. Maybe he was suffocating in our mythology.

C Here's a myth – happily ever after! Next time no mythology for me. Write me your letters, send me your flowers, piggyback me across the damn desert but not until you've figured out what you want to be when you grow up – Lick, drink, suck! *(they all do a shooter)*

B Maybe mythology isn't a bad thing, maybe it binds you. He knows me like no-one else. I'll never have that again.

C Yes you will and the next time it will be better, and the time after that it will be better than the time before and after that–

B No it won't.

C Yes it will! Sweetie it's hard, but it's over, now there's a whole world of great stories out there, new myths waiting to happen. Lick, drink, suck! *(they do another shooter)*

A Then why do you keep telling the same one?

C Hey hey hey, just 'cause he left you before you got it together to leave him–

A I had plenty of chances to leave. Plenty. Opportunities. Chances.

B I know.

A But I didn't.

B No.

A Y'know that? I didn't.

B No, you didn't.

A And y'know why? Y'wanna know why?

C Why?

A Because I'm honourable. I honoured what we had.

B You are.

A I am. I am. I honour… things. Sacred things. Love. And honour. I honoured… honour. Y'know?

B I know.

A But he, he–

B Well, he doesn't know what honour is.

C Clearly.

A He doesn't. He never did.

C Let's go key his car.

A I loved that car. I honoured that car.

C I miss Mountie boy's car.

A You honoured the Mountie's car.

B Mountie boy had a car you could honour. I don't miss Magic Man's car at all.

C We had a better marriage when we were poor, but…

B It was a K-car!

C …I looked so good in that car. I fit in that car.

B You did fit with his car…

C And his parents – geez, I loved his parents.

A Honour your parents. Honour the Mountie's parents.

C Let's go key the Coward's car.

A I don't honour the Coward's car. I honour the Coward's parents. He doesn't honour his parents. I did. I do. I honour them.

C That's a lot of honour. Where does he live now?

A A lot of honour. Who?

C The Coward.

A The Coward?

C Does he park on the street?

A No, in the lane – there's a lane. I don't think there's a garage. If there was, he'd be rehearsing with the band in there.

B He doesn't honour his car.

C I'd honour that car. I love that car. Not as much as Mountie Boy's car, but I'd look pretty good in Coward's car too.

A Let's go.

B What?

A He doesn't honour his car, neither should we.

C Yea, baby.

B What? What do you mean?

A *(brandishing keys)* Call us a cab, baby doll. We're movin' out.

B I'll be right there.

A and C leave the stage, leaving B alone for a moment.

GONE WITH THE WIND

B I've watched "Gone With The Wind" four times. Last week I watched this movie with Rob Lowe and Demi Moore called "About Last Night" and I cried and cried when they divided their stuff. But then he figured it all out and came back. And then I read the play the real play – it's called *Sexual Perversity in Chicago* and you know they don't even end up together again in the real play. I mean how could they, it's called *Sexual Perversity in Chicago* for god's sake. So I think why did they make them end up together in the movie? The play came first so why don't they leave the ending the way it is and not change it to pretty it all up and make it seem all happy and perfect. Of course I saw the movie before I read the play so now what am I supposed to think, that's it's not really a happy ending? Maybe nothing is. Maybe I did have the love story of my life and I'll never have it again. Just like the play, it ends and that's that.

Mummy

Voice offstage: "Mummy, why did you let Daddy leave?"

C Well, you see, Daddy and I spent a long time talking about this, and Daddy was very unhappy. Not with you, just very unhappy about a lot of things that he couldn't figure out. And he thought that maybe if he went somewhere and lived on his own for a while, that maybe he might be happier.

And then he realized that it was a little easier for him to live on his own – it made him feel better than he had before. So, he and I decided that it would be better for you to live with me in our old house and that way you would get to see a happy Daddy sometimes instead of an unhappy Daddy all the time.

You know what? More than anything else in the whole wide world, Daddy loves you. He loves you more than this. *(She holds her arms out wide.)* And the hardest thing that Daddy has ever done in his life was leaving our house where we all lived together. Because there is nothing in Daddy's life that he likes better than waking up in the room down the hall from you.

You know what? When Daddy first told me that he couldn't live here any more, I got mad, because I wanted him to stay living with us too.

It's a crummy thing for grown-ups to do to kids, change their world around. But it doesn't mean you don't have a Daddy, and it doesn't mean that he loves you any less, it just means you don't get quite as much of him as you used to. But that's okay – you can get mad at us about that. You're allowed. It's okay.

Keying the Car

A,B, & C are in the audience with flashlights.

B I don't like this. I don't like this at all.

A It's over here.

C I love this neighbourhood. Look at all these backyards. Even the garages are nice.

B This is not right. This is just not right.

A We haven't done anything yet. We're just walking in the lane here.

B At midnight. In the dark. With flashlights. Behind your ex's house.

C So?

B Look, I have serious is-sues about all this.

A What?

B I have is-sues.

A Ishues?

B Yes, is-sues.

C Ishues.

A Yeah.

C Say it.

B Is-sues.

A Ish-ues.

B *(repeating)* Is-sues.

C Say Ish.

B Ish.

A Yews.

B Yews.

C Ish. Yews.

B Ish. Yews.

A Ishues.

B Is-sues.

C Fuck!

A Ohmygod.

C What?

A It's Coward.

B Turn off your flashlight.

A I always told him to pull the curtains – I always said people could see in – he said, "what people?"

B Don't look – don't look! We're not peeping toms here… we haven't sunk that far…

C Yeah, yeah I came here to key his car, but I'm not going to spy on him?

B Don't you find that a little…

C What, unethical?

B Criminal.

A What he did to me was criminal.

C Shit.

B What.

A Who's that?

A drops to the ground. B crouches behind the car, C turns flashlight on again, stands up, then loudly…

C Who is that?

A I don't believe it. It's the Office Bitch.

B Didn't he leave you because he wanted to be alone?

A She's sitting on my end of the couch. That's my spot. She's sitting in my place.

C So is he, really.

B You let him have that couch?

A She's going to sleep with him. Why would she want to sleep with him?

C You wanted to sleep with him.

A He said he wanted to be alone. Alone. Not alone with other women. He said.

B Look, he's just falling into a rebound relationship. They never last. You are doing everything right, mourning the relationship, dealing with it. You can't learn to be in a relationship until you learn to be alone.

C Yeah, but while she's out getting big and strong and learning to be alone, he is clearly getting laid.

B Shhh! Look, he was bound to start dating sooner or later. Geez, he's looking over here—he hears us—guys let's get out of here.

C *(shining flashlight in her own face)* Hey! Asshole! That's her end of the couch.

B Stop that. Get down.

A *(in a heap on the ground)* My couch. My spot. Honour my couch!

C Yeah, you asshole – I've got keys here, how much do you like the finish on your cute little Beemer?

B Stop that. *(to house)* Sorry! I'm really sorry! Go back to what you were doing!

A No!!

C DON'T MAKE ME USE THESE!

Offstage Male Voice: "Hey! What's going on out there?"

B Geez. *(to voice, stage left)* Sorry! Sorry! Just leaving!

Offstage Male Voice: "People are trying to sleep here."

C People are trying to do a bit more than sleep here – people are talking about JUSTICE here! What is RIGHT. What is HONOURABLE. Do you hear me?

Offstage Male Voice: "I'm calling the police now."

B No! No! No police – we're going! I'm sorry. Get up *(to A)* GET UP.

A My boyfriend. My Coward. My couch spot. *(weeping incoherently)*

B *(turning to C)* Don't you go near that car. Give me those. Get hold of yourselves. Both of you. You are crazy. Both of you. Do you know that? Crazy. *(to voice)* Y'know what? Call the police, mister. Go ahead. Tell them to bring straitjackets. I am out of here. I am out of patience. You guys are nuts. Call me – when you are ready to be reasonable human beings and DEAL with this. All right? Reasonable. Human. Beings. Good night.

B leaves. Long pause.

C Geez. What got into her? *(She exits.)*

THE RANT

A is sitting on another moving box and throughout the rant pulls out props, ie: photos, handcuffs, a bridal veil.

A I have been dating for 16 years. In that time I have had no offers of marriage. In 16 years, I have lived with two men. Told at least six that I loved them, and meant it at the time. And I'm sure someone said they loved me back. None of them became major rock stars, a few are balding, one is a supermodel in Milan. So is his wife. She is younger than me, they have a child. My friend sent me his marriage announcement from the *Gravenhurst Times*. Underneath it she wrote: It was almost you babe! For the record, I broke up with him. I have slept with 20 people, it's not a lot, it's barely one a year. All, at the time, were attractive. I've never slept with an accountant or a businessman, which may explain the state of my finances. I've slept with too many musicians and not enough doctors, but the musicians were the ones who were around. Once I dated a cop and a criminal at the same time – but they weren't on the same case or anything so it's not like it was illegal. I don't just random date and dump. I don't usually sleep with other people's boyfriends. I inspire people you know. I have had three songs written about me and a piece of Japanese performance art. I am never envious when friends are happy with the little things like weddings and babies, I know my time will come. People keep telling me that I'm in my prime, that it'll happen when I least expect it. My phone gets cut off when I least expect it, I get a yeast infection when I least expect it, I get dumped, break out, laid off when I least expect it. When it comes to meeting Mr. Right, we always expect it. It's the unwritten thing to do in everyone's dayplanner – go for groceries, fix the sink, make the bed, meet Mr. Right. And then when he or she arrives, we substitute "meet" for "hold on to", "do not let go of"… I didn't hold on too tight, he let go of. I do not deserve this!

Maybe I

A Maybe we should

C talk. She got a great report card. Maybe I should

B call him. My stars feel really aligned right now. Maybe we

A should get together

C for a drink.

A, B, C Hi, it's me. What's your next Thursday like?

Reunion Sex

Lights up to reveal a hanging bed sheet. A & D are having sex behind it, their heads pop up.

D What are you doing?

A What do you mean?

D this, you, this–

A I'm riding you, screwing you, choking your chain–

D You're what?

A I'm straddling you. I'm banging you. We're making the two backed beast. *(making animal noises)* What's wrong? Why are you being like this? *(coaching him)* Just relax…

D Why am I? No, this is not like you…

He moves as if to get away from her – she doesn't let him go and continues to ride him.

A Yes it is, yes it is, it is, this is it baby, this is me, in touch and on top, oh yeah, you're not gonna get this anyplace else, do you like it like this, does the office bitch do it like this, does baby like it when I ride the purple python…

A goes down on him, and C pops up.

C Oh baby – Oh baby! Oh YES! *(She leans into him, then pulls from between them a suitcase.)*

D What – what is – what the hell is that?

C Your mother – my relationship with your mother. She calls you her baby doll and had an asthma attack when she walked into my apartment.

D I– *(fumbles towards her, arms around the suitcase, hands going "Come in Tokyo")*

C *(pulls out another suitcase)* Drinking – here's the drinking. Remember when you got trashed at my uncle's Christmas party?

D Uh…

C I love you honey I love you. *(another suitcase)* Oh no – your flirtation with Alex the lawyer. Or did you *(another suitcase)* ever sleep with her?

D waves arms desperately trying to be sexy – around all the suitcases.

AAAaaaah!!!! Smoking! *(another one)* Cats! *(another)* My brother! *(another)* The office party! *(another)* Body hair! *(another)* Oral sex! *(a huge one)*

D *(practically buried – muffled)* mmeye – mmmmwant – mmmyou – mmyou…

C and D go down together. We hear B and D building to climax behind the sheet.

B Oh god, oh god, oh god *(B and D pop up)* OH MY GOD! How come it was never like that before?

D I don't know.

B Maybe it was because we were too inhibited.

D Maybe.

B By the pressures of it all.

D Yeah, but…

B And now we can just be free of all that.

D Free?

B God it feels good! We can just be…

D What?

B Together.

<u>**Answering Machine**</u>

Answering machine beeps.

D *(voiceover)* Hi, uh, it's me, uh.… How are you? Uh, um, listen, about last night… I think it's so great that you're getting past this, past us, and moving on and I don't want you to get the wrong idea, I don't want to mess up your process – I don't want to be unfair to you – that's the last thing I would want to do to you. So, like, you take care of yourself and we'll see you around somewhere. Sometime. All right? All right. I'm sure you feel the same way. Let's not make the same mistake twice, eh? *(awkward laugh)* Yeah. Bye now. It was – good to see you. Bye.

Dialtone.

<u>**Breakups Anonymous**</u>

A,B, and C have a ceremonial passing of a rainstick.

A, B, C Sister goddess, Mother Moon, show me that I will heal soon

Before each bittergirl talks, she turns the rainstick over and holds it in front of her against her chest.

A Love songs tell us that the nights are the hardest to get through, but nights are the easiest. At night you can lie in the dark and cry. At night you are alone with your thoughts and there's no pretense of being capable, of doing a job, of being in a conversation, of being present. I decide to emerge from my cocoon and enter the world again. I am about to make my first appearance as a solo artist. I arrive and I am so alone. I am alone in a room full of people. But I will be okay. I tell stories that make people laugh, I talk about how busy we are at work, busy, busy, no time for myself, I barely had time to slip into this fabulous dress, I toss my hair, another funny story, smile, somebody else says something and everybody laughs. I am dying here. I want to look across the room and meet his eyes and know we're thinking the same thing. I want to be in the middle of a conversation and feel his hand on my back. I want to talk in "we's" again. I want to read him stuff from the newspaper that I know will make him laugh, I want to flirt while we do dishes. Instead I am standing here alone at a party full of friends. Will we ever be us again?

The other women clap and thank her, exchanging supportive looks.

C He left me. He left me. Every time I say it, it gets a little easier. Every time I say it I cry a little less. I have nine years of happy memories and six months of awful ones. I am no longer permitted to share the happy ones.

My wedding dress lives in a cardboard coffin from the dry-cleaners underneath the spare bed in my parents' house. Will my daughter want to wear it? Or is it tainted?

Marriage took me by surprise. I never even wanted to get married. He wanted it, wanted it desperately. Wanted the wife, the house, the kid the whole nine yards. Then he changed his mind and oops! he's single and I've got… the house and the kid and the whole nine yards.

How did I get here?

The other women clap lightly and supportively.

B When it comes down to it, it's not that I was too strong for him, that I was too creative, that I was too healthy, that I was too perfect, it's that I spilled my tea when I poured it, that I put the toilet paper roll down instead of roll up, that I always put chapstick on before I went to bed even if he was going to kiss it off. These are all the things he fell in love with in the first place, but at some point he chose not to. Love is a choice and he chose not to.

It's not about the leaving – that's not it. It's not even about him anymore. What it is about is that part of me that I can't find anymore, that precious kernel of myself he took when he walked out that day. That he carries it around with him and doesn't even know he has it – that is what this is about. I've retraced our entire four years together and now I have this map in front of me of where we ended up, I still can't figure out how we got here. Was there one word, one moment, one gesture, one day when things started to change? Will I ever get past this?

A, C Yes.

A Oh, I have something!

C Please share.

A Today, I found the nape of another man's neck sexy.

C Today, I woke up before my alarm clock.

B Today, I realized that I don't want to understand football.

A Today I bought my own garlic press.

C Today I shaved my legs.

B Today I took him off my speed dial.

A Today, I didn't drive past his house once!

B Today, I only read my horoscope.

C Today, I had a mar…

B …martini at

A …Franco's.

Franco's 2 – The Return

The three women are once again in the café from the opening scene. D runs in, notices them out of the corner of his eye and turns to avoid them, but they have seen him.

A, B, C Hi!

D Oh, hi. How are you?

A Busy.

B Fine.

C Okay.

A *(to B & C)* Smile, be funny.

B *(to A & C)* Don't cry, don't cry, don't cry.

C *(to A & B who do the actions as she says them)* Sit up straight, suck in stomach, make arms look thin.

D You look great.

A I feel great.

B Really?

C Yeah.

B So

C do

A you.

They gesture for him to sit down The last word of the following three lines are repeated five times each.

A He's got a paunch!

B Has he always had a monobrow?

C He looks like a lizard.

A, B, C So…

B how

C are

A you?

D *(as he speaks the three women nod their heads to the rhythm of his speech)* Busy. Good. Good busy.

A So much for slowing down,

B listening,

C being alone.

D Sorry?

A, B, C Nothing…

A I am Wonder Woman, Joan of Arc. *(She does a superhero gesture.)*

B *(singing dreamily)* Somewhere over the rainbow…

C *(with great conviction)* I am a rock, I am an island.

A So how's the band?

D What?

B So, did you get your magic back?

D Uh, ye… I… uh… yeah.

C So can we talk about daycare?

D *(looks at watch, makes the gun gesture)* Uh, I'll call you.

A, B, & C lean back in their chairs.

A Wow.

C Wow.

B Wow.

A I am

C Over

B Him.

A Franco arrives

B with my

C martini.

A, B, C Hey Franco.

The women smile sweetly and wave at Franco. D turns around and realizes that Franco no longer wants him in his restaurant.

D I should…

A, B, C Yeah, you should…

D …go. I'll call you.

A, B, C No.

B I'll

C call

A you.

B Bye.

C Bye.

A Bye.

The three women wave at him and in turn breathe a huge sigh.

Bittergirl Manifesto

They stand up and make a singing trio formation, with B in the middle and A & C flanked on either side as the backup singers. Throughout the final scene A & C perform corresponding gestures to their lines as B reaches out to the audience with their message.

B Everyone has their war story.

C Joe. Wouldn't let me eat in his car.

B Some have many stories.

A Fraser. Wore tighty whities.

B But there's always one.

C Patrick. Wore white tube socks. With black dress shoes.

B The one that we coin the breakup of all breakups.

A Ken. The couples' therapist with commitment issues.

B And everyone thinks that their story is the most painful.

C Brian. Gave me shoelaces for my birthday.

B "Nobody hurt like I did", we say.

A Geoffrey. Growled during sex.

B We thrive on it, we bond through it.

C Buzz. The name kinda says it all.

B Yet if someone takes our glory, if someone's story surpasses the pain and hurt of our tale, we dismiss it.

A Paul. Told me I was selfish in bed.

B Don't dismiss it.

C George. Stopped calling…

C, A …and I never noticed.

B We've all earned our scars.

A Matt. Cried at Celine Dion songs.

B But remember, when all hope is lost…

C Blake. Wouldn't memorize my phone number.

B When you feel there's no tomorrow…

A John. Asked if a pickle wash would be out of the question.

B You're walking in darkness and drowning in sorrow…

C Bobby. Whispered baby have I got a load for you.

B Remember…

A Gary. Had middle child issues.

B Yesterday's heartache is tomorrow's one-liner.

C Rick. Referred to my legs as nutcrackers.

B That's what we do. It's how we get through.

A I've

B Got my

C Story

A, B, C what's yours?

The end.

Mail-Order Annie

by
Carl C. Cashin

Born on "The Rock" (Newfoundland) and raised in Toronto, **Carl C. Cashin** abandoned corporate life in 1976 to open a summer resort on the Trent-Severn Waterway, near the town of Stirling, Ontario. Life at the resort provided the background for twenty-one published anecdotes entitled *The Janitor.* His love of theatre was kindled while working backstage at the Belleville Theatre Guild, on productions of *Angel Street, Harvey,* and *The Stone Angel,* where lighting, sound and stage management were his main focus. Bitten, he wrote *Pathways* and *Yesterday's Hero,* both one-act plays which won several awards and praise at the Eastern Ontario Drama League Festival. *Mail-Order Annie* reflects Carl's love of history and the imprint it leaves on us all.

INTRODUCTION TO *MAIL-ORDER ANNIE*

During the early 1900s thousands of Canada's "Lonely Hearts" hoped to find companionship, love and a future through advertisements in the *Western Home Monthly*, a nationally distributed magazine. Many a prosperous young farmer, with a half-section of prairie property used this, along with the cost of a train fare, as a vehicle to find himself a hardworking wife and companion – *Mail-Order Annie* tells the story of one such union.

Motivated by loneliness and dreams, plus the death of her one true love, we are introduced to Annie O'Ryan as she arrives at a barren harvest station in rural Saskatchewan. It is here that Thomas Rodger, a kindly yet concerned railway porter befriends Annie while she awaits the arrival of John Proctor, the man with whom she has corresponded. Concerned for her safety, both physically and emotionally, the porter engages in conversation with Annie and during its course she must face up to the fact that within the next forty minutes she will determine the course of her lifetime.

Playwright Carl C. Cashin's simple prairie setting reflects the isolation and marginalized position of Annie and other "mail-order brides". The desolation and solitude of the rail station parallels the loneliness of the female character Annie, whose inner turmoil is magnified by the porter's gentle urging to "get back on the train girl, go back to what you know – go back to where you belong. Find a nice young man..."

Annie becomes caught up in her dream world, one that has been fuelled by the letters of Mr. John Proctor. In sharing her letters from John Proctor with the audience, Annie paints a picture of John, which does little to prepare the audience for his entrance. His gruff and authoritative nature during his interrogation of Annie causes the audience to wonder if her farmer simply sees Annie as "free labour from back east!" Can her dreams sustain her sense of adventure, or will she succumb to fear once the reality of her situation sets in?

Annie's quest for change leads her to become a western woman who demands the right to think and act independently.

Marian Doucette

l to r: Joanne Hartman and Robert Lloyd
Photo by C. Cashin.

Mail-Order Annie was first produced at Belleville Theatre Guild's Playwrights' Summer Festival in August 1999 with the following cast:

Annie O'Ryan	Joanne Hartman
Thomas Rodger	Peter Perkins
John Proctor	Robert Lloyd

Produced by Phil Bowerman
Directed by Debra Tosh
Stage Managed by Denyce Nielsen

Mail-Order Annie received the following awards at the Eastern Ontario Drama League One-Act Play Festival, held at the Domino Theatre, Kingston, in November 1999:

Ottawa Little Theatre Award for Best Production
Academy Theatre Foundation Award for Best Director

CHARACTERS

Annie O'Ryan
Porter / Thomas Rodger
John Proctor
Clare Proctor

PLAYWRIGHT'S NOTE

A full-length version of *Mail-Order Annie* was selected by Theatre BC as winner of its 13th Annual Canadian National Playwriting Competition. Acts 2 & 3 follow the lives of John and Annie Proctor through the Great Depression and WWII. Scripts are available from the playwright: Carl C. Cashin, Box 378, Stirling, Ontario, K0K 3E0 Ph. 613-395-0996 hartcash@kos.net

IN MEMORY

This play is dedicated to the thousands of Mail-Order Brides who braved the journey to Canada's Great Western Plain, during the expansion period of 1905-1925. Some came in search of adventure and romance, others, a simple home and family. Whatever their reasons, they shaped the future of a nation. The *Western Home Monthly*, a Winnipeg-based magazine with a national circulation, featured a lonely hearts correspondence column, receiving as many as 1500 letters each month.

MAIL-ORDER ANNIE
by Carl C. Cashin

Dear Editor;

...I am a prosperous young farmer with a half section of land fully equipped with horses and machinery and my ideas of a good wife run something as follows. She should be a good cook, willing to feed and look after the poultry, pigs, calves, milk about five cows, keep the house clean, do the washing, ironing, weed the garden and be prepared to get lunch on the table for the occasional caller. Of course she should play the piano, go to town or mend the clothes in her spare time. Hoping you will be able to send me a photograph of a suitable young lady of light complexion...

—A Western Guy, April 1917, Saskatchewan

Dearest Sir;

...My tastes are varied and contradictory, so in the list, my dear unknown, you will probably find something that agrees with your own, and that would form a bond of sympathy between us. Are you a good sport? Well, so am I! I can ride, drive, skate, play tennis or hockey. I can run your motor-car too, if you have one. If you haven't, you will get one because we are going to prosper. Are you fond of social life? So am I! I play cards and love to dance. "We'll two-step through life," if you like. Perhaps you are fond of reading and of quiet evenings at home. Well, I can imagine nothing more pleasant. You in your big armchair beside the hearth... and I in my low rocker with my fancy work. You will read to me, or I will read to you, as you rest and smoke too, if you wish to...

—Honeybunch, March 1921 Toronto, Ontario

ACT I

A railway station in rural Saskatchewan. A wooden bench is against the wall – above the bench a calendar reads "AUGUST 1923". Several crates are stacked to one side. Sign on wall "CANADIAN – PACIFIC – 2735 Station B". We hear the train approach and arrive at the station.

Enter baggage porter with trunk on dolly. Young woman follows behind.

THOMAS Over here Ma'am?

ANNIE Pardon me?

THOMAS I said, do you want your trunk put down over here? *(motioning toward a wooden bench)*

ANNIE Yes.... Yes that will be fine. Thank you. Thank you very much.

THOMAS Meeting someone?

ANNIE Pardon me?

THOMAS I said, are you meeting someone. I mean, you know, is someone coming to pick you up?

ANNIE Yes.... Yes, I'm being picked up, thank you.

THOMAS Not being nosy, understand, just that's what I've been trained to ask. Well, what I'm *in training* to ask I guess you'd say. You're the first person I've ever actually asked.

ANNIE I'm sorry, what did you say?

THOMAS Ma'am, if you don't mind my saying, you seem, well, just a little distracted.

ANNIE I'm sorry... Mr...?

THOMAS Thomas, Ma'am. Thomas Rodger. And I'm wondering why you didn't get off back in Weyburn. There's people in Weyburn.

ANNIE I'm sorry, Mr. Rodger, but there really isn't any cause for your concern. *(opens handbag, removes letter, reads aloud)* Let's see... Arrive: Station 2735 B: 9:10PM, this first day of August, 1923... Correct?

THOMAS *(takes letter in hand and reads)* Well, that's where we are... and we're running prit'near on time... so that part seems okay Ma'am. But you see...

ANNIE There we are then. That's settled. Here I am. Right place. Right time. I'll just sit down over on that bench and wait. I'll be fine. Thank you, Mr. Rodger.

THOMAS Well, not quite. You see, Ma'am, rules say we're not supposed to just drop... well you know, just drop "you ladies" off unless someone is actually waiting right there in the station.

ANNIE *(indignantly)* And why not?

THOMAS It's unsafe by a lot. You see, this is what we call a "Harvest Station". About the only time it's ever used for passengers is when we bring a load of workers from back east in late summer. We pull in and the men they get off the train and line up along the platform. Farmers, or anyone in the area needing hands, pick out the ones they want and the rest get back on the train. Then we head for the next place and do it all over again. There's nothing within a days walk of this station and I don't see any provisions. There's been a lot of sad things happen along this route in the past while and people are just trying to make sure them things don't happen again, that's all.

ANNIE Like what things?

THOMAS Well Ma'am, sometimes "you ladies"... well, sometimes people don't get picked up. Sometimes people just forgets them. Or maybe the person gets sick and can't find someone else to go. Or maybe their wagon breaks down.... Or their motorcar.... Lot of things, Ma'am.

ANNIE "You ladies"! For heaven's sake, why do you keep saying, "you ladies"?

THOMAS Well now, I don't mean any disrespect you understand, but I'm assuming... well, I'm assuming you've never met the man who's picking you up.

ANNIE His name is Mr. John Proctor. And if I haven't?

THOMAS If you haven't... well again now, I'm just assuming... you're what we on the railroad call a "mail-order".

ANNIE A what?

THOMAS A "mail-order", Ma'am. A "mail-order bride". That's what we call them because, well... because everything's done, you know, through the mail. Why, since they passed that "Soldier Settlement Act", and the Western Plain seems to be God's new beginning for so many folk, we see lots out this way. Some months maybe a dozen. That's why the new policy. Too many were coming to no good.

ANNIE Mail-order. I... you.... How dare you infer...

THOMAS Please Ma'am. I didn't mean to offend. Just that... well, you asked what could happen.

ANNIE Thank you for your concern, Mr. Rodger, but I'm quite sure I'll be all right.

THOMAS Well Ma'am, you see, that's the problem. As I've been saying, new CP policy is to not drop *anyone*, especially… well, especially *ladies*, at rural unmanned stations without they have proper escorts. Ma'am, unless your person arrives before the train pulls out, I'm afraid you'll have to get back on.

ANNIE Get back on! Get back on the train! That's preposterous! Out of the question! Do you have any idea how far…

THOMAS I'm sorry Ma'am, but you have to understand how barren…

ANNIE *(angry, yet almost at the point of tears)* You don't have to remind me where I am. I know where I am. I know exactly where I am! And I've been looking out that window at rock and wilderness for only God knows how long, and now you tell me this? Where's the Conductor? I wish to speak with the Conductor!

THOMAS That would be Mr. Sullivan, Ma'am. Jack Sullivan. Now, he's the one told me to *make sure* you knew what was what.

ANNIE You can't possibly make me get back on the train. I won't do it!

THOMAS Ma'am, I don't make the rules. But, well, in this case I kind of agree with them.

Pause.

ANNIE How long before you pull out?

THOMAS Well now, that depends. We've got water to take on and the brakeman has to run a check. Probably no more than forty minutes.

ANNIE If no one's here by then can you… you know, stall or something?

THOMAS I'm sorry Ma'am.

ANNIE Forty minutes?

THOMAS Yes Ma'am.

ANNIE walks over and sits on the bench. THOMAS busies himself with his clipboard at the crates. A few moments pass.

ANNIE *(quietly)* Is that how you see me? Like something from a catalogue?

THOMAS It's an expression, Ma'am. Nothing personal was meant.

ANNIE All the same, I never once saw it that way. Or thought for one second that others did.... *(talking to herself)* Mail-order bride. How many people in the last few months have thought the same? How many have thought, "There goes ol' Annie, the desperate spinster. Can't find a man here so she's mailing herself halfway across the country." My God, the train fare like postage.

THOMAS Ma'am, I think you're being a little hard on yourself.

ANNIE Annie. My name is Annie O'Ryan, Mr. Rodger. I'm twenty-eight years old and one of eight born in Belleville, Ontario to Meagan and Sean O'Ryan, formerly of Kilkenny County, Ireland. Five years ago I moved to Toronto and went into service with a lovely family in Kensington, the Abrams.

THOMAS Ma'am, you don't have to...

ANNIE I graduated school, Mr. Rodger. And I am... well... *was*, gainfully employed. I'm not an... an... opportunist, if that's what you're thinking.

THOMAS You don't have to apologize to me or anyone else. It's none of my business.

ANNIE I wasn't apologizing. I was...

Long awkward pause. Neither knows what to say. THOMAS goes back to checking tags on crates.

ANNIE What are you doing?

THOMAS Freight, Ma'am. This station is used regularly for shipping and such. See, out here people's lives are governed by the weather rather than an appointment book like back east. Sunshine means you work the land; rain means you do your catch-up. For instance these crates. Some are from quite a distance. A man can't always afford to give up a day's work just to meet a train, so they come when they can – leave them here – we pick them up and deliver them. Drop stuff off too.

ANNIE That's remarkable. But who pays?

THOMAS The person who picks it up. It's a new thing called C.O.D. – Cash on delivery. Works for letters too.

THOMAS loads small crate on dolly.

ANNIE I answered a letter in the *Western Home Monthly*. Each issue has letters from gentlemen, who, for whatever reason…

THOMAS I know the magazine Ma'am. All us on the railroad do.

ANNIE I know what you're thinking. The "Lonely Hearts Club Guidebook"! I was only looking through it for fun. In fact, some of the letters were quite funny… then I saw the letter from Mr. Proctor…

THOMAS Ma'am don't feel you have to…

ANNIE I don't, Mr. Rodger. It's just that… so far it's been such a great adventure. But now… now that I'm actually here, sitting in this station, I'm having a little trouble catching my breath. To be truthful, I can't believe I've come this far. I'm feeling rather awkward… or nervous or… *(fighting back tears)* Oh Mr. Rodger, I'm so scared.

ANNIE takes a handkerchief from her purse. THOMAS puts aside what he is doing and sits beside ANNIE on the bench in a fatherly manner.

THOMAS Now, now, there's no need for all this. Tell me now… Miss O'Ryan was it?

ANNIE Annie.

THOMAS Tell me now, Annie, what would make a lovely young girl like yourself, gainfully employed as you said, haul up stakes and move out here to this wilderness, and make no mistake about it, this *is* wilderness. What would make you think there was something better waiting for you here?

ANNIE Dreams, I suppose.

THOMAS But dreams have to be based on some sort of reality Annie.

ANNIE Where are *you* from Mr. Rodger?

THOMAS Me? The Ottawa Valley. You being from Belleville, Annie, you'd know where that is.

ANNIE Indeed I do. My Father's brother, Uncle Mick, lives not far from Perth. When I was fourteen my sister Alice and I spent a glorious summer on the farm with him and Aunt Mo. We learned how to milk and tend the stock. We planted and hoed and weeded and watered and picked and sweated and… and we laughed…

THOMAS There's a world of difference between the Ottawa Valley and the Saskatchewan Plain. Trust me, Annie, it was your family that brought you that happiness – not the farm. Think hard, it's a demanding life to say the least. I've seen women come this way before. They arrive fresh – like spring rain, only to leave with broken spirits in tired eyes. Life on the Plain is hard Annie, with few rewards. Get back on the train girl, go back to what you know – go back to where you belong. Find a nice young man…

Pause.

ANNIE *(reflectively)* Yes, a nice young man…. Michael came to my tenth birthday party. It was the first time I'd met him. He was twelve and wore a tie. He seemed so grown up…. Michael's Mother was new to the Women's League and Mom invited him 'round, not stopping to think that the *last* thing I wanted at my party was a boy! It didn't matter to him though, nope! He walked right up – stuck out his hand – and said, "Michael Corby, pleased to make your acquaintance." *(big smile)* Did you know that ten-year-olds can have heart flutters Mr. Rodger? From that day on, we were rarely apart. Michael and Annie, Annie and Michael – Oh, how the wags would gossip…. See that scar? *(shows THOMAS her finger)* I was fifteen. We were sitting by the bay. I cut his first – then mine…. Oh, he was such a baby! *(pause)* Michael was in the first wave at Vimy Ridge. Almost four thousand dead in only a few hours… they told me it was a great victory for Canada. Our finest moment. The Somme, Passchendaele… thousands more… and for each dead soldier – one woman must live her life alone.

THOMAS I'm sorry Annie.

ANNIE It's all right, Mr. Rodger, God put his mark on my generation, but with good reason. Michael's death wasn't in vain. This war ended all wars. It'll never be repeated – so you see, the end *has* justified the means.

THOMAS I guess only time will tell, Annie. Time will tell.

ANNIE *(trying to cheer up)* So, how long have you worked on the railroad?

THOMAS Thirty-seven years this fall.

ANNIE And do you have a family Mr. Rodger?

THOMAS My Emily's been gone, let's see, nearing eight years now. But we were blessed with three fine sons. Good boys they are, always looking toward their Dad.

ANNIE Do you miss them? I mean when you're travelling like this, do you miss seeing them?

THOMAS Every mile of every track. Especially when they were small. I'd get home and Em would be catching me up. "Charles did well on his tests," she might say, "And Patrick finished up his assignment at the Boy's Club. But Andrew, now there's a lad needs a talking to, Tom." *(smiling proudly)* Andy was the oldest. Quite the lad he was. Once him and that little rascal Willy Randall had been pestering the life out of Eddie Cook's two daughters. One afternoon the boys nipped by Warner's pond for a quick swim and the girls sneaked up and took their clothes. All of 'em, right down to their red flannels! Yes sir! Didn't bring them back either. Nope. Andy, twelve I think he was at the time, and young Willy had to sneak back the four miles from the pond to home buck naked. Tree to tree… What a tale that is to hear!

ANNIE My kind of girls!

THOMAS Hardly a Christmas goes by without that story being told.

ANNIE That's what I want, Mr. Rodger! When I'm old, I want to tell stories like that.

THOMAS Then no one should deny you, Annie. You deserve as much. But why here? Why not Toronto – or Belleville or anywhere back east? Anywhere you're familiar with?

ANNIE gathers her thoughts.

ANNIE Carpe diem.

THOMAS Carpe what?

ANNIE Carpe diem. It's Latin. *"Seize the day and accept what tomorrow brings."* It was an expression of Michael's. "Sometimes you just have to take a chance, Annie," he'd say. "Rely on your instincts and listen to your heart." *(pause)* Shortly after word arrived about Michael, Uncle Mick stopped by on his yearly trip to Toronto. When he left next morning I was in the back of his new Ford. A new day – a new life. I started with the Abrams that September. The Abrams were wonderful people. I did "upstairs" work mainly, you know, linen and beds and such for over two years. Little Rebecca was five at the time… my little Rebecca…. Mrs. Abrams, well let's say she loved children but loved her social life a notch better, she just didn't have the time for the little angel and, well… decided to hire a full time Nanny. When I heard that news I was at her door in a second with my letters of reference, few as they were. "Annie," she asked, "What makes you think for one second that you're qualified to raise my two children – and over some very experienced applications I might add." I stood there feeling silly and awkward. I couldn't think of what to say so I blurted out, "Rebecca doesn't like fur, especially on scarves… it scares her and keeps her awake nights. And Hermy, he'd be toilet-trained by now if everyone would just leave him alone. Poor little guy has more pressure on him than a cat in a room full of rocking chairs." Mrs. Abrams laughed, then looked at me… she looked at me strangely, and said, "I thought only *I* knew those things." Next thing I knew I had my own room in the main house! *(laughing)* Imagine that!

THOMAS And a grand choice I'm sure you were, Annie O'Ryan!

ANNIE The Abrams, they were Jewish you see…

THOMAS Yes Annie, I'd guessed as much.

ANNIE *(looks puzzled for a moment)* Oh Mr. Rodger! *(laughing)* I'm sorry… *Abrams*… of course.

THOMAS But you're Christian!

ANNIE Roman Catholic, actually.

THOMAS Even more so! I'm surprised you'd take a job in their employ – even more surprised they allowed you to be their nanny!

ANNIE I'm ashamed to admit I thought that way in the beginning too, but I needed the job and in a very short time I'd learned a big lesson in life. I learned that different isn't wrong – it's just different. And the more you learn about someone different, the less afraid you become. It's the kind of lesson we should be teaching in the classroom and preaching from the pulpit. The kind taught by everyday actions, everyday words. You see, to the Abrams, I was always just Annie O'Ryan from Belleville. No one else.

THOMAS Noble thoughts. Easily said, difficult to live.

ANNIE It should at least be in our hearts to try.

THOMAS I suppose…

ANNIE Anyway, the Abrams were from Germany but spoke flawless English. From old money, Mrs. Murray the housekeeper said… very hush hush… apparently their lives were threatened and they were forced to leave, and only because they were Jewish. I can't imagine a place like that. Can you? Anyway, Mr. Abrams was in paper sales, not newspapers but "paper" as in "newsprint". He was away a lot making big deals in places like New York City and Chicago but when he got home it was always "family party time". Mrs. Abrams would invite a few select friends and have the table set with the *most* delicious things to eat and the children would be dressed in their finest. And a place was *always* set for me. "Miss O'Ryan, sit here with the children," Mr. Abrams would say, and stories of my growing up in Belleville were welcomed. I was *never* just "The Nanny" to the Abrams – I was *always* referred to as Miss O'Ryan. *(reflectively)* I understood that gesture and always returned their respect. Anyway, during dinner Mr. Abrams—who Mrs. Abrams said secretly wanted to do Vaudeville—would entertain us with the funniest riddles a body ever heard. For instance…. A cowboy rode into town on Friday and left three days later on Friday – How did he do it?

THOMAS He rode into town on Friday…. Three days later… I give up. How'd he do it?

ANNIE His horse was named Friday!

THOMAS *(shakes his head laughing)* Oh my.

ANNIE How many months have 28 days?

THOMAS That's easy. Just one, February!

ANNIE *(bursting out laughing)* Nope. All of them!

THOMAS Enough already!

ANNIE One more – just one more. What does a 200 pound mouse say?

THOMAS I give up. What *does* a 200 pound mouse say?

ANNIE *(deep voice)* Here, Kitty, Kitty!

They both laugh together.

After dinner everyone would retire to the parlour. Someone would always try a little poetry, but mostly we would sing and play music on the gramophone. Mr. Abrams always brought home the newest records. And we would dance… *(ANNIE stands up and does a little twirl)* Oh, how we would dance… it was lovely. Do you dance Mr. Rodger?

THOMAS Well, not much I guess…

ANNIE *(ANNIE holds out her hand)* Come on, Mr. Rodger! Come here and I'll show you their dance. Come on it's fun!

THOMAS No…. Really, Annie I can't…

ANNIE *(grabbing his arm and playfully spinning him around)* You see…. You can do it!

They dance around the stage laughing, until finally THOMAS stops – out of breath.

THOMAS Few have a zest for life like yourself, Annie. But, I warn you, the Plain will surely crush it – as easily as one would a spark from a woodstove. Protect it. Take it with you. Go back to Toronto…

ANNIE To what? A life in service to someone else?

THOMAS You said you loved them. You said your life was wonderful.

ANNIE I did – and it was! But it was *their* life, don't you see?

THOMAS Go back to what you *know* then! Who is this John Proctor really? Do you have any idea?

ANNIE I have his letters. We've corresponded. And I know… I know…

THOMAS You *know* nothing! Only what he wants you to *know*. Go home Annie! Go home or you'll die on the Plain!

ANNIE *(quietly and forcefully)* No Mr. Rodger, you're wrong. I'll make it. Wait and see... I *will* make it.

THOMAS pulls his watch from his vest pocket.

THOMAS The choice may be left to God. *(looks at watch)* Twenty minutes.

ANNIE Twenty minutes.

THOMAS loads a crate and exits. ANNIE sits back down.

(closing her eyes in prayer) Lord Jesus, in your mercy, spare a moment if you can to look down upon your servant Anne Frances O'Ryan. My journey has been long Lord, but with your help and blessing I'm nearing the end. John Proctor is a good man, of this I'm sure and in this I believe. In your wisdom, it is he whom you have chosen for me. *(aside)* Oh my, at least I'm hoping you've been paying attention. *(back to prayer)* It seems at the moment, dear Lord, that Mr. Proctor is guilty of the sin of tardiness. It's not the sin itself which worries me at this moment but rather its timing...

ANNIE shuffles through her handbag and produces several well-worn letters.

(reads aloud) Mr. John Proctor, Weyburn/Saskatchewan. *(wistfully)* John... such a good Christian name for a good Christian man. One thousand acres. I can't imagine a farm that big. Mr. Proctor says he plants the lot in grain. "Wheat", he says, "Miss O'Ryan we have fields so vast they disappear over the horizon. And at harvest time they become seas of liquid gold, filling the granaries to overflow with the wheat to feed our new Nation." So poetic. Surely these are just a man's fancy words to his betrothed. To have fields that large would offend the Almighty Himself. Just the same though, it'll be a sight to see. And the house, "The finest on the Western Plain," he says, "A house to be admired by many." I'll bet it's stone! Yes, a house built of fine cut stone shipped from afar...

Now Annie girl, don't let your dreams take over your head. Be just as proud of one built of strong timbers – one with the floors sanded enough to take some polish when the neighbours come to visit. A house filled with dancing and laughter. Or maybe the Father, when he takes his rounds will make it his regular stop, a house he knows to cherish Christian values. A house of God.

(over dramatic) Oh Saint Anne, Saint Anne, hear my prayer. Thank you for listening to this poor soul's wretched cry and guiding me to this place today. A place far from a life of servitude and thankless toil. Far away from the poisonous city. Far away from the chains of…. Oh my, Annie girl… calm yourself! Thankless toil? Poisonous city? Where did that come from? *(looks up)* Sorry, Saint Anne, but you know me. And I'm in a bit of a situation here and if… well, I'm not sure how much influence you have, but if you can help out a bit, I would be most grateful. *(afterthought)* Thank you.

ANNIE looks through her purse and holds up a photograph.

I don't remember his nose being quite that big… and he's not really what you would call handsome, but I guess he'd pass with a shove – especially with those broad shoulders…. *(stares intently)* In fact, *very* broad shoulders. Almost *too* broad. I wonder if the coat was padded? No…. No, Mr. Proctor is a forthright man. A man who, from what I read in his letters, would not suffer the sin of vanity well… and no beard. Merciful Lord, I'm thankful of that. I don't like beards. They always seem to have little bits of last night's dinner caught up in the edges…

Being a farmer, he *must* be tall or at least of normal height. I read somewhere that they don't let short people operate farm machinery, something about their feet not touching the pedals…. And those eyes – oh my, without a doubt his strong point. He said in his letter they're blue…. Yes, I can tell, they're blue! I read once that a person's eyes are a window to their soul. I believe that. And in them I see… I see strength. Yes, I see strength of character and great determination. Someone with focus. Someone with a clear vision of the future and of what they wish to achieve…. *(wistfully)* Am I part of your vision John Proctor? *(continues to stare intently)* But there is something else in your eyes. Weakness? No, more a gentleness. A gentle side you hide because you *perceive* it as weakness. A side that wouldn't allow you to openly present me with spring flowers, but rather, leave them on the kitchen stoop for me to find. But you needn't fear, I'll keep your secret from the other men, lest they tease and pester you when they come 'round Sunday afternoons to talk about things like livestock or crops. I'll be the proper wife – make sure you get your respect as a man *and* receive your due as head of the house…. Mother always said, *(Irish accent)* "A man's home is his castle. Keep the king happy and everything else will fall into place! Order and Happiness, Annie, they go hand-in-hand"… *(looks back at picture and utters a long sigh)* …and children, are they part of your vision? A supper table circled with round shiny faces and not an empty chair to be had. We bow our heads while you give thanks – then the room is filled with chatter of the day's adventures. And at night when the last one is tucked in… *(holds picture to her breast)* …and you take my hand… *(shocked by her own words)* Annie, calm yourself girl! *(fans herself while raising her eyes in prayer again)* Saint Anne, Saint Anne, it's me again. Let me not be dragged to hell's doorstep with lustful thoughts. John Proctor is a man of honor, a man of stature in his community, surely these are the qualities important in life, not a person's appearance. John Proctor is a man deserving of the love and respect only a wife and caring woman can provide. I will love John Proctor unconditionally… till death do us part. Providing he gets here of course.

There is a shuffling from the wings. ANNIE looks toward the door in anticipation. Enter JOHN Proctor. He is wearing a fedora hat.

JOHN You Annie O'Ryan?

ANNIE Yes.

JOHN Well, don't just sit there. Stand up! Let me get a look.

ANNIE Mr. Proctor? I'm pleased to make your…

JOHN Stand up, girl! Like you're told.

ANNIE Yes sir.

ANNIE stands up and JOHN looks her up and down for a while.

JOHN Not as much to look at as I'd hoped for. But I guess a sight better than what Stu Jackson got. *(looks toward trunk)* That all you brought?

ANNIE *(very quietly)* Yes sir.

JOHN I said, is that all you brought?

ANNIE Yes sir!

JOHN walks over to the trunk and lifts one side.

JOHN Feels like just clothes.

ANNIE *(starts speaking softly)* Yes, mainly. My other things…

JOHN Speak up girl!

ANNIE *(visibly startled, speaks louder)* I was hoping to have my other things sent on later. After I'm settled.

JOHN *(extracting a list from his pocket and reading from it)* You mean the china and silverware?

ANNIE Yes. But not the tea service – you see, my sister Alice was married only seven weeks ago – I think I mentioned it in one of my letters? Anyway, when she and Mother came to Toronto to visit, I just naturally…

JOHN And who's supposed to pay for all this?

ANNIE Well I… I…

JOHN Never mind. I should have expected as much.

While JOHN refers back to his list, THOMAS enters with his loading dolly, takes a long look at the scene before him and is visibly not pleased.

How are your teeth?

ANNIE My teeth?

JOHN Yes woman, your teeth. How are they? I'd rather face the trials of Job than be snowbound in January with a woman with a tooth ache.

ANNIE Well, they're… they're… they don't hurt… they…

JOHN Open up then and let's have a look.

ANNIE Open up?

JOHN Yes! Yes! Come on, hurry it up!

ANNIE opens her mouth wide while JOHN peers in.

JOHN Hmmm…. Good. Very good, actually.

ANNIE *(meekly)* Thank you.

JOHN How about ailments? Do you have any back pain or arthritis?

ANNIE No.

JOHN Arches okay?

ANNIE Yes.

JOHN Let's see… how about cold sores, do you have anything like that – something that keeps coming back?

ANNIE *(embarrassed with head down)* Oh no, Sir! Nothing like that.

THOMAS has been carrying on with his duties but is becoming visibly upset at what he is witnessing.

JOHN *(referring to the letter)* You said you had farm experience. Did that include dairy or just mixed? And have you handled cream – for retail that is…

ANNIE *(cheerfully)* Well, when I was fourteen I spent the summer at my Uncle Mick's farm. He milked two cows so I guess you could call that dairy, but mostly Alice and I worked in the market garden. We'd be right out there with Aunt Mo and have a day's work done by breakfast…

JOHN You're joking, right?

ANNIE No.

JOHN You're telling me that your "Farm experience" consists of a single summer at your uncle's? *(angrily)* Good God, woman! I've got 17 Holsteins on their way from Regina. If this is an indication of what I'm getting…

THOMAS See here, I've heard enough! Don't let him talk to you this way, Annie. Remember, you're *not* from a catalogue.

ANNIE It's okay, Mr. Rodger.

THOMAS It's *not* okay! I'm not going to stand here and let this misguided dirt farmer insult you!

JOHN Who in hell are you?

THOMAS *(bravely advancing toward JOHN)* I'm… I'm her friend!

ANNIE *(guiding THOMAS back to his crates)* It's all right, Mr. Rodger, really. Thank you. But I guess he has a right to ask these questions. Everything will be fine.

ANNIE walks back to JOHN and stands with her head down.

ANNIE I'm sorry about that, Mr. Proctor. You were saying?

JOHN I have 300 acres in wheat and another 150 in oats, and by this time next year I'd hoped to break another 80. I'm taking 25 bushels of grain per acre. Normally that would bring a handsome sum of money, but since the war the market has been flooded and prices have bottomed out. Well managed, the Holsteins could bring $100 a month in cream alone – and milk is going 45 cents to the gallon. I was counting on *you* to handle the herd while I worked the fields. Now you tell me this…

ANNIE I'll work very hard, Sir. I promise you that. And I'm a quick study. Maybe you could just hire someone for a while – to "show me the ropes", so to speak.

THOMAS Why pay someone when you can order up free labour from back east!

JOHN glares at THOMAS – then back to ANNIE.

JOHN *(referring to his list)* Can you read and do sums or is that another tale?

ANNIE I graduated high school showing promise in bookkeeping. My last employer, Jacob Abrams, engaged my skills for simple household finances, paying tradesmen and such. I'm not stupid Mr. Proctor if that's what you're wondering.

JOHN Yes, well, that's yet to be determined.

JOHN reaches into his pocket and takes out a Bible.

JOHN Here, read me a passage from the good book. Any passage, I don't care.

ANNIE takes the Bible in hand and opens it. She hesitates, then looks at the inside cover.

ANNIE Mr. Proctor! This is a "King James" version!

JOHN And what did you expect?

ANNIE God's word Mr. Proctor, not the King of England's! Are you not Catholic then?

JOHN Presbyterian.

ANNIE Oh, Holy Mother. *(ANNIE crosses herself)* You knew of my faith. I distinctly said in my letter I was Roman Catholic.

JOHN I know, but I didn't think it would matter much. After all, Christians are Christians. We all bow to the same Lord.

ANNIE But it does matter – it matters very much! Do you even *have* a Priest out here?

JOHN We built a small church with what little we had. Everyone shows up Sunday morning, and if there's a Minister—doesn't matter what denomination—he does the service. If not, one of us "reads". Works out well. But if that ain't good enough for you, there's a Catholic church over in Weyburn – Father D'Angelo. Road's rough. I'll take you once a month.

ANNIE turns away and tries to adjust to this new situation.

Well?

ANNIE *(to herself with eyes closed)* Saint Anne, it's me again. Things aren't going so good. I know different isn't wrong – it's just different. But Presbyterian? *(crosses both her fingers)* Carpe diem. *(turning back to JOHN)* Every two weeks!

JOHN Done. *(consulting his list)* I guess that leaves just one thing.... *(clears his throat)* Are you a "Lady", Miss O'Ryan?

ANNIE What do you mean?

JOHN Are you a "Lady"? You know, in the *proper sense* so to speak.

ANNIE *(aghast)* Am I a "Lady"?

JOHN Yes. I know it's rather personal, but I feel I have a right to know.

ANNIE A right to know? You feel you have a right to know?

THOMAS Mr. Proctor! This has gone far enough...

ANNIE It's okay, Mr. Rodger! *(turns to JOHN and stands erect—shoulders back—fighting back tears)* Sir, I left behind my family and friends and travelled nearly two thousand miles to stand before you today. I've sold most of my possessions except for the few I had hoped to share with you. I stood before you and without protest accepted your... your interrogation. I had hoped to begin a new life with you here on this Plain, but Sir, I find now that I cannot. Please accept my apologies for any inconvenience I may have caused you. *(turns to THOMAS)* Mr. Rodger, please collect my trunk. I'm going home.

THOMAS Yes, Ma'am!

THOMAS flashes a winning grin at JOHN, then loads the trunk on the dolly and exits. JOHN is visibly shocked by this unexpected turn of events.

JOHN What are you doing? You can't leave. Go home. Just like that!

ANNIE And why not?

JOHN We have an agreement, that's why. Plans have been made.

ANNIE If plans have been made, Sir, they are your own. Plans I've certainly not been privy to. And as far as an *agreement* is concerned... if one *did* exist it is *you* that has not lived up to it. I at least tried to let you see who *I* was, but you... you misled me from the beginning! You are rude, calculating and arrogant, and I do not intend to spend the rest of my life as your chattel. I could have stayed in Toronto and been paid for what you wish me to do. I may have my whole life ahead of me Mr. Proctor, but you know, that's not very long. Goodbye! *(turns to walk away)*

JOHN Miss O'Ryan, wait!

ANNIE stops.

Maybe I'm not exactly the man you expected – whoever he might be, but I assure you I've tried to be honest. If you've fostered some other image of me—some girlish notion of a knight in shining armour who's come to save you—it's not my fault if I don't live up to those expectations. And as for the questions—my "interrogation" you called it—this is the Western Plain you've come to girl, not some farm back east that's been tilled for generations. Out here the soil is being broken for the first time. Roads are being cut through virgin wood; communities springing to life overnight. It's not a place for the weak of body *or* spirit. Wanting to be part of this growth is not enough, you have to be physically capable of surviving it!

ANNIE But I answered those questions and more in my letters.

JOHN Begging you pardon, Miss O'Ryan, but some things… well, some things are too important to be left to chance. Now, you take Stu Jackson for example…

ANNIE Mr. Proctor, do you have anything *else* to say? If not…

JOHN Just that, well…. Living by themselves, a person can get used to their own company and over the years sometimes forget how to be civil. Forget how to treat another person with respect – not just on special occasions but in every day talk. Mostly you don't know you've done it until someone's giving you a stare – like right now…. You just try each day to get done what has to be done and you forget how to act around folks – you don't use extra words, only the ones you need. *(He removes his fedora.)* I apologize, Miss O'Ryan. If I offended you it wasn't on purpose – fact is you got company… I offend a lot of people.

ANNIE I accept your apology, Sir. And I thank you – but it changes nothing.

Again ANNIE turns to walk away.

JOHN Just one more minute, please! The farm, why it sits on some of the best acreage in the Province. Russell's Creek—well, it's a little *more* than a creek in spring—runs through it from one end to the other. And with close to 100 acres in pasture, the Holsteins should do well. You know, I'm thinking you're right. Grant Sutter's boy is nearing sixteen and out of school. He'd be a good one to come work for us a while. The boy knows dairy for sure. And I've planted a good-size garden in the 'lee of the barn. With proper tending extra produce could be sold… I don't know, maybe some chickens…?

ANNIE It doesn't matter anymore.

JOHN And the house, well, the house it ain't much, just three rooms, but I've ordered milled planks from Hartman's in Weyburn with the intention of adding on. A parlour if it suited you.

ANNIE It's not stone?

JOHN Stone?

ANNIE Yes, stone! You said it was, "The finest house on the Western Plain, built amid fields of wheat so vast they disappear over the horizon."

JOHN The finest on the Western Plain? What else did I say?

ANNIE That, "The fields were seas of liquid gold, and the granaries"... you didn't write that letter did you?

JOHN *(quietly)* No.

ANNIE Who wrote it then?

JOHN Kathleen, my sister. Sending the letter was her idea. In fact she had it sent before I knew anything about it. "Living alone like you do isn't natural," Kathleen would say, "John, you need a wife and children or else when you die – no one will ever know you lived." *(weak laugh)* And by the sounds of the words in my letter, she wants to see me married more than most. *(pause)* I've been happy with my life – never felt the need to share it with anyone. I enjoy the solitude of my home and don't "suffer fools gladly" as some say. But, it seems because I like my own company I'm a failure to most. So I guess when I first saw you standing there – that's what you were – someone else's answer to a problem I didn't think I even had. I hadn't asked you here. You were an intrusion. But now... I don't know... seeing you standing here.... Look, I'm not the best with words, but I'm trying to be honest with you, Miss O'Ryan...

ANNIE I'm surprised you know how.

JOHN I'm doing my best.

ANNIE That's yet to be determined. *(pulling the picture from her purse)* She sent this picture.

JOHN Oh God! Look at that would you. Regina Fair 19 and 10. Thirteen years ago... guess I've changed a bit.

ANNIE More than a bit! *(aside)* The coat *was* padded too.

JOHN I've not had one taken since. If you knew Kathleen, you'd know she meant no harm with her exaggerations. *(with unexpected tenderness)* Kathleen is... well... she's my sister.

ANNIE She lives nearby?

JOHN Next section to mine. Her an' Marty and the two boys. Daniel's ten and Jeff, why he must be almost fifteen now… Amy, their oldest, would have been seventeen next month but we lost her to the Spanish flu in 19 and 18.

ANNIE I'm sorry.

JOHN It was a terrible plague. Lot of folks lost loved ones that year.

ANNIE *(quietly)* Yes, a lot of folks lost loved ones that year.

Long pause.

JOHN So…. Do you think you might reconsider, Miss O'Ryan?

ANNIE I'm sorry, but this has all been a bad mistake. I know now there's nothing here I didn't leave behind. You need a cook, bookkeeper and field-hand wrapped into one. The Plain doesn't have a monopoly on working dawn to dusk, I can do that anywhere. Hire the Sutter boy – he can do as much or more than me and you needn't worry about his teeth. The fact is John Proctor, you've not given me one good reason to stay.

Enter THOMAS.

THOMAS All aboard! Come on Annie, it's time!

ANNIE I'm coming Mr. Rodger!

THOMAS exits. Train whistle. ANNIE walks toward exit.

JOHN Miss O'Ryan! Please, you're wrong. I know what you're saying…. Look, when Kathleen first showed me your letters and told me what she'd done, I was very angry. In fact, I did everything to get your address from her but she stood firm. "Think hard about it, John," she said, "And if in thirty days you decide against Miss O'Ryan coming I'll give you the address and you can tell her yourself!" I slammed out of her house that Sunday with black in my heart, but as the thirty days progressed I admit I got to thinking selfish. I began planning what you could do or how much work you could handle. But now, with you standing here, I can put a person to the face… you're not just a picture… I know now I need much more.

The porter was right, I *am* just a dirt farmer and not that white knight you expected, but I work hard and I'm proud of my farm – proud of what I've accomplished with my life. I don't know if I'm making any sense, but I read once that neither joy nor sorrow exist without someone to share them with. I didn't know what that meant until this very moment. And I'm not talking about just the big things, I'm talking about walking in your door at night and saying, "Guess what I did today," or maybe just sitting on the porch together in the rain. Do you know what I'm saying? It's like when you wake up and you know you've been dreaming but you can't remember what about. You sit on the edge of the bed – trying to remember – and it's *so* close, oh *so* close – but it never comes – and in the end you know you've missed your chance – a chance that won't come again, and you're left with emptiness.... That's how I'm feeling right now. Like I'm sitting on the edge of the bed, trying to remember my dream, knowing it's close, but all the while afraid I'm going to lose it.

Miss O'Ryan, I may live alone, but I'm around people a lot. I probably go to town twice a week – then there's church Sundays... there's always *someone* in my doorway. But loneliness isn't just the absence of someone near – it's the absence of someone to share with. *(pause)* So I guess that's what I'm standing here asking you, Miss O'Ryan... I'm asking you to please share your life with me.

ANNIE has been listening intently. She turns her back to JOHN and is now facing the audience. Train whistle. Sound of train leaving station. THOMAS enters.

THOMAS Annie! We're moving, come on!

JOHN Miss O'Ryan, please!

THOMAS Annie! Come on!

THOMAS exits. ANNIE raises her eyes to heaven, then turns around to face JOHN.

ANNIE Will you leave spring flowers on the back stoop?

JOHN Spring flowers? Miss O'Ryan... Annie... I promise to try.

ANNIE Then... let's go home John.

The sound of train leaving station. Train whistle.

The end.

Derailed

by
Emil Sher

Born and raised in Montreal, **Emil Sher** taught English at a secondary school in rural Botswana before returning to Montreal to pursue a degree in creative writing. Ever since, he has written professionally in a variety of genres, including stage plays, screenplays, radio dramas, short fiction and essays. He is particularly drawn to character-driven stories, narratives fuelled by individuals struggling to navigate their way through a world rarely of their own making. His works include *Mourning Dove*, a radio play about a father who kills his severely disabled daughter that Sher is adapting for the screen and stage. Several of his essays have been anthologized, and three of his radio plays were published in one volume titled *Making Waves*. *Café Olé*, a romantic comedy filmed in Montreal, was released in 2001 and honoured as one of the Top Ten scripts of the year by the Writers Guild of Canada. A playwright-in-residence at Necessary Angel Theatre Company in Toronto, Sher's current projects include the stage play *Semi-detached*, and *Bluenose*, a play for young audiences about three clumsy, colonizing pirates.

INTRODUCTION TO *DERAILED*

Emil Sher's *Derailed* is a challenging hybrid theatre-piece: a sharply detailed, often shrewdly comic exploration of collapsing relationships, packaged in a frenetic merger of physical theatre, music, and clown. Four frequently manic characters take a train ride that transforms their tawdry lives into vivid expressionistic extravagance. The piece depends heavily on deft and precise movement, rhythm, light, and sound, much of it scripted. Importantly, the intense physical theatricality is not an end in itself. Rather, it is a razor-sharp tool for psychic revelation, pushing the characters to open performance of their fears and desires, both conscious and unconscious.

This train ride along what Freud called the repression barrier is overseen by Victor the conductor, whose initial potential as a neutral observer is soon subverted by knee-jerk acting-out of his own "unspoken desires and dreams." As the journey begins, Victor's three passengers are defined by obsessive routine: Brenda, the devoted wife, carries George's shoe in her purse, and spit-polishes it over and over. Anya, George's mistress and colleague, tallies up sums on an old adding machine, while trying unsuccessfully to keep her leg from wandering out from under her. George, fleeing from financial scandal, furtively shreds paper in a kitchen blender. Later, even the details of George's disintegrating love life will smack of routine (and a stunted imagination): wife and mistress have received identical anniversary gifts, and have been taken to the same New York hotel room for identical romantic getaways.

Time and again, physical theatre generates the dramatic moment. The train ride literally throws people together, its jolts and jostles causing collisions and reconfigurations, some of them embarrassingly inconvenient, some of them luxuriously illicit. Transitions are achieved organically, for instance by sending the train through a tunnel (and into a blackout) at a crucial moment and revealing rearranged locations or pairings when the train emerges again into the light. The set itself consists simply of a pair of rails extending forward from the back wall. At the Factory Studio, they disappeared into a tunnel-like opening upstage centre. All features of the train's interior—the compartment, the dining-car, and the adjacent corridors—are created by the actors' constant arrangement and rearrangement of trunks and vintage suitcases. (The play is set in the 1950s.) These props also externalize the subtextual dynamics, trapping characters together or becoming the focus of their conflict. In one exuberant fantasy moment, Anya and Victor suddenly take off in the freedom of their imaginations, dancing blithely over suitcase-corridor walls as if they weren't there at all.

Poor George is an improbable love object – a laughably childlike philanderer whose superficial successes with women and work are rapidly being overtaken by his deep-seated talent for deception and failure. Not even his puerile suicide attempt is a success, except as black comedy. The women are much more sympathetically created. Brenda is touchingly (if incomprehensibly) loyal, clinging to the dream of real children George will never give her. Anya Rumkowski is the reluctant exotic (at least, she is exotic in George's white-bread mind). Rootless and longing for security, she is tired of living "out of a suitcase. Always moving. Always a different bed."

The moment when Brenda unmasks Anya, letting her know that her affair with George is no longer a secret, is wonderfully understated and exact. Speaking of George's coming disgrace, which she has just discovered, Brenda says:

BRENDA Did he mention it to you?
ANYA Why would he?
BRENDA Sometimes he talks in his sleep.
Both women look at each other, and then out the window.

Though their lives are not much changed at the end of the play, the women in *Derailed* are clearly survivors. The final beats are wonderfully ironic, in a tragicomic vein. Together Brenda and Anya tear up the (almost identical) suicide notes George has left them, and exit separately toward futures that may not be bright, but at least contain far fewer illusions. As for George, with all his lies laid bare, his attempt to hang himself is totally inept, and he is finally reduced to stuffing the loose end of his rope into his suitcase and shambling off with the noose still dangling around his neck. We move from sympathy at the fate of the women to laughter at the dismal incompetence of the man. And then Victor shouts "All aboard," and life's mad train ride starts all over again.

Skip Shand

l to r: Rena Polley, David Fraser, Blair Williams, Catherine Hayos.
Photo by Rob Gray.

Derailed was first workshopped by Stiletto Theatre Company at the Fringe of Toronto Festival in May 1994. It premiered at the Factory Studio Theatre in March 1995, with the following cast:

VICTOR	David Fraser
BRENDA	Catherine Hayos
ANYA	Rena Polley
GEORGE	Blair Williams

Written by Emil Sher
Created by Catherine Hayos and Rena Polley
Produced by Stiletto Theatre Company
Directed by Jim Warren

Stage Managed by Dina Wendler
Set, Props and Costumes by Julie Fox
Lighting Designed by Glenn Davidson
Train Sound Effects by John Roby

Production Notes

Derailed plays on three levels. The first level is the narrative of the play, where a love triangle disintegrates on a train journey. The second level explores the physical and clowning element in the script. The third level is a series of stylized vignettes interspersed throughout the piece. These vignettes—relying on music and movement—are the unspoken desires and dreams of the individuals.

All four characters remain on stage at all times. When a character exits he or she creates a corridor with the suitcases. The suitcases also turn into other elements in the fantasy vignettes. The setting and mood of *Derailed* is pure 1950s.

A Note to the Reader

Please keep in mind that physical theatre, clowning, music and rhythm work are integral elements of *Derailed*. The written words are but a part of the narrative, as the physical aspects of the show contribute greatly to character development and storyline. Movement scenes are described in as much detail as possible.

DERAILED
by Emil Sher

Suitcases are stacked at the apex of the train tracks upstage centre. Two trunks are balanced on a wood platform downstage. One light is beaming along the tracks.

VICTOR, the conductor, slowly walks down the tracks with a stopwatch in his hand counting down the seconds. He snaps the watch closed.

VICTOR All aboard! Last call! Watch your step. Watch your luggage. All aboard.

He begins to set up the train compartment arranging first the trunks as compartment seats. VICTOR exits upstage.

BRENDA enters with music playing, head in purse, looking through the purse, then pulls out a shoe. She spits on the shoe and urgently begins polishing. The shoe takes on a dance as she ends up chasing it to complete the polishing. She jumps over the tracks and continues polishing.

VICTOR enters again and continues to set up the train using the suitcases to define the corridors.

All aboard! Last call! Once we roll, we won't look back. This train runs on time. If you're not satisfied, we'll refund the scenery. All aboard!

VICTOR exits upstage. ANYA enters, adding figures on a large adding machine in a business-like manner. Her leg begins to wander out from her body. She quickly pulls herself together by pulling her leg sharply back in place. This continues and the pace accelerates until the force of this action pulls her up and over the tracks, where she continues adding figures.

VICTOR enters with suitcases, placing them along the tracks.

All aboard! Women and children first. Washrooms in the rear. We still can't find the engineer. Have no fear, 'cause Victor's here. All aboard!

VICTOR exits upstage. GEORGE enters with a kitchen blender in his hand. His pockets are stuffed with shredded paper. He furtively looks around and then takes the paper out of his pockets and places it in the blender. He turns the blender on.

VICTOR enters with more suitcases. GEORGE, BRENDA and ANYA start running on the spot as they continue their actions throughout VICTOR's next speech.

All aboard! Last call! Tickets ready. No standing in the aisles. No running between cars. No singing on the roof. Last call! All aboard!

VICTOR exits. GEORGE, BRENDA and ANYA stop. Simultaneously, they each discover a shredded paper: BRENDA discovers one in the shoe she is holding, ANYA finds one in her dress and GEORGE pulls one from the blender. All three look at it and drop it on the floor. They look out at the audience.

Blackout. Sound of train. Lights up on the train compartment.

BRENDA and GEORGE have just arrived and are settling in. The opening of this scene is a rhythmic interchange between BRENDA and GEORGE. BRENDA stakes out their territory by setting out their belongings as GEORGE scours a newspaper.

VICTOR is seated in the corner on a suitcase reading a book.

BRENDA I brought slippers. *(GEORGE turns a page.)* Ear plugs. Clippers. *(sprays air freshener)* Pine.

GEORGE Fine.

BRENDA New blades. Faberge. Lucky Strike.

GEORGE Right.

BRENDA Tissues. Mints. *Life.*

GEORGE Christ! *(quickly folds newspaper and puts it away)*

BRENDA Are you mentioned in the paper?

GEORGE No.

BRENDA Not yet. You will be. It's an important award, sweetheart. A special occasion. *(takes out her camera and begins to take pictures of GEORGE)*

GEORGE It's not the Nobel Prize. And I don't want my picture taken. You don't need a picture. I'm right here. In the flesh.

BRENDA I brought my red dress. Heads will turn. Tongues will wag.

GEORGE Let's not talk about the awards. There will be plenty of time for that. Now it's just you and me.

BRENDA I want to cover every inch of your body. Then put it back together again, piece by piece. *(continues to snap pictures)*

GEORGE Brenda, please.

BRENDA Train trips are so romantic.

GEORGE I'm all yours. *(takes the camera and puts it away, kneels down in front of BRENDA)* No steering. *(reaches for BRENDA seductively and then unlocks one of the latches on the trunk)*

BRENDA No maps.

GEORGE No traffic. *(unlocks the other latch on trunk)*

BRENDA You can keep your eyes on me instead of the road.

GEORGE We can take in the scenery together.

GEORGE picks up BRENDA seductively while trying to hide the newspaper in the trunk. BRENDA is straddling GEORGE and kissing him. GEORGE gets the newspaper in the trunk when ANYA enters. GEORGE's back is to the entrance. BRENDA sees ANYA.

GEORGE Ow! *(hits finger on trunk)*

ANYA Oh!

BRENDA Oh…

ANYA exits to corridor. Throughout the next scene she pulls out her makeup mirror and checks out her body from top to bottom before getting the conductor.

GEORGE, still on his knees, pulls out his hand and sucks on his finger.

GEORGE Who was that?

BRENDA I don't know. A woman. How's your / finger?

GEORGE / What woman? Who?

BRENDA I don't know. Show me your finger.

GEORGE *(obvious pain)* My finger's fine.

BRENDA I have something for it.

GEORGE I don't want anything.

BRENDA A first aid travel kit.

GEORGE I don't need first aid.

BRENDA You never know what can happen on a trip. *(opens kit)* Band aids. Band aids. Band aids. Would a band aid help?

GEORGE I'm fine.

BRENDA Let me see it.

GEORGE No.

BRENDA A quick look.

GEORGE No.

BRENDA I'll be careful.

GEORGE No.

BRENDA I won't touch it.

GEORGE No.

BRENDA I hate to see you in pain.

GEORGE I'm not.

BRENDA You don't look well.

GEORGE I am.

BRENDA is on her knees, kissing GEORGE's finger. ANYA returns with VICTOR, who is carrying her ticket. They see BRENDA and GEORGE and hesitate for a moment before

ANYA enters the compartment. GEORGE tries to block her entrance. Their physical encounter inadvertently turns into a dance.

VICTOR Sorry no dancing in the compartment.

GEORGE This car is full.

VICTOR I beg your pardon?

ANYA I was expecting…

VICTOR …the very best. You'll be happy here.

BRENDA We weren't expecting…

GEORGE We're full. Not an inch to spare.

VICTOR This passenger has a ticket.

GEORGE Victor, someone has made a mistake. You'll take care of it. *(He tips him.)*

VICTOR I don't book seats, Mr. Cummings. I seat passengers.

BRENDA My husband…

VICTOR …knows the rules.

BRENDA …needs ice.

GEORGE I am not a child. I don't need ice.

ANYA This is a very nice compartment. Thank you. *(gives VICTOR a tip and takes GEORGE's seat)*

GEORGE That's my seat.

VICTOR By journey's end, you'll all be friends. That's the beautiful thing about train travel. *(takes ANYA's ticket)* Miss Raum…

ANYA Rumkowski.

VICTOR I would have gotten it. I've seen worse. Miss Rumkowski, meet Mr. and Mrs. Cummings.

BRENDA/ ANYA/ GEORGE Hello/Hello/Hello.

VICTOR I'll get you your ice.

VICTOR exits.

They watch VICTOR exit. They turn, face each other, inhale, smile, and turn to look out the window. Each drops the smile on their face and reveals what they are really thinking.

Train sound and blackout as they enter a tunnel.

BRENDA Oh!

ANYA Ah!

GEORGE Ow!

Lights up. GEORGE has fallen on top of ANYA. ANYA's hat and purse have fallen to the ground.

ANYA Get off.

GEORGE Excuse me.

BRENDA Are you all right?

ANYA *(to GEORGE)* Give me my hat.

BRENDA *(picks up purse)* I'm sorry.

ANYA It happens.

Pause.

BRENDA This is my husband, George. I'm Brenda.

ANYA Anya Rumkowski.

BRENDA Rumkowski isn't a very common name.

ANYA In this country.

BRENDA George is off to accept an award.

ANYA Then I'm not interrupting a romantic weekend.

BRENDA Oh, no. We're married. Parkview Children's Hospital is honouring my husband. He's donated a lot of money.

GEORGE I'm accepting the award on the company's behalf, that's all.

BRENDA Sweetheart, you are the company.

GEORGE The award isn't in my name.

BRENDA It should be. *(pause)* Where are you going?

ANYA My lover sent me this ticket. He's going to meet me on the train at some point.

BRENDA How mysterious.

ANYA I'm not sure where he's taking me.

BRENDA You travel blindly?

ANYA It's exciting not to know where you're going.

BRENDA Isn't that romantic, George?

GEORGE Only if you like mysteries.

BRENDA George loves to tease me. Sweetheart, did you bring any chocolates?

GEORGE *(takes out a small box from his jacket)* Your favourite.

BRENDA These are no good.

GEORGE I bought them today.

BRENDA This is the wrong brand.

GEORGE They didn't have Durocher chocolates.

BRENDA Durocher is the only kind I can eat.

GEORGE Try one.

BRENDA shakes her head.

GEORGE Just one.

BRENDA shakes her head again. GEORGE tries to get her to eat one in ways that are very playful and sexual.

BRENDA Would you like one?

ANYA No thank you. Excuse me.

ANYA takes a cigarette case out of her purse and exits down a corridor.

BRENDA She looks familiar.

GEORGE I've never seen her before.

BRENDA I have. Somewhere.

GEORGE steps out.

BRENDA Where are you going?

GEORGE The washroom. My hand.

BRENDA The conductor is bringing ice.

GEORGE I don't need the conductor.

ANYA is in the corridor and takes out a cigarette. GEORGE is in a corridor on the other side of the compartment. BRENDA is tidying the compartment, resisting the temptation to look through ANYA's purse. VICTOR walks in, holding a compress.

VICTOR Where's the patient?

BRENDA Patient, he's not.

VICTOR A nervous traveller.

BRENDA I've never seen him like this. He seems preoccupied.

VICTOR Your husband's a busy man.

BRENDA Very busy. He's a company man, only he never keeps me company.

VICTOR You're lucky to have him. The other ones, they always seem to forget the wives they've left behind. Not him. Always buying you gifts. Classy boxes. Your husband has excellent taste. I can't imagine how much he paid for those pearl earrings.

BRENDA *(pause)* Neither can I.

VICTOR He's always thinking of you.

BRENDA He's a wonderful provider. We have a brand new washer and dryer.

VICTOR Congratulations.

GEORGE crouches past the compartment to get to ANYA on the other side. He comes up behind her.

GEORGE Anya.

ANYA Rumkowski.

GEORGE Anya Rumkowski.

ANYA Yes.

The train jostles. With each train jostle, all the characters, with the exception of VICTOR, are slightly thrown off balance and into each other. ANYA falls into GEORGE and gently pushes him away as she puts out her cigarette. BRENDA falls into VICTOR and they separate, feeling embarrassed.

BRENDA You're melting. *(beat)* The ice in your hand.

VICTOR sees the ice in his hand has begun to melt.

BRENDA Here. *(dries his hand with a tissue)*

VICTOR I guess he won't be needing this.

BRENDA He's very stubborn. But successful.

VICTOR I'm neither.

BRENDA I'm sorry.

VICTOR I'm satisfied.

Train jostle. BRENDA falls into VICTOR and again they separate. VICTOR exits and goes back to reading his book. BRENDA begins eating chocolates. ANYA and GEORGE fall into each other. They are now side by side in a narrow corridor.

ANYA What are you doing to me?

GEORGE I'm sorry. There was a mistake. You were supposed to be in another compartment.

ANYA This wasn't a mistake. I know your mistakes. What are you up to?

GEORGE I'm taking you on to New York.

ANYA With your wife?

GEORGE Brenda insisted on coming for the awards ceremony. I'm sending her home right after.

ANYA Don't feed me your lies, George. *(She picks up a suitcase and places it further down the corridor.)* I'll grow fat.

GEORGE *(follows her)* I'm sending her home. That's the truth.

ANYA What did you tell her?

GEORGE She's expecting a weekend in Montreal.

ANYA That's why she can't keep her hands off you. You tell her what she wants to hear. *(picks up the suitcase and slithers past GEORGE)*

GEORGE Come to New York with me. The Plaza. The same room.

ANYA You're wanted here by the police.

ANYA drops the suitcase, blocking GEORGE's exit, and walks past the compartment. She stops and looks in at BRENDA, looks back at GEORGE and crosses to the other side.

GEORGE *(whispering across compartment)* What do you mean? *(covers his face and sneaks by the compartment)* What do you mean?

ANYA The police. They've come to the office asking questions.

GEORGE What kind of questions?

ANYA Questions about you.

GEORGE Questions about us.

ANYA Questions only about you.

GEORGE Not you?

ANYA I'm part of the answer. What are you going to do?

GEORGE I have a plan.

ANYA Don't point the finger at me.

GEORGE Calm down. You're becoming hysterical.

ANYA Don't! I'm not your wife. *(throws suitcase at GEORGE)*

GEORGE If the bottom gives out, we both sink. You need me.

ANYA I need this job.

She grabs handle of suitcase and they struggle over it during the next few lines.

GEORGE I've given you everything you need. Your job couldn't pay for half of what you've got.

ANYA If I lose my job, I have to start over. From the beginning. I'm tired of always beginning.

GEORGE If we stay, we get caught. What did the police ask you?

ANYA I told you. *(lets go of suitcase)* Questions.

GEORGE What did you tell them? *(bangs suitcase to the floor)*

ANYA They didn't trust me. No one trusts people with names they can't pronounce. *(picks up suitcase and moves)*

GEORGE What did you say?! *(follows her)*

ANYA You need me. *(lifts leg and places it on suitcase)*

GEORGE I always have. *(caresses ANYA's leg and lifts it off suitcase)*

ANYA What am I supposed to do the rest of the trip? Stare at your wife?

GEORGE You're on a train. Soak up the scenery.

ANYA I hate train travel.

GEORGE Pretend you're somewhere else. Pretend you're with me.

Music – fantasy vignette. GEORGE draws ANYA into his arms. Throughout this sequence GEORGE and ANYA slowly pick up a suitcase each and begin dancing, wedged between the two suitcases.

ANYA I am with you.

GEORGE We're on a mountain. Having a picnic. Fresh bread. Cold wine. A dozen cheeses. I'm feeding you tangerines.

ANYA I love the smell of tangerines.

GEORGE You open your mouth like a bird.

ANYA You purr like a cat.

GEORGE I put the tangerine on your tongue.

ANYA I plant my lips on your neck.

GEORGE The sun is bright.

ANYA The wind is soft.

GEORGE Your eyes are closed.

ANYA Your hands are cupped.

GEORGE Your waist is good to hold.

On the other side of the train, BRENDA's longing for a child is manifested in a clowning piece where she takes a baby bundle out of a suitcase and begins to rock it. VICTOR appears from behind a suitcase and admires the baby bundle. As VICTOR disappears, BRENDA pulls back the baby blanket to discover one of GEORGE's shoes. She spits on the shoe and begins to polish it. Vignette ends.

BRENDA brings the shoe back to the compartment. This shoe matches the shoe from the opening scene of the play.

VICTOR interrupts GEORGE and ANYA.

VICTOR Any scars?

GEORGE What?

VICTOR Your hand.

GEORGE I'm fine.

VICTOR Doesn't look good from here.

ANYA We work together.

VICTOR I see.

GEORGE You're not a doctor. *(He takes out a bill and tips VICTOR.)*

VICTOR Cuts, bruises, babies. I've seen it all.

ANYA walks away.

GEORGE Look at that. What would you do to get your hands on her?

VICTOR I keep my hands to myself. That's why God gave us pockets.

Train jostle. ANYA enters the compartment and sees BRENDA holding a small glass dome that fills with snow when shaken. BRENDA has taken it out of ANYA's purse. It is a winter scene of children playing in front of a storybook house.

ANYA Do you like it?

BRENDA I'm sorry. I didn't mean to–

ANYA Please.

BRENDA hesitates, then shakes it. They silently watch the snow fall.

Peaceful. I take it with me whenever I travel.

BRENDA A good luck charm.

ANYA Calm. It makes me feel calm.

BRENDA Where did you get it?

ANYA A gift.

BRENDA I had one just like it.

ANYA As a child?

BRENDA George gave it to me.

ANYA Oh...

BRENDA For our first wedding anniversary.

ANYA How nice.

BRENDA It broke. I was cleaning it. It slipped out of my hand and fell to the floor. The water trickled out, carrying bits of snow and little children and the grey smoke that was glued to the chimney.

ANYA I love the chimney smoke.

BRENDA The children drowned. That's what it looked like. Like they'd drowned. I threw it out. George didn't notice it was gone. Not at first.

ANYA You can replace it.

BRENDA I didn't want another one. I'd always worry it would break. *(hands it back to ANYA)*

Train jostle. Throughout this next segment simultaneous action occurs in the corridor between GEORGE and VICTOR and in the compartment between BRENDA and ANYA. While two of the characters are engaged in conversation the other two characters are involved in physical actions that demonstrate their unspoken desires. Cut to corridor.

GEORGE How deep are those pockets God gave you?

VICTOR Deep enough.

GEORGE My pockets are deeper.

VICTOR Good for you.

GEORGE I give away more money than some people earn.

VICTOR That's very generous of you.

GEORGE I can't afford not to be generous. Charity is good for business.

VICTOR Charity begins at home.

Train jostle. Cut to compartment. During this scene GEORGE and VICTOR play a game of thumb wrestling. The snow dome is thrown in the air during the jostle and ANYA catches it.

BRENDA Do you mind if I take your picture?

ANYA I don't like getting my picture taken.

BRENDA Just one.

ANYA No. Thank you. I never appear the way I think I look.

BRENDA Someone as pretty as you?

ANYA You're very kind.

BRENDA I'd pay to have a complexion like yours.

ANYA I pay to have a complexion like mine.

Train jostle – corridor. During this scene BRENDA and ANYA check out the make and fabric of each other's dress and accessories to the point where they look like they are sniffing each other.

GEORGE You spend too much time on trains. You have to get out more often.

VICTOR Trains lead you into tunnels, not temptation.

GEORGE Miss Anya Rumkowski doesn't tempt you? You wouldn't give a week's salary to spend one night with her? Happiness is a two-car garage. Why have one woman when you can have two?

VICTOR Honesty.

GEORGE And you're an honest man.

VICTOR Occasionally.

GEORGE A regular Boy Scout. I'm not surprised.

Train jostle – compartment. During this scene GEORGE and VICTOR have moved up to a game of hand slapping.

ANYA That's a lovely outfit you're wearing. Is it a Dior?

BRENDA If only. It's just a little something I picked up in New York.

ANYA How often do you go to New York?

BRENDA I've only been there once.

ANYA Pleasant memories?

BRENDA Very. Does it show? It was like meeting him again for the first time. It's a husband and wife thing.

ANYA I can imagine. Where did you stay?

BRENDA The Plaza. George reserved a beautiful suite. Champagne, long stem roses. He really outdid himself.

ANYA The Plaza is a very romantic hotel, isn't it?

BRENDA Perfect. Where do you think he's taking you?

ANYA Who?

BRENDA Your mystery man.

ANYA Oh, I think we're going to New York.

Train jostle – corridor. During this scene, ANYA falls behind BRENDA and slowly puts her fingers through BRENDA's hair, ruining her hat and her coiffed hairstyle.

GEORGE I was a Boy Scout you know. Wanna know the best knot I ever made? It was at the end of a long rope hanging from a tree. I knotted the end so you could stand on it and swing. Ever swing on a rope?

VICTOR It's been years.

GEORGE Back and forth. Back and forth. That swing took me places I'd never been.

Train jostle – compartment. During this scene GEORGE and VICTOR's physical competition escalates to a game of arm wrestling.

ANYA How long have you been married?

BRENDA Seven years.

ANYA Any children?

BRENDA Not yet.

ANYA Seven years and no children? It's best to wait until you're ready.

BRENDA I am.

Train jostle – corridor. During this scene BRENDA reaches for a pair of scissors, crosses to ANYA, removes her hat, cuts a handful of hair and then replaces the hat on ANYA's head.

GEORGE How well do you know this route?

VICTOR Like the back of my hand.

GEORGE There's this tree.

VICTOR Lots of trees.

GEORGE I'm talking about a very specific tree. You can't miss it. This tree is a landmark.

VICTOR Depends on who's looking.

GEORGE There's a large green house with a weather vane on top. Right by the water tower. I grew up in that house.

VICTOR You're planning a visit.

GEORGE Near the house is a tree. A large, oak tree. Huge. Magnificent. You must have passed that tree a thousand times.

VICTOR I do remember seeing it.

GEORGE Then you know it. Keep your eyes open. *(tips VICTOR)*

Train jostle – compartment.

BRENDA Surely you must want to settle down. Make roots.

ANYA I was never one to plant roots.

BRENDA A husband and home could give you the security you need. An attractive woman like you could pick and choose.

ANYA I choose not to pick.

BRENDA What about the gentleman who sent you your ticket?

ANYA If I wasn't his lover, I'd be doing his laundry.

BRENDA Someone has to do the laundry.

ANYA Yes, I know. They're called wives.

During this scene GEORGE and VICTOR walk down the corridor. VICTOR pulls out two drinks and gives them to GEORGE. Train jostle. GEORGE enters compartment carrying drinks. The women lean back to avoid the spill.

BRENDA We were just talking about you.

GEORGE What were you saying?

ANYA Your wife suggested I do laundry more often.

BRENDA That's not what I said.

ANYA That's what I heard.

GEORGE I brought drinks for everyone.

BRENDA What did you bring?

GEORGE Cokes all around. *(hands drinks out)*

BRENDA *(peers into glass)* You've made a mistake.

GEORGE You love Coke.

BRENDA You forgot the ice. I can't drink it without ice.

GEORGE It's ice cold.

BRENDA That's not the same thing.

GEORGE I'll order a drink with ice in the dining car. We have a table with a beautiful view.

BRENDA Would you like to join us?

ANYA You're very kind, but I think I'll wait.

BRENDA Oh, I don't want you eating alone. It's always nicer to stare at a face than a plate. Come with us.

GEORGE We really should get going.

BRENDA What's the hurry?

GEORGE You're missing some great scenery. You can take a picture.

BRENDA I want to take a picture of you and Anya. So we'll remember this trip.

ANYA I can take a picture of the two of you.

BRENDA That's no fun. We know each other.

GEORGE calls to VICTOR in the corridor.

GEORGE I need ice.

VICTOR Again?

GEORGE For this drink.

VICTOR All right. I thought you folks might want a copy of today's paper.

GEORGE grabs the newspaper out of VICTOR's hand. During the following dialogue whoever is speaking grabs the paper.

GEORGE I'll take that.

VICTOR That's meant to be shared.

GEORGE I want to read it first.

VICTOR I can get you another.

GEORGE That won't be necessary.

ANYA I'd like one.

GEORGE No!

BRENDA George...

GEORGE She can borrow mine.

BRENDA She can have her own.

GEORGE She doesn't have to. One paper is all we need.

BRENDA You're not being reasonable.

VICTOR stops the game by grabbing the paper.

VICTOR Surely we can come to a civilized agreement.

GEORGE I've agreed to share the newspaper.

VICTOR You can't read it all at once. What is it you want to read first?

GEORGE Business.

VICTOR Well then, why not share the other sections. *(hands out sections of the paper to everyone)*

VICTOR There now. That wasn't so hard, was it? I'll go get your ice.

BRENDA and ANYA browse through the paper. GEORGE tears an article out of his section.

BRENDA What are you doing? *(pause)* It's about the award, isn't it?

GEORGE Yes.

BRENDA Let me see it.

GEORGE No.

BRENDA What did they say?

GEORGE It's embarrassing.

BRENDA Read it out loud.

GEORGE shreds the article into tiny strips.

I don't understand you. I'm proud of what you've done.

GEORGE I haven't done anything.

Music – fantasy vignette. GEORGE exits and goes to the end of the corridor. VICTOR is beside GEORGE, reading the article about him in the newspaper. VICTOR rips out the article and puts it in his pocket. GEORGE grabs the paper and puts it in a suitcase. BRENDA and ANYA tear an incriminating article from their respective newspapers. ANYA presents the article to GEORGE in the corridor. He grabs the paper, puts it in his mouth and begins a tango with ANYA. He dances her into a trunk and closes it. He meets BRENDA in the corridor who gives him the article she tore out of the newspaper. GEORGE lifts BRENDA up, twirls and throws her into another trunk, and closes it.

Vignette ends. GEORGE meets VICTOR in the corridor.

Tell me something, Victor. What games did you play as a kid?

VICTOR I was never a kid.

GEORGE You were born a conductor?

VICTOR I had to grow up quickly.

GEORGE You must have played some games.

VICTOR Some.

GEORGE Games with balls? *(bounces a ball to VICTOR)*

VICTOR Sometimes.

GEORGE How much would you pay for a ball if you were a kid?

VICTOR I'm not a kid. *(bounces ball back to GEORGE)*

GEORGE More than a nickel?

VICTOR Depends on the ball.

GEORGE Depends on the kid. Kids have changed, Victor.

VICTOR Kids are kids.

GEORGE Times have changed. There's money out there, Victor. Kids with money. *(throws ball to VICTOR)*

VICTOR Kids don't make money. *(throws ball back to GEORGE)*

GEORGE Kids make choices. They want or they don't want. I can make them want. You like kids?

VICTOR Some.

GEORGE I love kids. Kids are going to make me rich. Know what success feels like? Here, feel this. *(holds ball in VICTOR's hand)* Squeeze it. That's the feel of success.

VICTOR It's a ball.

GEORGE It's a campaign. It's a billboard. It's a television commercial. I'll package this ball so that every kid in the country wants one for his very own. What do you think of that?

VICTOR It's still a ball.

GEORGE It's not a ball! Look, it has a "B" on it.

VICTOR "B" for ball.

GEORGE That's right. Simple, isn't it?

VICTOR Very.

GEORGE Imagine every kid on the block has a ball with a "B" on it except you. How would that make you feel? I don't give people what they want. I give them what they think they want.

VICTOR And you think they want a ball with a "B" on it.

GEORGE Like everyone else, they want to belong. That's what we're selling. The opportunity to belong. *(beat)* Buy a ball and belong.

VICTOR Catchy slogan.

GEORGE Just made it up. Know what *slogan* means?

VICTOR Money.

GEORGE A war cry. *(bounces ball on VICTOR's chest)* A battle for your mind. There are a million choices out there. How're you going to choose? You can't. I point the way to the needs you never knew you really needed.

VICTOR If I never knew I needed them, how can they be needs?

GEORGE We know what we're doing, Victor, and we do it well. So well we're giving money away, for God's sake. To a children's hospital. We're saving children's lives. When was the last time you saved a child's life?

VICTOR Hasn't happened yet.

GEORGE I love kids.

GEORGE throws ball in air. VICTOR catches it. Blackout. Lights up on compartment. GEORGE is seated as BRENDA loops an assortment of ties around his neck. VICTOR is seated on a trunk down the corridor, squeezing the ball. He takes out the incriminating newspaper article and reads it.

What do you think of the name Edward?

BRENDA For a child?

GEORGE For me.

BRENDA What's wrong with George?

GEORGE I've always wanted a middle name.

BRENDA George is all you need.

GEORGE George Edward Cummings.

BRENDA What's wrong with what you have?

GEORGE What's wrong with wanting more?

BRENDA has tried a succession of ties. GEORGE suddenly rises. BRENDA pulls him back by pulling on the tie.

BRENDA I'm not finished.

GEORGE We can do it later.

BRENDA We'll be eating soon. In the dining car. I want you to look your best.

GEORGE I'll choose my own tie.

BRENDA I make better choices, George. You know that. You may wear the pants in the family, but I choose which ones.

BRENDA loops another tie around GEORGE's neck. The following exchange unfolds like a tug-of-war, as GEORGE struggles to walk away while BRENDA tries to reel him back.

GEORGE Later.

BRENDA Now.

GEORGE Later.

BRENDA Later will be too late.

GEORGE You're hurting me.

BRENDA You're hurting me. *(releases him)*

GEORGE What do you mean?

BRENDA You can't sit still anymore. Not with me. It makes me wonder.

GEORGE About what?

BRENDA That there's something wrong with me. That I've done something wrong. That I've done something to deserve this.

GEORGE You haven't done anything.

BRENDA Why can't you sit next to me for five minutes?

GEORGE I can. I have.

BRENDA Even when you're with me, you're not here.

GEORGE I keep your picture on my desk.

BRENDA You're drifting away. Smaller and smaller.

GEORGE And one in my wallet.

BRENDA Soon you'll be a dot in the distance.

GEORGE I'd like one for the car.

BRENDA I don't want a dot for a husband.

GEORGE How many husbands have pictures of their wives sitting on their dashboard?

BRENDA I don't want to sit on a dashboard, George. I want to sit next to you. I want you to sit next to me.

GEORGE finally sits down.

GEORGE I'm sitting.

BRENDA I miss you, George. Come home.

GEORGE We're going home. After the awards ceremony.

BRENDA realizes she's not getting through. She rises, chooses a final tie, then exits. She passes ANYA in the corridor. ANYA enters the compartment. GEORGE is inspecting the cuffs of his shirt.

What do you think of Edward?

ANYA Who's Edward?

GEORGE Edward may be me. I'm thinking of changing my name.

ANYA Why?

GEORGE To add a touch of class. Monogrammed initials would look good on my cuffs. What's your middle name?

ANYA I don't have one.

GEORGE Make one up. Natasha. Anya Natasha Rumkowski.

ANYA No thank you.

GEORGE To add a touch of mystery.

ANYA You said you don't like mysteries.

GEORGE I like you.

He pulls her towards him. ANYA avoids GEORGE's touch and crosses to the other side of the compartment.

ANYA I like watching men put on ties.

GEORGE I never liked ties.

ANYA Why wear them?

GEORGE I'm a business man. Business men wear ties. It's good for business.

ANYA What was in the paper? *(adjusts GEORGE's tie)*

GEORGE What paper?

ANYA The newspaper you tore into small pieces.

GEORGE What pieces?

ANYA George… *(tightens GEORGE's tie and chokes him – parallels tie scene with BRENDA)*

GEORGE It was nothing.

ANYA It was something. You tore something up.

GEORGE Yes.

ANYA Something you didn't want seen.

GEORGE Not yet.

ANYA When?

GEORGE remains awkwardly silent, takes out a small piece of paper from his pocket and hands it to ANYA.

GEORGE Read this.

ANYA What is it?

GEORGE Just read it.

ANYA As I walked out one evening
Walking down Bristol Street
The crowds upon the pavement
Were fields of harvest wheat

And down by the brimming river
I heard a lover sing
Under an arch of the railway:
"Love has no ending."[1]

GEORGE Do you like it?

ANYA Beautiful. I didn't know you wrote like this.

GEORGE A man can't write slogans all day.

ANYA How long did it take you to write?

GEORGE Not long.

ANYA What inspired you?

GEORGE It's something I've always wanted to do.

ANYA You should do more.

GEORGE You can't make money writing that. I wish…

[1] W.H. Auden, *As I Walked Out One Evening*

ANYA You wish...

GEORGE I wish you would read it again. *(tries to grab ANYA)*

ANYA Later.

GEORGE Just once.

ANYA Later.

GEORGE Now.

ANYA Later.

GEORGE One verse.

ANYA I want to read it to myself.

GEORGE It's meant to be shared.

ANYA With whom?

GEORGE With... with another.

ANYA Share it with me.

She hands the poem back to GEORGE for him to read. He doesn't take it.

You wrote it. Maybe you should have spent more time writing poems, and less time at the company.

GEORGE Why?

ANYA Maybe you wouldn't be in trouble.

GEORGE I'm not in trouble. I'm on a train. I know where I'm going. I know what I left behind. I know what I have to do.

ANYA What did the paper say?

GEORGE Lies. All lies.

ANYA Did they mention my name?

GEORGE I love your name.

ANYA I'm scared.

GEORGE You're safe.

ANYA A name can be a target. You don't know what it's like to live out of a suitcase. Always moving. Always a different bed. Friends. A permanent address. These were luxuries.

GEORGE Luxuries?

ANYA That's what I love about you, George. The life you've lived is the only life you've known. That must be very comforting.

GEORGE I haven't thought about it.

ANYA You haven't had to. You've never tasted uncertainty.

GEORGE And never will.

ANYA Our pasts are so different.

GEORGE The future is ours.

ANYA The future is my past, George.

GEORGE I don't understand.

ANYA And never will.

Blackout and train sounds as they enter a tunnel. Lights up: dining car.

GEORGE is seated on a suitcase; BRENDA and ANYA each sit on a trunk. Each has a plate and silverware on their laps. Using the sounds of eating (cutlery moved across a plate), BRENDA starts a rhythm that is slowly picked up by ANYA. GEORGE punctuates their sounds by sawing with his knife and fork on his plate. BRENDA and ANYA's rhythms merge while GEORGE's eating is off-rhythm and urgent. This builds in speed and sound until BRENDA speaks. During this scene VICTOR has set up his own dining area up in the corridor. He opens a lunch bucket and places a small table cloth on his lap. He takes out a boiled egg.

BRENDA Slow down, George. You'll choke on your food.

VICTOR rhythmically taps an egg with a spoon, GEORGE saws with his knife.

George, do you remember the gift you got me for our first anniversary?

GEORGE I've given you many anniversary gifts, dear.

BRENDA It was a glass ball filled with water. Children playing in front of a house. When you shook it, snow fell to the ground.

GEORGE Oh, yes. Falling snow.

BRENDA Anya has one just like it.

GEORGE Good for her.

BRENDA *(to ANYA)* Would you mind if I showed it to George? *(takes the ball out of ANYA's purse and hands it to GEORGE)* See?

GEORGE shakes it, absorbed by the scene despite himself. BRENDA and ANYA continue to eat.

I know where I've seen you before. At the company picnic.

ANYA It's a very big company.

BRENDA You wore an emerald dress. Emerald always makes me look pale.

ANYA You would look good in red.

ANYA and BRENDA wipe their forks on their knives as if they are sharpening their weapons.

BRENDA That's what I wore at the company picnic. When's the next one?

ANYA August.

BRENDA We'll have to sit together. The three of us.

ANYA Yes, we should.

Each slams her knife and fork on her plate.

GEORGE You named them.

BRENDA What?

GEORGE The children in the ball. You named them. Don't you remember? I came home early one day and found you in the living room, talking to yourself. Talking to this ball. You.... You were calling them in for dinner. *(imitating BRENDA)* "You've played outside long enough. Time to come in. Time for some hot chocolate." What were their names again?

BRENDA Grace, J.J. and Michael.

ANYA I named them, too. The children.

GEORGE I see.

ANYA What's wrong with naming them?

GEORGE Nothing. There's nothing wrong. I never said it was wrong. I always liked the name Grace.

BRENDA His mother's name was Grace. George was close to his mother.

GEORGE Brenda, please.

BRENDA When she died, he wilted.

GEORGE Brenda.

BRENDA He had the look of a lost child.

GEORGE I did not.

BRENDA You know that lost child look. Those bottomless eyes. It's heartbreaking.

GEORGE I wasn't lost.

ANYA Why apologize for loving your mother?

GEORGE I'm not apologizing.

ANYA We're always children. Until our parents die.

GEORGE I am not a child. I'm a busy man.

ANYA I think family is important.

BRENDA So do I.

GEORGE So do I.

BRENDA You've never been a family man.

GEORGE We don't have a family.

BRENDA George is married to his work.

ANYA A faithful worker.

BRENDA Very. Loyal to the company.

ANYA I know.

BRENDA I think it's important. Being faithful and loyal.

ANYA So do I.

GEORGE Excuse me. *(rises)*

BRENDA Where are you going?

GEORGE I have to rehearse my speech.

BRENDA We haven't had dessert yet. The meal isn't over until we've had dessert.

GEORGE I don't want dessert.

BRENDA It's your favourite.

GEORGE I'm not in the mood.

GEORGE exits. VICTOR packs up his dinner and begins to read.

BRENDA He loves apple pie.

ANYA Take a piece back to him.

BRENDA I couldn't. Too many crumbs.

ANYA We're always cleaning up after them.

BRENDA They're like children, the way they eat.

ANYA And the way they dress.

BRENDA Yes! No sense of colour or coordination.

ANYA Socks that don't match pants.

BRENDA Pants that don't match shirts.

ANYA Shirts that don't match ties.

BRENDA Ties that are too loud.

ANYA Too thin.

BRENDA Too wide.

ANYA Too bold.

BRENDA Too bland.

BRENDA I buy George all his ties.

ANYA He dresses very well.

BRENDA I'm worried about him. He hasn't been himself lately.

ANYA Pressure at work?

BRENDA You tell me.

GEORGE is in the corridor, writing in a tiny notebook.

Is George in trouble?

GEORGE rips a page out of the book.

ANYA Yes.

BRENDA Big trouble.

GEORGE rips another page out of the book.

ANYA Yes.

BRENDA I should speak to him.

ANYA Yes.

BRENDA Did he mention it to you?

ANYA Why would he?

BRENDA Sometimes he talks in his sleep.

Both women look at each other, and then out the window.

At least I have someone to wake up to every morning.

ANYA Your life is yours to live.

BRENDA I have freedom in routine.

ANYA I prefer the routine of freedom. *(turns to BRENDA)* I have empty nights. You have empty days.

BRENDA We're even.

Both women stand up. ANYA grabs BRENDA's plate.

ANYA What about the crumbs?

BRENDA I'll manage.

BRENDA takes the plates and exits looking for GEORGE. ANYA goes to her purse to get her cigarette container. She exits.

GEORGE is in the corridor and approaches VICTOR from behind to see what VICTOR is reading.

GEORGE "He swept her up in his brawny arms and carried her across the threshold."

VICTOR quickly closes book and puts it away.

GEORGE You'll let me know.

VICTOR About what?

GEORGE The tree. I don't want to miss it. Neither do the two ladies. They'll see something they've never seen before.

VICTOR You want to surprise them.

GEORGE A big surprise. It'll be a good feeling swinging again.

VICTOR And you can't get enough of good feelings, can you?

ANYA walks by the corridor looking for GEORGE. She sees him with VICTOR and turns around.

GEORGE See her? I had her, you know. On a train to New York. Back and forth. Back and forth. Guess how she likes it.

VICTOR That's no way to talk about her. How would she feel if she heard you talk that way?

VICTOR goes to the compartment to collect the dishes. GEORGE follows.

GEORGE She loves the way I talk.

VICTOR I was brought up to respect women.

GEORGE What do you call this?

Pulls book out of VICTOR's pocket. VICTOR tries to grab it back.

VICTOR That's... that's harmless. Those are just stories. Adventure stories. Women are safe. And saved. In good hands. No one gets hurt.

GEORGE You don't have to apologize, Victor. I know how these stories make you feel. They take you places you've never been.

At this point BRENDA and ANYA meet in the corridor. Each refuses to move. They take a step backwards, sideways and forwards together. They pause and ANYA flips BRENDA in the air until she is behind her. They instantly regain their composure and continue walking down the corridor in opposite directions.

I used to read them, too. When I was a young. It's a good feeling. And you can't get enough of those, can you?

VICTOR Not when the feeling's at someone else's expense.

GEORGE We all have a line we'll cross, Victor. A line that puts our feelings ahead of everyone else. Where's yours?

VICTOR pulls the incriminating article out of his pocket.

VICTOR I know what you've done.

GEORGE I haven't done anything.

VICTOR You've been accused of some nasty things.

GEORGE Are you threatening me, Victor?

VICTOR I only wanted you to know that I know.

GEORGE And now that you know, what will you do?

VICTOR I haven't decided.

GEORGE slides the book back into VICTOR's pocket. They both look at ANYA as she walks by the compartment.

GEORGE You shouldn't stare. It's rude.

VICTOR exits. GEORGE is alone in the compartment and takes one of the sheets of notebook paper out of his pocket. He kisses it and puts it into ANYA's purse. He takes the second sheet out of his pocket, kisses it and puts it into BRENDA's bag. BRENDA enters with a piece of pie.

BRENDA I brought you some pie.

GEORGE doesn't reply. BRENDA begins to feed him.

What can I do for you? There must be something I can do, something I can give you that no one else can.

GEORGE I never really learned to ask.

BRENDA I'll teach you.

GEORGE It's easier to take. *(opens mouth for more pie)*

BRENDA Give and take. We're supposed to be here for each other.

GEORGE I'm here.

BRENDA Tell each other things we wouldn't tell anyone else. *(puts the pie down)*

GEORGE I'm listening.

BRENDA I'm listening, waiting to hear whatever it is you want to tell me.

GEORGE I tell you everything.

BRENDA You tell me nothing! We can fix what's broken. Tell me and I'll do it.

GEORGE I told you all there is to know.

BRENDA I know you're in trouble.

GEORGE I don't want to burden you.

BRENDA Being kept in the dark is more of a burden.

GEORGE Sometimes it's safer in the dark.

BRENDA What can I do for you that I haven't done? *(spits on his shoe and begins to polish it)* I'll try anything. I'll do anything. Tell me. Tell me what you've done, and I'll show you what I'll do. Show and tell.

GEORGE We're too old for show-and-tell.

BRENDA Give me something, George

GEORGE I've given you everything you've always wanted.

BRENDA A morsel…

GEORGE A washer…

BRENDA A tiny bit of yourself.

GEORGE A dryer.

BRENDA Let me love you.

GEORGE What do you want?

BRENDA The truth.

GEORGE The truth…. The truth is everything will turn out for the best. You're just tired.

GEORGE climbs into BRENDA's arms like a child and lays his head on her shoulder.

BRENDA Rumkowski. I didn't think you had it in you. What would they say at your golf club?

ANYA enters. BRENDA is rocking GEORGE, asleep in her arms.

Sshhh!

ANYA Is he sick?

BRENDA You wouldn't understand when he gets like this. You think you have to be naked to be intimate.

ANYA Some water?

BRENDA He's tired, not thirsty.

ANYA I meant for you.

BRENDA No, thank you.

ANYA puts her cigarette case back in her purse.

There's more than one reason to have a man in your arms.

ANYA They all want the same thing.

BRENDA There's satisfaction in doing something for others. You wouldn't understand that. I'd rather be wanted than desired.

ANYA I want to be desired.

BRENDA So do I. But not at any cost.

ANYA I have nothing to lose. *(starts to leave)*

BRENDA Would you like to rock him? You can if you like. He wouldn't notice the difference.

ANYA No. Thank you.

BRENDA You've never rocked him, have you?

ANYA He never asked.

BRENDA I'd like to be rocked. A train is the perfect place. Back and forth. Back and forth. Wouldn't you like to be rocked?

ANYA No.

BRENDA I'm not surprised. You don't trust anyone enough to let them rock you. That's what rocking really is. A sign of trust.

ANYA And you think George trusts you?

BRENDA You know he does. He trusts me because I trust myself.

ANYA Excuse me.

She exits. BRENDA continues to rock GEORGE. ANYA walks down the corridor and sees VICTOR sitting on a suitcase, looking out the window.

Train life can be lonely.

VICTOR I've been riding these trains for fifteen years.

ANYA Everyone's a stranger. You can't get close to anyone.

VICTOR I see a lot of the same faces. Regular passengers. It's like a family.

ANYA You don't understand. That's what I like: you can't get close to anyone. Do you have a family?

VICTOR rises.

VICTOR No, Ma'am.

ANYA A handsome man like you. Passengers must propose to you all the time.

VICTOR Hasn't happened yet.

ANYA I'm surprised. You seem like the faithful type. Women find that very attractive in a man. Are trains your whole life?

VICTOR They keep me occupied.

ANYA I never liked trains much.

VICTOR Sorry to hear that.

ANYA Trains leave no room for choice. A train goes where the tracks lie.

VICTOR I trust the tracks.

ANYA You're a very lucky man, Mr.…

VICTOR Stanton.

ANYA Mr. Stanton. You sleep well at night, don't you?

VICTOR Trains are like a cradle at night.

ANYA Night time is lonely, Mr. Stanton. That's when I feel most alone. When I'm lying next to someone.

VICTOR Excuse me.

VICTOR begins to walk away. ANYA and VICTOR touch bodies as he tries to pass her in the corridor. He walks away.

ANYA Wait.

Music. Fantasy vignette. VICTOR and ANYA stare at each other. VICTOR reaches out his hand and ANYA takes it. He pulls her in. She twirls into him and they grab each other by the waist and shoulders. They begin to dance as VICTOR lifts ANYA in the air. She kicks her legs up and spins in the air. She lands, begins to run and leaps on top of the trunks where BRENDA is still rocking GEORGE. She lands and VICTOR follows, hurdling over the trunks. They meet in each other's arms as VICTOR spins ANYA around. VICTOR picks up ANYA and carries her over the tracks, kicking an imaginary door open as though carrying her over a threshold. He puts her down on the tracks and they lean over trying to kiss one another. ANYA swoons and VICTOR catches her in his arms. He throws her into the air again and she lands arms outstretched.

Lights up. Fantasy vignette ends.

Do you have the time?

VICTOR Seven forty-two.

ANYA Thank you.

BRENDA slides out from under GEORGE, leaving him in the cradle position. She takes one of GEORGE's cigarettes and exits to the corridor. VICTOR passes her and stops to light her cigarette.

BRENDA You wear many different hats.

VICTOR You have to on a train.

BRENDA What happens when you step off the train?

VICTOR I take off my hat.

BRENDA smokes her cigarette. VICTOR returns to his adventure book and starts to rip out the pages.

ANYA enters the compartment. She looks at GEORGE and knocks him off balance. He awakens.

ANYA Pleasant dreams?

GEORGE You starred in all of them.

ANYA You always have a line, George. You're like a fisherman, reeling everyone in with your lines.

GEORGE You should see the one that got away.

ANYA I don't want another line. I want the truth.

GEORGE The truth is, I'm a wanted man. I'd rather be desired.

ANYA realizes GEORGE was awake during her conversation with BRENDA. She tries to slap GEORGE but he grabs her arm.

ANYA Why did you bring us together?

GEORGE I told you. After the awards, I'm sending her home. Then we're off to New York.

ANYA Don't lie to me.

GEORGE I've lied before.

ANYA What are you really up to?

GEORGE I'm leaving you.

VICTOR rips a page from his book.

ANYA I don't believe you.

GEORGE For good.

ANYA Back to Brenda?

GEORGE I'm leaving her, too.

VICTOR rips another page from his book.

ANYA You have nowhere to go.

GEORGE I'm going to start over. Reinvent myself.

ANYA I've been doing that all my life. It's tiring.

GEORGE You can help me.

ANYA You said you were leaving me.

GEORGE We'll both start over. We'll rise out of the ashes.

ANYA No one comes back from ashes.

GEORGE This is your chance to change your name. You once told me you wanted to be a Jane.

ANYA My name is Anya.

GEORGE Jane.

ANYA Anya.

GEORGE Richardson. Jane Richardson.

ANYA Rumkowski.

GEORGE I'll change my name to Roger.

ANYA Anya Rumkowski.

GEORGE Roger. Over and out.

ANYA George and Anya.

GEORGE Roger and Jane.

ANYA It won't last.

GEORGE We'll never get caught. Jane. Leave Anya behind.

ANYA I can't. I've tried.

GEORGE Try again.

Cut to corridor.

BRENDA Do you have high expectations, Mr. Stanton?

VICTOR Not anymore.

BRENDA Why's that?

VICTOR High expectations are a recipe for disaster.

BRENDA When does one start lowering one's expectations?

VICTOR When disappointment becomes your daily bread.

Throughout the preceding dialogue GEORGE and ANYA are doing a seductive dance of pushing and pulling. They end up on the trunk wrapped around each other. VICTOR approaches the compartment to let GEORGE know his tree is coming up. He sees GEORGE and ANYA together. BRENDA approaches; VICTOR struggles to pull her away and cover her eyes. They begin to struggle and realize they are in an embrace. They stop and separate. BRENDA takes VICTOR's hand and puts it to her breast. VICTOR pulls away.

Train sounds and blackout as they enter a tunnel. Lights up. ANYA is smoking frantically and GEORGE is sitting opposite her. BRENDA is standing at the entrance of the compartment. She enters, takes the can of pine air freshener out of her bag and begins to spray the compartment. ANYA puts out her cigarette.

ANYA I'm so sorry.

BRENDA It's not the smoke.

An awkward silence follows. ANYA and GEORGE both look away.

Now I know what you talk about when it's over. *(looks at ANYA)* I feel sorry for you.

GEORGE Don't embarrass yourself, Brenda.

BRENDA I'm not blushing, George.

GEORGE You need a drink.

BRENDA I need to know when you think it will end. You know me, George. I like to be organized. Once I know when it will end, we can make plans. I like to plan ahead.

GEORGE I've made plans.

BRENDA Do they include me?

GEORGE Of course.

ANYA gets up to leave.

BRENDA I'm so sorry. Was it the air freshener? Would you like a drink?

ANYA I need some fresh air. Excuse me.

ANYA exits. She goes to a corridor. Her leg begins to wander and she pulls it in to keep herself from falling apart.

BRENDA I know you're in trouble George. She told me.

GEORGE What does she know?

BRENDA You've broken the law.

GEORGE Don't worry. I won't get caught. *(goes over to BRENDA)*

BRENDA Don't touch me.

GEORGE I have a plan. A way out.

BRENDA Do what you have to do.

GEORGE paces back and forth, chewing the words he so desperately wants to say.

You're going to wear out your shoes, George.

GEORGE I want you to know…

BRENDA begins to rearrange her makeup bag.

BRENDA Know what?

GEORGE I know what you've done.

BRENDA I haven't done anything. You're the one who's in trouble, not me.

GEORGE That's not what I… I want…

BRENDA What is it you want, George?

GEORGE I don't want anything. I need…

BRENDA What is it you need? *(BRENDA begins to put on lipstick.)*

GEORGE You should know that.... That's a beautiful colour. On you. You look good in that colour. It makes your lips... I've never seen you wear that colour before.

BRENDA I've never worn it before. I bought it for the awards ceremony. A special occasion.

BRENDA begins to brush her hair. GEORGE goes over and very tentatively runs his fingers through her hair.

George, please. My hair.

GEORGE retreats, but takes a pair of makeup scissors with him.

GEORGE I know why I married you.

BRENDA I should hope so.

GEORGE I've always known. Sometimes you forget what you've always known.

BRENDA You're not making sense. You're making me nervous.

GEORGE takes a sheet of newspaper and folds it in half. He begins to cut out a shape with the scissors.

GEORGE We make choices. You and me. We chose each other.

BRENDA We fell in love, George.

GEORGE That's right. That's exactly right. We did.

BRENDA And then we married.

GEORGE Each other.

BRENDA Yes.

GEORGE That's what I mean. We're married. To each other. We exchanged vows.

BRENDA "'Til death do us part."

GEORGE If we part before then we've broken our vows.

BRENDA I haven't broken anything. Not in seven years. Except for that little glass ball with the children in it.

GEORGE unfolds the sheet of newspaper. By cutting a figure out of a folded sheet, he has created two figures. They are identical, linked at the hands, child-like. He holds them up, behind BRENDA, who's now standing at the compartment door.

GEORGE He loves her.

BRENDA Who does? What are you talking about?

GEORGE Nothing. No one. Never mind.

BRENDA exits. ANYA enters, holding GEORGE's poem in one hand.

ANYA *(drops note in front of GEORGE)* You didn't write it.

GEORGE I might have written it. If I'd had the time.

ANYA Even your words of love are lies.

GEORGE I borrowed the words. The feelings are mine.

ANYA begins to leave.

Wait! I have two…

ANYA You have to what, George?

GEORGE remains silent, then finally speaks.

GEORGE I have two poems.

ANYA That you borrowed?

GEORGE That I've written.

ANYA Let me see them.

GEORGE No. *(beat)* Not yet. *(beat)* Trust me.

ANYA How much longer?

GEORGE How much longer?

Train whistle as GEORGE steps into one of the trunks and closes the top over him.

Spotlights rise on BRENDA, ANYA and VICTOR as they speak. The three are in their own worlds. VICTOR enters and places a suitcase on the trunk. Throughout the following scene he opens the suitcase, changes his jacket for another identical one, closes the suitcase and repeats this action.

VICTOR How much longer? That's what I ask myself before every run. I shave and put on my uniform. I walk downstairs. Two pieces of dry toast, a cup of black coffee. I'm at the station by 7:42. I step onto the train. There's nothing like the silence of an empty train. I stroll down the aisle, touching the tops of the empty seats. No one sees me. No one tugs at my sleeve. No one knows my name.

BRENDA enters with two suitcases, tugs at them and puts them down. Throughout the scene, she sits on one suitcase and rocks the other one in her arms like a child. She then stands up again as if addressing her children.

BRENDA I don't know how much longer, sweetheart. As soon as we get there I'll buy you all some ice cream. Vanilla for Michael. Chocolate for Grace. Strawberry for J.J. I love you too, sweetheart. Michael, I wish you wouldn't do that. Because I'm your mother, that's why. Mommies make rules.

ANYA enters with a suitcase and puts it down.

ANYA I'm looking for a place to stay. Until I find something more permanent. First, a job. Then a house to come home to. Forgive me. I'm jumping ahead. A job is all I need. This suitcase is all I have. *(beat)* Rumkowski. Anya Rumkowski.

ANYA puts leg on suitcase, seductively puts it down, then draws her other leg back in.

VICTOR Then they climb on. The passengers. Like cattle. Like peasants. They push. They shove. They sweat. I can't believe what I've had to clean off this uniform.

ANYA Anya Rumkowski. *(lifts suitcase to her chest as if it is armour)*

BRENDA I'm going to count to ten, and when I get to ten, I want everyone to zip their mouths shut.

ANYA R-U-M...

BRENDA One...

VICTOR Shit.

BRENDA Two…

VICTOR Drool.

BRENDA Three…

VICTOR Gum. This jacket has seen it all.

ANYA K-O-W…

BRENDA Four.

VICTOR Booze.

BRENDA Five.

VICTOR Blood.

BRENDA Six.

VICTOR Lipstick. Every stain is another story.

ANYA S…

BRENDA Seven.

VICTOR Ashes.

ANYA K…

BRENDA Eight.

VICTOR Tears.

BRENDA Nine.

ANYA I.

VICTOR I can't come to work with day-old heartache running down my sleeve.

BRENDA Ten. I said ten. Ten, ten, ten!

ANYA Rumkowski.

VICTOR At night I set out a fresh uniform.

BRENDA Time for a story.

ANYA I don't know how long I'll be staying.

VICTOR Some evenings, I wish the night and the tracks would never end.

BRENDA We'll begin at the end, so we'll know how the story turns out.

ANYA I'll know when I've arrived.

VICTOR Sunrise leaves me cold.

ANYA I'll see the falling snow.

BRENDA And they lived happily ever after.

Blackout. Train sounds. Lights up slowly. GEORGE is holding the emergency handle and VICTOR enters. Throughout this scene BRENDA and ANYA are on opposite sides of the compartment, sitting on suitcases. They both begin to rock back and forth.

GEORGE We're almost at the tree.

VICTOR Almost.

GEORGE I need your help. I need you to stop the train.

VICTOR I can't do that.

GEORGE Yes, you can. When you see the tree, pull the cord. It's that simple.

VICTOR And you think I'm a simple man.

GEORGE You play by the rules and rules are meant to be broken.

VICTOR I go by the book.

GEORGE Then read between the lines. I need to get to the tree. What I plan to do is a gesture of love. But I can't do it without your help. Pull the cord when we get to the tree. Please.

VICTOR I don't have the power.

GEORGE You have more power than you realize. Feel the power, Victor. It's a good feeling.

VICTOR I'd get into trouble.

GEORGE What are you afraid of? It will be a good feeling. And you like good feelings, don't you?

As GEORGE releases his grip he places VICTOR's hand around the cord.

GEORGE Feel the power. Pull the cord.

VICTOR hesitates, then pulls the cord. Sound of a train screeching to a halt. Lights fade to half.

The two women fall off their suitcases and collapse to the floor. GEORGE stands there.

Train sound stops in mid-screech. VICTOR methodically turns over suitcases and creates the aftermath of a train grinding to an unexpected stop.

VICTOR I'll lie. I'll tell a simple lie. Simple and sweet. I've never lied before. It's so easy.

VICTOR throws ANYA over a trunk that is standing upright. BRENDA is thrown onto another trunk and a suitcase put on top of her. VICTOR then continues to turn over suitcases.

Train sound continues until it comes to a halt. Lights up to full. GEORGE is standing with a noose around his neck which he has pulled out of his suitcase. ANYA and BRENDA climb down from their trunks and discover the suicide notes in their bags. They read silently as GEORGE recites the contents of the notes.

GEORGE "Sweet Anya. As I walk down Bristol Street, I… I see you. I see you walking away. I call out your name. Anya. Anya Rumkowski. You keep walking. You never turn back. You're a dot in the distance. You were always ready to leave. One hand on your bag, one foot out the door. I was always looking forward. You were always looking back. Now look at me."

"Dearest Brenda. As I walk down the driveway, towards the front door, I see you. I see you through the window. You're setting the table for five. Mama Bear, three babies and a new Papa bear. I want you to be happy. Don't despair. Don't doubt my integritty. You made sacrifices. Now I understand what that means. I was always looking to take. You were always looking to give. Now look at me."

BRENDA and ANYA both look at GEORGE and then at one another. They look at the note and they rip it in half.

BRENDA He misspelled integrity.

ANYA He usually dictates.

They drop the shredded notes.

BRENDA Where will you go?

ANYA I'll follow the tracks and make my own way.

BRENDA What if you get lost?

ANYA I'll survive. I always do.

ANYA turns, takes the glass snow dome out of her purse and places it on one of the trunks. She exits upstage.

BRENDA I'm going home, George, but I can't go back.

BRENDA opens a suitcase and dumps a pile of GEORGE's shoes on the ground. She drops the suitcase, takes off her shoes and exits along the tracks.

GEORGE looks up, grabs the loose end of the rope and tries to throw it up in the air. Each time it falls limp on the floor. After three attempts he puts the loose end of the rope in his suitcase, snaps it shut, and exits with the noose still around his neck. Lights fade.

VICTOR enters, pumping a can of steam. He picks up BRENDA's shoes.

VICTOR All aboard. All aboard, please. Our apologies for the delay. A young girl was playing on the tracks. I saw her in the nick of time and did what I had to do. She's a bit shaken up, but safe. Keep your hands behind the windows. *(places shoes on trunk)* Watch your step. All aboard…

As VICTOR leaves, he finds the glass dome, takes it in his hands, shakes it and exits upstage.

Lights fade as a single beam of light shines down on the tracks.

The end.

Bellies, Knees and Ankles

by
W.A. Hamilton

W.A. Hamilton is founder of Theatre in Motion, a Sault Ste. Marie-based troupe created to give voice to northern Ontario stories. Other plays include: *MindLands* (Theatre in Motion, 1998; Theatre Aquarius, 2000; *The Canadian Theatre Review*, Winter 2002), *Hitchhiking to the End of the World* (Theatre in Motion, 2000) and *The Lions and the Lambs* (The Sault Theatre Workshop, 1999). *Bellies, Knees and Ankles* was written three pages at a time over the rehearsal process, with the original cast providing their own names and back stories prior to beginning writing. W.A. dedicates this publication to those original cast members with the hope that Lena, Maude, Karen and Emma will meet at the Talisman Café in many future productions.

INTRODUCTION TO *BELLIES, KNEES AND ANKLES*

Women talking to women. It seems so ordinary; the conversations just emerge, encircle, probe, embrace the similarities and analyze the differences. You don't even have to know each other – your femaleness and the desire to converse unite you. It can happen on a bus, in the grocery store, or as in *Bellies, Knees and Ankles* it happens mid-afternoon in the Talisman Café, a small Main Street "Good Eats" coffee shop that's become a trendy eatery.

It is here that we are introduced to four women, three of whom are middle-aged plus one in her early twenties. In her stage notes, playwright Wendy Hamilton reveals the etymology (that is, the derivations) of her characters' names. And during the course of the play the audience realizes that each name has been carefully selected to coincide with the respective personality.

First of all we encounter Maude ("Mighty battle maiden") the feisty, yet sensitive waitress at the Talisman engaged in a conversation with Jerry, the café cook whom we never meet. As she moves about the minimalist set, Maude is discussing the raging mood swings she is experiencing with her first pregnancy at age forty. In succession we are introduced to three female customers, Lena ("She who allures") who is a secretive woman alone, plus Emma ("Universal one") a twenty-two-year-old in search of her birth mother, and her supportive yet reserved mother, Karen ("Pure one") who frequented the Talisman in her youth.

We learn that everyone in the script has secrets. Maude, in the opening line of the play, alerts the audience to this when she states "I see things I don't want to see. I face things I don't want to face." Over the course of the play the audience discovers that each of these four women must face up to the fact that she is engaged in her own etymological quest – a search for or study of her personal self. Hamilton combines this theme with that natural female tendency to engage in the dance of conversation to exhibit her talent for creating meaningful dialogue and characters. One of the most powerful examples occurs during a three-way conversation between Maude, Karen and Emma; structured as a word association game, the individual responses revealing just how connected these women really are.

The complexity of each of the characters contrasts sharply with the minimalist set: three tables, five chairs, plus a workstation and stool. The fourth wall consists of an imaginary window and main door. This script plays out in "real time", so a prominently positioned clock is pre-set to mark 3PM at the top of the performance. Lena, Karen and Emma all enter from the house, passing through the audience – symbolizing, for me at least, that opportunities for conversation stem from and constantly surround us.

Hamilton's play affords us an opportunity to observe this customary practice of conversation and witness first-hand the extraordinary changes, discoveries and realizations that are possible when women talk with women.

Marian Doucette

Lorraine Mackie as Lena.
Photo courtesy of William Slingsby.

Bellies Knees and Ankles was first produced at Fringe Nord, Sudbury, Ontario, August 1997 in the Palladium Ballroom of the Ramada Inn with the following cast:

MAUDE	Susanne Myers
LENA	Lorraine Mackie
KAREN	Anna-Lee Potvin
EMMA	Sandra Iles

Directed by W.A. Hamilton
Stage Managed by Tamar Ritza and Tamarind Spender
Lighting Designed by Dominick Grace
Set Designed by the Cast and Crew

Musical compositions for this production were courtesy of Sault Ste. Marie artists The Wailing Aztecs from their CD "It's Only Human" and the students of Sir James Dunn Collegiate and Vocational School from the CD "Dunnplugged".

CHARACTERS

MAUDE Aileen Beattie: Old German: Mat-hilde. "Mighty battle maiden." Age 40. Waitress at the Talisman.
LENA Maidanski: Latin: Lena. "She who allures." Age 41. A woman alone.
KAREN Wilson: (see Catharine) – Greek: Katharos. "Pure one." Age 51. Emma's mother.
EMMA Margaret Wilson: Old German: Imma. "Universal one." Age 22.

SETTING

All action takes place in The Talisman Café, a small main street establishment that has only recently been transformed from a coffee shop to a trendy café. For forty plus years The Talisman was a bustling Good Eats establishment. If the walls could talk, The Talisman would have a thousand secrets to tell.

This piece has been written for a minimalist set. Three tables, five chairs, and a workstation and stool for Maude are the only set pieces required. An imaginary picture window and main door front the café. Lena, Karen and Emma first enter from the house, passing through the audience and crossing downstage to represent the main street. Wing space either stage left or stage right is required, representing a doorway to the kitchen and public washrooms. Since the action plays out in "real time" it is suggested a wall clock be prominently positioned and pre-set to mark 3:00PM off the top of the performance.

BELLIES, KNEES AND ANKLES
by W.A. Hamilton

This play script represents half the action. The other half is Lena's silent journey – the woman alone who overhears too much.

The time is 3PM, a weekday afternoon. The Talisman Café is empty. All the tables are in order except one, which has just been vacated. Music, set at ambient restaurant level, plays over the sound system.

We find MAUDE clearing the table. During the following dialogue she comes and goes from the kitchen, carrying on a conversation with the café cook, Jerry. We can see she's in a strange mood, preoccupied. In fact her mood should flip/flop noticeably with every entrance and exit. She might remove her shoes; forget window cleaning supplies; suddenly feel unsafe on stool.

MAUDE Like in that movie "Sixth Sense"?—where that little kid says he sees dead people?—well that's what it's like for me. I see things I don't want to see. I face things I don't want to face.

Exits to kitchen and re-enters.

Oh yeah and I suppose you thought that Mike Myers thing, what, "The Spy Who Shagged Me", was great. What an exercise in intelligence that was.

Exits to kitchen and re-enters.

So – everybody has their moods – what's your problem? *(beat)* For pete sakes Jerry. Give me a break from that music will you? You would think that after all these years that a smart guy like you would be able to figure out what my problem is.

Standing on step stool; cleaning the picture window.

My God. You and Doris, good Catholics that you are, eight kids and you can't figure out where my mood swings and morning sickness comes from? Just like Howard – sweet, sensitive, maddening with his one word answers. Why do all the men in my life clam up like a steel trap whenever anything is wrong. Just ignore it. It'll go away. Well not this time. *(yelling)* Jerry change the tape!

Looks out picture window.

Oh my God. I can't believe it. Hey Jerry. Those teenagers are back. You know the little one? The one with the dyed black hair and eyeliner? She's got my top on.

Jerry changes the CD in kitchen to new country.

One I gave to the Salvation Army last spring. *(smiles)* Looks good on her.

Starts singing, cleaning to music.

Hey Jerry. Turn it up will you? I like that one.

Dances to workstation – where her stool, ashtray and cigarettes are. Sound of music up. Turns automatically for a cigarette, but stops herself, leaving it neatly on the side of the ashtray. She sings and dances with growing abandon, fighting the urge for a cigarette, fighting her mood until she actually becomes lost in the music. LENA walks across downstage, looks in the Café window. She watches MAUDE, subtly dancing along with her until MAUDE suddenly turns and sees her. She is mortified. LENA laughs and heads for the entrance.

(yelling over the music to JERRY; rushing to put away cleaning supplies) Jerry – Jerry! Turn it down now please. Jerry, are you in the john? I think we've got a customer.

LENA enters just as MAUDE is about to exit.

MAUDE *(yelling over music)* Hi.

LENA Hi.

MAUDE Sit anywhere. I'll be right with you.

LENA Alright. Thanks. Uh, you are open, aren't you?

MAUDE Oh yes. *(beat)* Anywhere. Something to drink?

LENA Yes. A cup of *(music down)* tea?

MAUDE Regular tea or herbal?

LENA Regular's fine.

MAUDE Milk with that?

LENA Yes milk. Uh, actually, could I have a pot of tea?

MAUDE One pot of tea coming up.

MAUDE exits. LENA moves to the table in the picture window. She settles into her chosen spot in the cafe. She watches the action on the street. She waits. MAUDE can be heard in the wings absently singing to herself.

(entering, bringing pot of tea) There you go. *(referring to street kids)* You know those kids?

LENA No.

MAUDE Do you have any kids?

LENA *(beat)* No. *(beat)* Do you?

MAUDE What? I'm sorry – you–

LENA Children. Do you have any children?

MAUDE *(beat)* No.

LENA I never expected to see street people up here. I don't know why I thought–

MAUDE Street people. They're just kids. Somebody's kids.

LENA Oh. I see.

MAUDE I've never ever seen anybody give them food before.

LENA Really?

MAUDE Smart idea I guess though eh? They ate them.

LENA Typical teenagers. They were hungry.

MAUDE Yep. Should be at home, raiding the refrigerator. Would you like some banana bread to go with that tea? I made it this morning.

LENA Actually. A sandwich maybe? Those looked good.

MAUDE Well you've come to the right place. We make the best sandwiches in the whole world here. *(giving LENA a menu)* You'll have a hard time choosing.

LENA *(not looking at menu)* Could you make me a tomato and cheese sandwich?

MAUDE Swiss or American. *(LENA chooses)* Toasted? *(LENA)* White, brown, rye? *(LENA)* Lettuce? *(LENA)* Butter?

MAUDE & LENA Mayo.

MAUDE Salt and pepper? *(LENA)* Dill pickle? *(LENA)* See, we can satisfy any craving here. *(recites back order)*

As MAUDE recites back order, EMMA and KAREN, approach window.

EMMA *(abruptly; immediately heading for cafe entrance)* Let's go here.

KAREN *(peering in window; unsure)* Here?

KAREN and LENA inadvertently lock eyes through the picture window. KAREN runs to catch up with her daughter.

MAUDE You picked the display table.

LENA I picked the–?

KAREN joins EMMA who waits impatiently to open the door, tugging on EMMA's skirt or top in an habitual maternal gesture. EMMA opens the door and they enter the Café.

MAUDE Display table. It's the spot in the window that draws in other customers. *(to KAREN and EMMA)* Hi.

KAREN *(to MAUDE)* We're just having herbal tea. Is that okay?

MAUDE No problem.

EMMA *(quickly choosing a table upstage of LENA's)* Could I have a menu please?

MAUDE Just one menu, then? And two herbal teas?

KAREN Yes thank…

EMMA A café au lait for me thanks.

MAUDE One café au lait and one herbal tea.

KAREN You know what? I think I'll have a café au lait too.

EMMA Have a tea. That's what you ordered.

KAREN Well yes but a café au lait sounds good. I'd like to try one.

EMMA Alright.

MAUDE That's two café au lait then. *(exits)*

EMMA Sorry Mom.

KAREN For goodness sakes Emma. We've been having such a nice day. I've had fun. You and that sales clerk trying to talk me into that leather outfit.

EMMA We weren't lying to you. You should have bought it.

KAREN Mm. I'm still amazed by the ring in that clerk's tongue. How does she eat? *(noting the cigarettes and lighter EMMA has placed on the table)* Are we in the smoking section?

EMMA *(reading menu)* Mm hmm.

KAREN The Talisman. I haven't been in this place for years. Pretty dead isn't it. I wish you wouldn't smoke.

EMMA Mm hmm.

KAREN You're going to have something to eat then?

EMMA Poutine. How can anybody eat that. Think about it.

KAREN Okay. I'm thinking about it–

EMMA French fries, gravy and cheese.

KAREN I think it's a French Canadian uh, speciality.

EMMA I think it's gross. Besides, the French didn't invent the french fry. You're stereotyping.

MAUDE brings coffees to KAREN and EMMA's table.

MAUDE Excuse me. Here you are. Ready to order?

EMMA No. Not yet.

MAUDE *(to herself, exiting)* Okay.

KAREN If you're going to eat maybe we could sit at that table away from the smokers.

EMMA Mom, you said it yourself. It's empty.

LENA and KAREN inadvertently exchange a look.

What does it matter where we sit. Did you say you've been here before?

KAREN Oh I have. It's changed a bit since then but, I have. Lois Smith, Bonnie MacQuarrie, Kathleen Delaney – four cokes and a plate of french fries please.

EMMA *(seeing KAREN almost hit her coffee cup)* Mom–

KAREN The Talisman had the best french fries.

EMMA Mom. Your coffee.

KAREN This place has been around for years. In fact I think your Gramma Blake used to date the owner.

EMMA *(trying to initiate what she has to say)* Mom.

MAUDE Have you decided?

EMMA Oh. No. Nothing thanks.

KAREN What was his name?

MAUDE Roland LeBlanc.

KAREN Roland LeBlanc. That's it. He's not still alive is he?

MAUDE No. He died last year. His son and daughter still own the place though.

KAREN *(awkward silence)* Aah. *(MAUDE still doesn't go away.)* Well then.

MAUDE *(just as EMMA is about to speak)* Rollie's wife Audrey is a super lady. Do you know Audrey?

KAREN No, I didn't know Rollie personally. I uh, just came to his restaurant.

MAUDE Hmm. *(to EMMA, just as she is about to light her cigarette)* You know a nice big slice of banana bread would be good with that coffee.

EMMA I'm sure it would be but I'm not hungry. *(flicks her lighter)*

MAUDE Sure?

EMMA Sure. *(drops unlit cigarette in ashtray)*

MAUDE Mm-kay. *(exits)*

KAREN She must think you need fattening up honey.

EMMA Maybe.

KAREN Oh well, when you and Chad get to Montreal it will be nothing but the best restaurants.

EMMA You are in a good mood today aren't you?

KAREN Why wouldn't I be? My daughter invited me to spend the day with her. Besides, you know I don't believe in that whole thing about moods anyway.

MAUDE brings sandwich to LENA.

All these people with depression... PMS...

EMMA Well in some cases it is genetic you know. It's a medical fact.

KAREN Oh genetics. Please. I think too many people use it as an excuse that's all.

EMMA I got a letter from Joe Capelli. I have to–

KAREN Joseph Capelli. The lawyer? Whatever about?

EMMA About my birth mother.

KAREN Your bir– you didn't mention to me that – I thought–

EMMA You thought–?

KAREN I – We just hadn't discussed this since...

EMMA I haven't been keeping anything from you Mom. I was just waiting till I was – ready.

KAREN And now you're ready. *(dismissively)* Well I've told you everything I know about it. They don't give out names you know.

EMMA Are you alright?

KAREN I'm fine. I'm fine. And I support you in this Emma. I've always said that haven't I? I understand completely.

EMMA I have to tell you what was in the letter now.

KAREN Oh I'm sure everything was in order. Joseph Capelli is a meticulous lawyer. Your father's always said that about him. Completely above board. Scrupulous. Oh yes we knew you'd come to us by the letter of the law. Never a hint of shady dealings. Everything legal. Emma Margaret Wilson. Our baby. From the moment you were born. *(looking for MAUDE)* Where's the – *(to MAUDE)* Oh yes can I uh, can I – *(to EMMA)* You want more coffee? *(to MAUDE)* We'll have more coffee. *(to EMMA)* All this caffeine. I don't know why I didn't order decaf. I'm sure to pay for this.

EMMA The washroom's right over there Mom. Behind you.

KAREN I know where the ladies' room is Emma. How old do you think that waitress is? She looks about forty. Don't you think she looks forty? I'll bet she has four kids and a husband who's a – an auto mechanic. That's it a mechanic. And not one of her children will have a horse when she's sixteen, or the education you could have had.

EMMA No. I've been blessed. I've had all the opportunities…

KAREN Not that I blame you for leaving university Emma. Not all women are cut out for a career. But Dad and I always wanted you to have choices other girls, in different situations, don't have. And now you've met this lovely man, and you're moving to Montreal–

MAUDE brings coffee carafe and two butter tarts.

What's this? Butter tarts. Oh my God. Butter tarts.

MAUDE With raisins.

KAREN With raisins! I remember. There used to be a big sign on that wall that said–

MAUDE Rollie's big fat tarts.

EMMA We didn't order these.

MAUDE I'll take them back then–

KAREN Oh, no no. No you can leave these tarts right here.

EMMA is about to light her cigarette.

Try one Emma. Go ahead. Take a bite.

EMMA reluctantly puts down her unlit smoke and tries the butter tart.

Well? Good isn't it?

EMMA *(chewing, politely)* Mmm.

Both KAREN and MAUDE "ah" and laugh. LENA, who has been trying to choose her moment.

LENA Excuse me.

MAUDE Ope. *(to KAREN)* Well you eat those butter tarts. They're a source of natural sugar. Good for energy.

EMMA I've got to tell you Mom.

MAUDE *(to LENA)* You haven't touched your dill pickle.

LENA Oh don't worry. I will. I'm just a slow eater. That's all.

KAREN Why here Emma?

MAUDE More tea? Banana bread?

KAREN Why in a public place?

LENA Oh you would have made a great mother.

EMMA Because I–

LENA No. Just a glass of water.

EMMA Because I can't talk about it at home.

MAUDE If you don't mind me asking, you're not from here are you?

LENA No. I–

KAREN But why?

MAUDE Oh wait now. Don't tell me. Let me guess.

EMMA I don't know why. I wanted somewhere neutral.

MAUDE Toronto.

LENA Hey. Are you psychic?

MAUDE Yes I am. I do tarot cards. Thursday nights at 9.

LENA *(uncomfortably)* Really.

MAUDE Have you ever had your cards read?

LENA Mm. *(shakes her head no)*

KAREN Maybe you should have your cards read.

LENA Did you see what the kids are doing?

KAREN You like that kind of thing don't you?

MAUDE Well will you look at that.

EMMA Yeah I – Mom. Please – *(fighting tears)*

MAUDE They're putting on a show. Oh that little girl can dance. She's good isn't she. *(spontaneously welling up with tears)* Well you eat that pickle now. *(exits quickly)*

KAREN Emma. Oh don't do that honey. No, not here. I'll get the bill.

EMMA No. I need to tell you what was in the letter! I know he can find her you see. He has a letter, a letter from her, saying if I come looking for her she–

KAREN *(resignedly)* She what.

EMMA She's looking for me too. The letter's dated 1997 *(8 etc.)* Ten years ago. But you know all this anyway don't you.

KAREN She was old enough to know what she was doing when she gave you up.

EMMA Nineteen. She was nineteen.

KAREN Twenty-two years ago that was plenty old enough. In all fairness to her she was smart enough, and old enough, to know she couldn't give you a decent life.

EMMA Is that why? Do you know that for a fact?

KAREN No I – I just believe that.

EMMA Are you sure?

KAREN Yes I'm sure. Your father and Joe looked after all of it. It was all about legal things and, forms and, paperwork. It was all so impersonal.

EMMA Impersonal?

KAREN Adopting a child isn't easy Emma. You're at the mercy of the legal system and the whim of the biological mother. I knew you were mine eight weeks before you were born. I had months to pray night after night that nothing would go wrong. That no big hand would reach out and take you away from me before I even got to hold you in my arms.

The sound of a telephone rings in the kitchen. It's picked up after two rings.

EMMA I think, this is the first time, I ever heard you admit to feeling insecure. Ever. About anything. *(no response from KAREN)* You do know Mom, that she was probably feeling exactly the same thing. *(again, no response)* I mean, doesn't every pregnant woman pray that her baby's going to be born with ten fingers and ten toes? She's just a person Mom. A person I need to meet.

KAREN I know.

MAUDE enters hurriedly, trying to get away from the phone, talking as she enters. Everyone looks up.

MAUDE No Jerry you just tell him I can't talk right now. Tell him I'm– *(sees everyone looking)* – working. *(not sure which table exactly, to address her question to)* Oh I'm sorry. You wanted something didn't you. You wanted–

LENA Water.

MAUDE That's it. Water. *(exits)*

EMMA Her parents were Catholics. She's from a big family. Maybe she was pressured into giving me away.

KAREN Giving you away. That's a funny expression.

EMMA She has three sisters and two brothers. And you know what, her mother had, or has—I don't know—asthma.

KAREN Sounds like me.

EMMA Like you. You don't have asthma.

KAREN No but I have seven sisters and brothers don't I. And your Auntie Jackie has allergies doesn't she. So did your Great Uncle George. That's why you really should stop smoking Emma. You're only mildly asthmatic now but as you age – well. Uncle George died with emphysema.

MAUDE *(from off to on stage)* Never mind why. Just take a message if he calls back.

MAUDE brings the water to LENA. The sound of the phone starts again. It is picked up in middle of third ring.

MAUDE I'm going to be forty tomorrow.

LENA That's okay. I'm forty-one.

EMMA I want to switch seats.

KAREN You what?

EMMA Here. Here. You take this chair.

KAREN Okay. But–

EMMA I just can't stand looking at you from the same direction all the time. It's like how we sit at the dinner table. Me on one side, you on the other and…

KAREN And Daddy right here.

EMMA jumps up again, moving her chair upstage, to Daddy's place.

EMMA I always look at you the same way. I just, need to see you another way.

MAUDE *(offstage, on phone)* Of course I'm happy. Did I say I wasn't happy? So maybe I'm not happy. Maybe I'm scared. Maybe I'm worried. Maybe there's just a whole bunch of things to consider here that you're not considering.

EMMA *(over MAUDE, after "So maybe I'm not happy.")* Mom. Remember the contract? When I went through that really bad time? When I was so mad because I didn't come out of your stomach like they showed us at school? The contract? The contract you and Dad gave to me? Karen and Robert Wilson hereby declare that we choose Emma Margaret as our child to love and care for forever and ever no matter what. I can't remember you telling me I was adopted, it was like I always knew, did I always know? How did you decide when I should know? Was I three, or six?

MAUDE *(entering, still on phone, trying to talk out of range of Jerry in the kitchen)* Oh don't you start on that now. Don't start on about miracles.

KAREN You drew a picture to illustrate that contract. It was very creative.

EMMA I did?

KAREN It was a field of flowers and on each little flower you drew a face and you gave each flower a name. Then you drew two stick figures but instead of lines for the bodies you printed out our names – Karen on one, Robert on the other.

MAUDE Alright. How about work. Are you ready to support three of us on your pay cheque?

KAREN *(overlapping MAUDE)* And the two stick figures were picking the flower with your name on it. We were picking the Emma flower. It was very creative.

EMMA I won't go behind your back Mom. I'm going to tell you everything. We've always told each other everything. I couldn't handle keeping secrets.

MAUDE *(overlapping EMMA at "secrets")* And what if it's born with problems? How can we manage that?

KAREN Oh don't be ridiculous. Everybody has secrets.

MAUDE What do you think I mean by problems. *(exiting)*

KAREN What is that woman going on about?

EMMA You don't want to know then? When Joe lets me know where and when?

KAREN Why? Are you planning on meeting her?

EMMA That's the process Mom. He contacts her and sets up a meeting.

KAREN She could be anywhere. That letter's ten years old. She may not even live in Oshawa anymore.

EMMA Oh I'm not sure she ever did live in Oshawa. Toronto. She's in Toronto.

KAREN Well you were born in Oshawa.

EMMA I know but she's originally from the Sept Illes.

KAREN *(correcting EMMA's pronunciation)* Sept Illes.

EMMA Sept Illes. So maybe she went to Oshawa to have me. Away from the family.

KAREN Have you given any thought to what you might find Emma? You could be very disappointed. I doubt she has a house like you grew up in.

EMMA I think about it all the time. *(staring absently at LENA's back)* Not what she looks like. I have no way of knowing, but of what I want her to look like. When I see her.

KAREN What you want her to look like. What. You think this is some fantasy? You think this is some doll you can take out and dress up the way you want? This is life my sweet Emma. This is those children sitting on that street corner out there, begging change and sleeping in – in– *(sudden realization)* You didn't even see those children did you. You didn't even notice them.

EMMA *(unconvincingly)* Sure I did.

KAREN We've spoiled you.

EMMA What a revelation.

KAREN We've spoiled you. You have no idea do you. No idea. You are completely out of touch with – oh my God. My God. Emma. Listen to me. If I could see that you were ready to deal sensitively with anything you find I'd–

EMMA I am ready. I – I don't care what her house is like, or her, life I – I just want to know about me. What happened with me. I want to–

KAREN Want want want? This is something that has nothing to do with what you want. This is – this, is about people living their lives before you were born. Before. It's about heartbreak and, fear, and pain. It's about something that should be absolutely beautiful turned into confusion and disappointment. It's about growing up in a great big hurry and making a decision so selfless, or selfish, you, Emma, couldn't begin to understand what it took to make it.

LENA bolts for the door.

EMMA What was that?

KAREN I don't know. She didn't take her bags.

EMMA Should we do something? Should we go see?

KAREN Alright. Just, take a peek. Just to the door.

EMMA tentatively looks out the door, then out the window.

KAREN Is she there?

EMMA Yes, she's right there. Maybe she's getting some air, or, I don't know. She looks upset.

KAREN Well what's she doing?

EMMA She's just standing there, against the wall. *(mirrors LENA's stance)* Like this.

KAREN Well it's none of our business. Nothing to do with us. Come back to the table Emma.

MAUDE *(entering)* Did someone just come in?

EMMA No. The woman who was sitting here just–

KAREN Yes. She just got up and left.

MAUDE Did I miss something? Did something happen?

KAREN & EMMA No no. Nothing.

LENA re-enters and EMMA immediately goes back to her table.

MAUDE *(to LENA)* Everything alright?

LENA I think, I would like, some of your banana bread now.

EMMA Could I have some banana bread too please.

KAREN starts eating a butter tart.

LENA Where's the washroom?

MAUDE Back there. Turn right past the kitchen.

LENA *(exiting)* Thank you.

MAUDE Two banana breads. *(beat)* Thank you.

MAUDE is about to exit when the sound of the phone starts again. It rings four times. She picks up her smoke instead. MAUDE and EMMA simultaneously flick their lighters when–

KAREN Don't light that cigarette.

They both oblige.

EMMA *(noticing clock)* What time did we get here?

KAREN I don't know. Three?

EMMA We've been here for half an hour. Doesn't it feel like we got here yesterday or something? *(to MAUDE who is now frantically cleaning anything)* Uh, aren't you going to get the banana bread?

MAUDE *(still cleaning)* Absolutely. Ab-so-lutely.

EMMA Oh-kay then.

MAUDE *(to KAREN)* You're not married to a doctor by chance are you?

KAREN *(still eating)* Mm mm.

EMMA She's married to an accountant.

MAUDE *(indicating LENA's table)* Do you think she's married to a doctor?

EMMA I don't know. Maybe she's a doctor.

KAREN I thought you read cards and all that. Can't you see, or feel or however it works?

MAUDE Sure I can. My vision's a little clouded right now but – she definitely has some kind of knowledge aura. Most likely a professional of some sort.

EMMA Your vision's a little clouded?

MAUDE Hormones. Surging. Roiling.

EMMA Clouding your vision.

MAUDE Telephones.

EMMA Ringing.

MAUDE Ringing. Jangling my nerves.

EMMA Voices.

MAUDE Clamouring.

LENA returns from washroom.

EMMA Commanding.

MAUDE Muffling my ears.

EMMA Senses. Heightened. Suspended.

MAUDE Lost in the...

KAREN Clouds?

EMMA & MAUDE No. No.

KAREN Fog?

EMMA Mm. Not, *some*thing enough.

MAUDE Yes, it's got to be – *some*thing.

KAREN Life's a bitch and then you die?

MAUDE Two orders of banana bread then. *(exiting)* Fresh this morning. Coming up.

KAREN Well she's evidently pregnant. Baby number five on the way.

EMMA Honestly Mom. You confuse me. One minute you're giving me royal hell for being so insensitive, or naive or, whatever it is exactly you think I am, and the next minute you're passing judgement on people like that waitress.

KAREN Lower your voice Emma.

EMMA You don't know anything about her.

KAREN I've seen both sides of the tracks. I know.

EMMA Yes but when you say things like that, like that "she's evidently pregnant", are you sympathizing or criticising or envying or–?

KAREN I'm – worrying.

EMMA Worrying for who?

KAREN For you. For her. *(to herself)* For me.

EMMA For her. The waitress.

KAREN No. For her. For that woman who had to give you up.

EMMA What. You think she might not like me?

KAREN Emma. Don't you ever say anything like that again.

EMMA Well? *(pause)* You know I like that waitress. I think you're wrong about her. I think she's a poet, probably. She's probably completely the opposite of what you think she's like.

KAREN You're entitled to your opinion but–

EMMA I think she grew up on a farm, with horses, and she married her childhood sweetheart and, they don't have any children because, they chose not to, because they like animals, but not people and her husband's really good with his hands, he's a craftsman.

KAREN Playing dolls again Emma? Dressing them up?

EMMA I think you're wrong.

KAREN And I think you're wrong.

EMMA And I think you make too many decisions before you have the facts.

KAREN Facts. Ha. Just wait till you're my age and then you'll know the difference between fantasy and fact.

MAUDE enters with three orders of banana bread and goes to LENA's table.

LENA *(to MAUDE)* I have to ask you something. It's very rude, I have to ask though. Are you expecting a baby? She thinks – well I just need to know if she's – if she's right. That girl's mother. Is she right?

MAUDE She's right.

LENA She's probably right about a lot of things – this girl's mother.

MAUDE Seems so doesn't it.

LENA How does she look – to you?

MAUDE Rich.

LENA Does she appear, attractive? – to you? Does she look, motherly?

MAUDE She looks empty. Like she's starved for something.

LENA She must be feeling very offended.

MAUDE I'm feeling a little offended myself.

LENA *(rising)* I need to apologize to her. I want to say I'm sorry.

KAREN stands, ready to do battle.

MAUDE *(easing LENA back into her chair)* Sure sure. I'll tell her. I'll apologize for you. You eat up now. That banana bread's loaded with potassium. Good for you.

LENA Yes – banana br– But she *was* right.

MAUDE crosses to KAREN and EMMA's table.

KAREN What is going on here? I have never–

MAUDE She says she's sorry.

KAREN So I heard.

MAUDE Strange. Being talked about isn't it.

KAREN But I haven't exchanged a word with the woman. We weren't talking about her.

MAUDE So I heard.

EMMA So do you have other kids? Four, kids?

MAUDE Four. No. This would be my first. You ate those butter tarts.

MAUDE's attempts to exit the conversation are continually thwarted throughout the following.

EMMA And what does your husband do?

MAUDE He's a mechanic. Over at Terry's Auto.

KAREN So you've never had any other children. This is your first.

MAUDE Yes. Except for the miscarriages.

KAREN Oh. My. I won't ask how many. *(starts eating banana bread)*

MAUDE No. I wouldn't bother to ask how many.

EMMA & LENA *(loudly)*
(softly) I would.

MAUDE But you might hurt my feelings.

EMMA I might? *(beat)* Well then I'd have to risk it. I believe in facts, not fantasy.

KAREN *(still eating)* Hah.

EMMA *(to KAREN)* How else am I supposed to do it? There are things I want to know. Things I have a right to know.

KAREN I, I, I.

EMMA *(to MAUDE)* She just said I should face up to reality. *(to KAREN)* Well then, I have to *see* reality don't I?

MAUDE I couldn't agree with you more.

EMMA *(to KAREN)* It's not easy making a decision that affects the people I love. *(to MAUDE)* But that's life isn't it? That's the cold hard facts of life.

MAUDE Cold hard facts. That's what I need right now.

KAREN Maybe, the fact is, I always thought she and I were more alike than we are.

MAUDE Is this typical mother/child syndrome?

EMMA No. It's called only child syndrome. The only person I've had to war with is my mother.

KAREN Ah. I see. Now we're at war. I had no idea.

MAUDE May I be excused now?

EMMA My mother doesn't believe in arguing. She'd rather live in a make-believe world where the sun always shines.

KAREN Life is what you make it.

EMMA Life's what Dad makes it. You just live in it.

KAREN I beg your pardon?

MAUDE finally makes it to the sanctuary of her workstation.

EMMA Well, Dad's the one who makes all the money. Except for Jeannie all your friends are Dad's clients. All you do with your time is volunteer and entertain and go to the "club".

KAREN I can't believe this.

EMMA You're always doing stuff for him and his business and when you're not you're doing stuff for me. You never do anything for yourself. It's like you don't have any – identity or something.

KAREN I see.

EMMA You see? You see what?

KAREN I see. I see what you think of me.

EMMA But I want to know what you see. What *you* think. Do you see an adult woman you like? Really, someone you like, as a person? Or do you see a spoiled brat who never finishes anything she starts. I want to know. Do you think we get along Mom? Do you think we're okay – you and me?

KAREN Why don't you talk a little louder Emma. I don't think the woman at the next table heard every word.

EMMA Good good. I'm glad you're mad at me. Seriously, I'm glad. I finally got a reaction out of you. Finally, you're not just saying "oh that's alright honey I understand." You're always saying that. Like school. You just let me quit. Just let me come home. You should have made me stay. Weren't you disappointed or, pissed off or, did you just not care?

KAREN *(to LENA)* I'm beyond mortification now. Feel free to join in, voice an opinion, whatever.

EMMA No Mom. Don't. Don't stop arguing now. Don't stop.

KAREN I don't want to argue. I don't even know what we're arguing about.

EMMA So, just, keep arguing. Keep arguing until we find out.

KAREN I surrender.

EMMA It started with the letter from–

KAREN I surrender.

EMMA So – what? We just go home and not talk about it anymore?

KAREN I think it's better that way. If I don't get involved. Enough's been said.

EMMA I can't tell if you're with me or against me. I can't tell I can't tell!

KAREN It will all work out for the best.

EMMA And we'll all live happily ever after.

KAREN I'm sure it will all be fine.

EMMA I thought you said this was life. I thought it was me who still played with dolls.

KAREN Whatever. I'm tired Emma. You're a big girl now. You pick your world and I'll pick mine. Okay?

EMMA Okay fine.

KAREN Alright then. Fine.

Mother and daughter stare intently at LENA's back for what starts to seem an eternity until–

(to MAUDE) I think we'd like our bill now please.

MAUDE Fine.

KAREN *(to LENA)* So you're from Toronto. Do you have family here?

LENA No.

KAREN Just passing through then? On vacation?

LENA No.

EMMA *(stopping on her way to the washroom)* Well what then?

LENA What then? I'm – here for a job interview.

EMMA exits.

KAREN Really. Where?

LENA At the university.

KAREN The university. My. What department?

LENA Department of anthropology.

KAREN Anthropology. How exciting. It's always so nice to see women in professions. You had your interview this morning did you?

LENA Yes.

KAREN I suppose it's been a very stressful day for you then. I hope my daughter and I have been an entertaining diversion for you.

MAUDE *(delivering bill to KAREN)* Rollie's big fat tarts are on the house.

KAREN Thank you but I'd rather pay. Just tell me how much. Don't bother to change the bill.

MAUDE The tarts are on the house.

KAREN But I don't like– *(acquiescing)* You're certainly going to make a very good mother. You are impossible to say no to. *(to LENA)* Don't you agree? Isn't she a very persuasive person?

MAUDE *(at LENA's table)* You didn't eat your pickle and you didn't finish your banana bread.

EMMA enters.

Still eating?

The sound of the telephone rings off stage. It rings four times and is picked up in the middle of the fifth ring.

EMMA There's that nerve-jangling telephone again.

MAUDE It's my husband.

KAREN Is he thrilled at the prospect of being a father?

MAUDE Oh he thinks it's a miracle. Excuse me. I'll be right back for your bill. *(exits)*

KAREN What did you do with your hair?

EMMA I let it down. It was giving me a headache.

KAREN It looks nice Emma. I like it like that.

EMMA Emma. I bet that's going to be strange for her. She probably thinks of me by the other name.

KAREN How do you know about that?

EMMA I saw it. On that report you gave.

KAREN What report?

EMMA The one about me. When I was a baby.

KAREN Where?

EMMA I don't know where. I just found it one day. It was a long time ago.

KAREN It certainly was. I can barely remember it myself. Is that the description of your first year?

EMMA At one month she smiled socially. She cut her first tooth at five months. It's the form the birth mother gets.

KAREN And your name wasn't on there. It didn't say Emma anywhere on it.

EMMA No. Don't you remember any of this?

KAREN Vaguely.

EMMA You really didn't have much to do with my adoption did you?

KAREN Well I must have given someone that information. Your father wouldn't have known anything about that sort of thing.

EMMA It's all she knows about me I guess. Unless Joe's not telling me everything. Unless you sent her more, later.

KAREN No one asked me to, that I recall. If I'd been asked I certainly would have.

EMMA But you knew about her letter.

KAREN Of course I knew.

EMMA I'm going to wait until we move to Montreal. It's only another six weeks.

KAREN That's a wise idea.

EMMA Maybe he won't be able to find her right away. She could have moved.

KAREN She could have, yes.

EMMA But if she moved and didn't give him her change of address that means she doesn't want me to find her anymore.

KAREN A lot can happen in ten years. It's hard to say.

EMMA So we won't talk about it anymore.

KAREN No. We'll leave it for now.

EMMA I wonder where she went.

KAREN You don't know that she's gone anywhere yet.

EMMA What? No Mom. The waitress. I was talking about the waitress.

KAREN Oh. On the phone with her husband most likely. *(beat)* She'd be what. Forty, forty-one now. *(beat)* Where do you think you'll meet her? In Toronto? At her – home?

EMMA I don't know. It's scary. Maybe somewhere neutral would be easier.

KAREN You could meet her at the Talisman. You could have her come here.

EMMA You're joking.

KAREN We really are nothing alike you and I. Are we.

EMMA Of course we are.

KAREN How?

EMMA I don't know. A zillion people have told us we are. Maybe it's that we're both social. We both like to shop and decorate and we're both neat freaks. My friends can never get over how neat I am. I'm the first one to pick up after a party. You know how you can't stand dirty dishes laying around. I'm the same. Ugh. Clutter. I can't stand it.

KAREN Like my mother's house.

EMMA Oh yeah. Gramma's is always such a mess. But, genetics, blood. I kind of think you can't escape it.

KAREN I'm neat and my mother's a slob. Of course with nine people in that house. Seven kids. Those brothers of mine were horrendous. Just, horrendous.

EMMA I might have brothers, and sisters.

KAREN *(bravely)* Yes. You might.

EMMA She didn't tell the guy – the – father. Why didn't she tell him?

KAREN He likely didn't mean much, in the greater scheme of things.

EMMA Yeah. Wham bam thank you ma'am.

KAREN and EMMA start to giggle.

KAREN Up. In. Out. 'N over.

MAUDE enters during this exchange, unsure about approaching to collect the bill. She fusses around LENA's table.

EMMA *(trying to think of another expression)* He, he, uh–

KAREN Doin' the horizontal mamba.

MAUDE *(from LENA's table)* Just pulled in for a quick lube. *(approaching)* Sorry. Mechanic's humour.

EMMA My Daddy was a miner.

MAUDE Well that happens. People are always making babies too young or, too old.

EMMA No. He was a miner. You know, hard hat, little light, works underground?

MAUDE Oh, he was a *miner*. *(beat)* Well no wonder then. He was used to squeezing into tight places.

EMMA Yeah yeah and – working in the dark!

KAREN *(gamely)* Oh I'm sure he kept his hard hat on honey.

This last effort breaks the mood and the laughter fizzles. EMMA reaches for a cigarette and MAUDE takes her hand, looks at her palm, while casually putting the cigarette back in the ashtray.

MAUDE These are strong hands here, for such a little girl.

EMMA Yeah and size eight feet to match.

MAUDE See this spot at the base of your ring finger? It means you have a love of the beautiful. And here? At the base of the wrist? That's the Luna mound. It indicates a dreamy disposition.

KAREN What about her lifeline? Is it strong?

MAUDE Hm.

EMMA What?

MAUDE Eight seems to be your number.

EMMA I'm going to live to be eighty?

MAUDE Let's hope so because you're going to have eight children.

EMMA Eight children? No.

MAUDE And money. Whoa. Lots and lots of money.

EMMA Eight kids?

MAUDE *(releasing EMMA's hand)* Yes, and eight husbands. *(beat)* I'm joking. Three. Three major loves over your lifetime.

EMMA *(holding out her hand)* No – I have a question. Can you see if I'm – happy? Can my hand tell you that?

MAUDE You are going to make some change, some discovery in your middle years that will give you a whole new life. You're a searcher for sure though it looks like the first part of your life is pretty clearly defined. *(turning EMMA's hand over)* Right now you need more calcium in your diet. See these ridges in your nails? That indicates a calcium deficiency. Try yogourt.

KAREN Yogourt.

MAUDE Plain. *(exiting with bill)* Mixed in with fresh fruit for vitamin C. *(to LENA)* You okay there?

LENA Okay.

KAREN Eight children. Size eight shoes. Ah well. *(beat)* I need a nap. I am exhausted.

EMMA Have you ever thought about what a coincidence it is that you both come from big families?

KAREN Oh Emma. She was just acting. Like on those psychic chat lines on TV? Heed the warning. For entertainment purposes only.

EMMA Can you imagine being that old and giving birth? She could be in her sixties when her baby's my age. An only child with aged parents. That would be a real bitch.

KAREN *(taking her compact out)* Fifty's plenty old enough for me.

EMMA Fifty-one Mom. You have such blonde hair and such green eyes. And look at your skin. It's white.

KAREN Well so it is.

EMMA And you're so tall. You're as tall as Dad.

KAREN No. Daddy's taller than me. He's six foot.

EMMA Eight kids and three lovers.

KAREN I'd advise you not to tell Chad.

EMMA Just a little bit different than your life eh?

KAREN *(putting compact away)* Mm.

EMMA You're so tall.

KAREN Is there a reason why you're dissecting me Emma? Is this about physical dissimilarities?

EMMA Yes.... No. Maybe.

KAREN I accept you want to meet the woman. I hope you find her. But for God sakes don't hold my blonde hair, eye colour and height against me when you do.

EMMA As if I'd do that.

KAREN Well – I just don't know what comes next. I'm not used to this, unknown. It's unsettling. And you start staring at me like I'm a stranger! I don't like it.

EMMA I don't get my eyes from her either. They're from Mr. Wham Bam.

KAREN What colour are her eyes?

EMMA Blue. Grey.

KAREN So what is it then? What makes you want to start this so badly? Because once it's started you can't turn back. *(beat)* Do you want to make her feel regret?

EMMA Jesus Mom.

KAREN Do you want to make her love you so she'll suffer for her sins?

EMMA Stop it Mom. She's a complete stranger.

KAREN Well what then? Curiosity?

EMMA I guess.

KAREN Curiosity about what?

EMMA Do I have any sisters or brothers? Nieces? Nephews? If I do I'd like to meet them as strange as that may seem.

KAREN Blood.

EMMA Blood. And knees.

KAREN Oh God no. Not your knees.

EMMA Well. I was given these stupid lumpy, bumpy, wrinkled, knobby knees that – come from somewhere!

KAREN No. No.

EMMA It may sound stupid to you but I want to see if we have the same knees – where are you going?

KAREN *(rises shakily)* To the bathroom. *(bumps LENA's chair)* Excuse me.

EMMA Do you want me to go with you?

KAREN exits without answering. The sound of the telephone is picked up after the first ring.

MAUDE *(on phone, outside kitchen door)* Yeah I'm alright. I'm alright. No don't worry. I'll walk like always. What? Well yeah, okay. Sure. maybe we can go to that new Chinese restaurant and then pick up a movie. "The Spy Who Shagged Me". Sure. Sure. I don't mind watching it again. Okay. Five o'clock. See you then. No. I feel fine. I am… I got my hand on it right now. Yeah I know. Don't fool with mother nature. I gotta go. I have customers. We'll talk later. See you at five. *(to LENA and EMMA)* Sorry about that. Didn't mean to make you eavesdroppers. *(exits to kitchen, then re-enters)* Your change. I'm just not with it today. Hormones. *(exits)*

LENA *(to EMMA)* Hi.

EMMA Hi.

LENA You had your palm read.

EMMA Yes.

LENA She's quite the gal isn't she. The waitress.

EMMA Yeah. I like her.

LENA Me too. Your uh – mother isn't feeling well? I don't know what came over me I – I couldn't help but – listen.

EMMA My mother's having a hard day. Nice ankle bracelet.

LENA Oh. It's so old but I can't seem to get out of the habit of wearing it.

EMMA No. It's sexy. I have a tattoo on my ankle.

LENA A tattoo! What of?

EMMA A bell. It's for my guardian angel. Her name's Lilith.

LENA That's what I have on my ankle bracelet. Bells.

EMMA Really?

LENA Yes. I used to be into all that. Angels. Drugs. Rock n roll. Being sexy. *(mortified that she has said this to EMMA)*

EMMA Hm. You were a hippie I guess then eh?

LENA Some people tell me I still am. Can I see your – tattoo?

EMMA I guess. Sure.

LENA and EMMA both rise to meet.

(baring her ankle) It's pretty small. I don't know if you can–

LENA *(bending to see; angling herself side by side with EMMA)* Oh. It's so cute!

EMMA Yeah, he did a pretty nice job.

LENA Your – I – your knees. I'm sorry – I'm afraid I overheard – but your knees – they look like – like mine.

EMMA Maybe. I can't tell they–

Just then KAREN returns from the bathroom. MAUDE enters with change right behind her. KAREN falls, collapsing, not moving.

Oh my God. Mom. Oh no. Mom.

MAUDE Don't move her.

LENA No. Don't move her.

EMMA She's not speaking.

MAUDE What's your Mom's name?

EMMA Karen.

LENA Karen. You fell. Do you think you broke something?

EMMA She's not answering. Why isn't she answering!

MAUDE Maybe she bumped her head. Let's get something under it.

They place something of LENA's under her head.

EMMA Careful. Careful.

MAUDE That's alright. She's got her.

EMMA Is she – breathing?

LENA Yes. See? Her belly's going in and out.

EMMA It's all my fault. I forget how old she is. I–

MAUDE I'll call an ambulance.

KAREN gasps.

EMMA Mom? Are you okay? I'm right here Mom. I'm right here.

LENA Karen. You've fallen. You're okay, but you've fallen.

EMMA Don't move Mom.

LENA Do you feel pain anywhere Karen?

MAUDE exits.

EMMA Why isn't she answering? I did this. I upset her. I–

LENA Is she diabetic? Epileptic? Does she take any sort of medication?

EMMA Estrogen. But she's been taking it for years. Oh. Oh. My Dad's never going to forgive me for this. Never! He's going to think–

LENA Ssh. Calm down now. Everything's going to be fine.

EMMA I have to call my Dad. Yes. I'm – I'm going to call my Dad.

LENA In a minute.

EMMA No. No I need a phone. I heard a phone. It's in there. I heard it in there.

LENA You can call your father. Just come sit here for a second and hold her hand. Come on. Come sit.

EMMA Okay.

LENA That's it. Now she knows you're here. *(beat)* Your name is – Emma? I'm Lena. You know I have a sister who used to take fainting spells. I remember how much that would scare me. One minute we'd be playing and the next minute she'd be on the ground. And then – up she'd get. Good as new.

EMMA What would make her faint?

LENA Actually, we never knew. It could be the heat, or if she got over-excited. Sometimes she just fainted dead away because somebody said something mean to her.

EMMA Because somebody said something to her?

LENA Oh yes. My sister didn't like confrontations. She'd do anything to avoid one.

EMMA I made her argue. My Mom hates arguing.

LENA Sometimes things just need to be said though eh?

EMMA Sure but there's lots of ways to say something. I should have been more respectful. She's my mother.

LENA Even mothers can't be right about everything.

EMMA Excuse me but you don't know. Actually my mother is right about a lot of things. Most things. What's wrong?

LENA Nothing. Just a cramp in my knee.

MAUDE enters with a sweater and a cold cloth.

MAUDE Any change?

EMMA Is the ambulance coming?

MAUDE Yes it's coming. I brought a cool cloth and a sweater to put under her head.

EMMA *(taking sweater)* I'll do it. She's just fainted.

KAREN opens her eyes, not moving.

She's waking up! Hey Mom. Can you hear me?

KAREN Emma. Where are we?

EMMA We're at the Talisman Café. You fainted.

KAREN *(seeing LENA and MAUDE)* There's something wrong with my leg.

MAUDE Which one?

KAREN My left. I think I've broken something.

EMMA bursts into tears.

Oh Emma. Shut up. *(to MAUDE)* Could you give me a hand please. I'd like to get up.

EMMA I'm sorry Mom. I'm so sorry.

KAREN Well that's good to hear but at the moment, I couldn't care less.

MAUDE Put your full weight on me. Don't try to use that leg. *(to LENA)* Can you give a lift here?

EMMA Is it broken? Is her – leg – broken?

LENA's attempts to help are rebuffed by KAREN.

MAUDE It's your ankle isn't it.

KAREN Yes. It's throbbing like a toothache.

MAUDE I think it's a sprain. We'll get that shoe off in a second.

KAREN Ooo. It's starting to swell up already.

EMMA The ambulance is on its way Mom. You fainted.

KAREN The ambulance! You called an ambulance?

LENA You weren't moving. We thought we'd better.

KAREN I blacked out. *(to MAUDE)* For how long?

LENA Three, four minutes.

KAREN *(uncomfortably)* I don't remember a thing.

LENA You gave Emma here quite a fright.

KAREN Really. She was worried was she.

EMMA What are we going to tell Dad? He's going to be so mad at me.

KAREN *(to MAUDE)* Quite the afternoon we've given you. I owe you an apology.

MAUDE Hey. My name is Maude. Short for Mathilda. It means "mighty battle maiden." You came to the right place.

KAREN Maude? *(extends her hand)* Mighty nice to meet you Maude. I'm Karen.

MAUDE *(taking KAREN's hand)* Katherine. Pure one.

KAREN Be optimistic Maude. Ursula Andress did it. Sophia Loren took to her bed to give birth to her children.

MAUDE *(rising)* Yeah but somehow I don't think they were on their feet ten hours a day. You won't need that ambulance.

LENA Melanie, maybe you should call your fa–

KAREN What did you say?

LENA I – I just wondered if you'd like someone to call your husband.

KAREN No. Thank you. I need an X-ray. This ankle's been bothering me for a while.

EMMA You called me Melanie.

LENA I did?

KAREN Yes. You did.

LENA Oh that's – that's my sister's name. The one who used to have fainting spells?

EMMA Is it?

LENA Yes Melanie. I named – she – was named after the singer, Melanie? I was telling Emma about my sister who used to have fainting spells. I thought it would – make her feel better.

EMMA I've never met anybody with that name.

KAREN Emma. Come here. Help me move out of this lady's chair.

EMMA But–

KAREN Come on now. Come help me.

EMMA helps KAREN from LENA's chair back to her own. LENA doesn't move a muscle.

Excuse me.

LENA slowly rises, holding out the chair for KAREN.

EMMA This is– *(to LENA)* I'm sorry. I've forgotten your name.

LENA Lena.

EMMA This is Lena, Mom. She explained you'd fainted. I thought you were dying or dead. She made me feel a lot better.

KAREN Lena. Such a pretty name. Is that French?

LENA Yes.

KAREN I thought so. Thank you for comforting my daughter Lena. She's not well equipped for emergencies. She's led such a pampered life.

EMMA Mom!

KAREN My shoe Emma. And you'll have to take my purse with you. And the shopping bags.

LENA stands confused, locked in a silent exchange with KAREN, while EMMA gathers up KAREN's shoe, tries to locate her purse. Unnoticed by EMMA, LENA impulsively removes her beloved ankle bracelet.

EMMA I can't find your purse.

KAREN What?

EMMA Your purse. I can't find it.

KAREN Oh. I must have left it in the ladies room. Go see.

EMMA *(exiting)* In the ladies room. That's not very safe.

LENA *(too late – holding out bracelet)* Emma?

KAREN It'll be fine.

All three women remain silent. LENA looks around her, to KAREN, to MAUDE. Then she goes to her table, leaves money, collects her bags and heads for the door.

KAREN *(to MAUDE)* Is there someone else here? Someone in the kitchen?

MAUDE Yes. The cook.

LENA suddenly turns on her heel and places the ankle bracelet by EMMA's coffee cup. She leaves.

KAREN How strange. For some reason it felt as if there was just us. A man?

MAUDE I guess you could call him that. I call him Jerry.

KAREN *(picking up ankle bracelet)* Do you think she'll be back?

MAUDE Oh yes. She'll be back. Everybody comes back to the Talisman. You did didn't you? How's the ankle.

KAREN Throbbing. Ba boom ba boom. How's the belly?

MAUDE Ba boom ba boom.

KAREN That little girl out there is surrounded by boys. Waving around a tambourine. Cigarette in her mouth.

EMMA *(entering)* Really Mom. You should be more aware. You're lucky we came to an empty restaurant.

Sound of MAUDE's New Country Music.

MAUDE *(looking out window)* Hey little girl. Where's your mamma?

Lights down.

The end.

Suffering Fools

by
Herman Goodden

Born and raised in London, Ontario where he still lives today with his wife and three children, **Herman Goodden** is an award-winning playwright for radio and stage, as well as a freelance print, radio and television journalist, and magazine editor. His seven published books include two novels, a collection of short stories, three collections of essays and a ground-breaking history of theatre in London which was tied in to a 1993 historical exhibition at Museum London which Mr. Goodden also curated.

Of the six plays he has so far written (encompassing everything from a children's play to a musical, to a dark meditation on a London hostage-taking incident), *Suffering Fools* has received the most productions, including some by student and amateur groups. His 1990 radio adaptation of the script, broadcast twice over CBC Radio, won the gold medal for best script at that year's New York International Radio Festival.

INTRODUCTION TO *SUFFERING FOOLS*

In some ways, Herman Goodden's *Suffering Fools* is a familiar play. Its direct theatrical self-presentation, along with its staged resurrection of the dead and gone, have distinct flavours of *Our Town*. Its central figure, the developmentally challenged Rodney Kincaid, could be an early study for "Forrest Gump." *Suffering Fools* was first performed in 1988, six years before we met Forrest. But interestingly, 1988 was also the year of Dustin Hoffman's "Rain Man." The topic was in the air.

That topic, also familiar, is society's careless forgetfulness when it comes to the real humanity of the developmentally challenged, the tendency not only on the part of official institutions, but even among family and friends, to treat the Rodney Kincaids of this world as objects without feelings, lower beings without human worth. To Rodney, this forgetfulness is full-blown betrayal, and Goodden's play draws strong energy and poignancy from Rodney's anger and his hurt, his despair and his dreams, and perhaps especially from his remarkable self-awareness.

The situation is simple. In the aftermath of a failed suicide attempt, Rodney's unfailingly loyal friend Bob has decided to exorcise some of Rodney's demons, and to enlighten some of his past and present tormentors, by turning Rodney's life into a memory play, performed by the actual figures from his life story. The characters in Rodney's play, the living and the dead, are seated in a semicircle upstage, coming forward to play their scenes as they are called. Some are made to witness the damage they have done. A few, like Bob's mother, are quietly honoured for the care they have shown. All are led toward new knowledge of a fully-feeling human being whom they have not properly considered.

The play, then, is constructed from an intense series of reconnections among Rodney and the real-life characters in his play, all managed by Bob. Together we return to humiliating grade school incidents, we taste Rodney's raw anger at having wasted 23 years in a sheltered workshop, we feel the poignancy of his romantic devotion to a woman who has never noticed him. Dramatic conflict is everywhere – in the collisions between Rodney and the world around him, and in Rodney's own traumatized reluctance to relive some of the scenes Bob requires of him. As in real life, some of Rodney's stories end in enlightened contrition and reintegration on the part of the people among whom he has lived, while others, perhaps more, lead only to defensive self-justification or to indignant rejection.

But this is not a despairing play. *Suffering Fools* moves to a triumph of personal wish-fulfillment, a suggestion like those in Shakespeare's last plays, of the powerful capacity of the imagination to heal a broken world. In the last beat of the action, Rodney's wounded relationship with his late father is recuperated through a moment of reconciliation (is it imaginary? is it real?) that reaches both back through death and ahead into the future:

RODNEY	I don't want to go out that door. I know what happens. It just gets worse and worse. You die and Mom dies and I start living alone and the only time anyone ever talks to me is at the workshop.... Please, Dad. Can we just talk a little?
MR KINCAID	*(Beckons him over, RODNEY sits with him on the cot.)* We'll end it here and then we'll have our talk. All right? *(RODNEY nods his assent, MR. KINCAID looks out to some invisible technician.)* Okay – if you could bring down the lights, this is how we're going to end the show. (*MR. KINCAID takes RODNEY into his arms as the light slowly fades to black.*)

Skip Shand

Suffering Fools was first produced at the McManus Studio of London Ontario's Grand Theatre in May 1988, with the following cast:

Chris Potter
Alistair McGhee
Eleanor Ender
Anna Khimasia
Bill Meaden
John Turner
Julia Webb

Directed by John Gerry
Lighting by Karen Wright

CHARACTERS

RODNEY KINCAID: About 35, Rodney sorts screws for a living in a workshop for the mentally retarded. He's no "drooler," doesn't "look" retarded at all, but gives himself away in the vehemence of his conversation, his impulsiveness, his weird enthusiasms. The more he talks, the more the uninitiated will start to wonder. Rodney dresses like a mama's boy – clean, "Sta-Prest" pants with a crease, leather shoes, long sleeve shirt with a subtle pattern buttoned right up to the neck, hair neatly trimmed and always in place. Most of the time Rodney's manner comes in one of two gears. He either holds himself back, a man of few words and softly spoken, or, when he cares enough, he gets pushy and feisty, even obnoxious. Bob holds the key to a more considered middle gear.

BOB PALMER: One year younger than Rodney, Bob is a gravedigger by trade and temperament and lives in work clothes; shirt tails out, faded jeans, well-worn sneakers or boots. He can be a bit of a slob. His manner is confident and affectionate. He's a man of considerable curiosity, well read, quite eloquent and thoughtful. He naturally fulfills G.K. Chesterton's dictum that, "The real mark of wisdom is not to suffer fools gladly but rather to enjoy them enormously."

MRS. PALMER: Bob's mother, mid 60s, a woman who loves and enjoys her children and their friends but has no illusions that any of them are candidates for sainthood. A fundamentally good soul, sensitive enough but not paralyzingly so.

GARY PALMER: Bob's older brother. A little tougher than Bob, visibly uncomfortable with the part he knows he played in Rodney's life. Underneath it all, quite fond of Rodney and ashamed of what he did to him.

ANDREW KINCAID: Rodney's father, mid 60s, a stern yet passionate man, consumed by self-loathing for the betrayal of his son.

JOAN KINCAID: Rodney's mother, mid 60s, a weak and disappointed woman who always meant to do the right thing but could rarely summon the fortitude to carry through on it. A worrier and a whiner.

MARY McPHERSON: Rodney's old public school classmate who quite unintentionally became the foremost object of his desire. A decent woman, she feels sorry for the guy but is intensely uncomfortable with the position he's put her in.

BERTHA WINTERS: Director of the workshop for the mentally retarded. About to retire after a long and frustrating career of trying to do the right thing for hundreds of clients that nobody wants anything to do with. Her ideals have taken a beating, she's had to close her eyes to a lot but she's fulfilled the impossible challenges of her job to the best of her abilities and won't be denigrated for her efforts.

DENNIS MULLER: Mary's husband, a pompous, dull-eyed twit, almost completely oblivious to what's going on around him.

Some of the above characters can be doubled up—Gary/Dennis; Mrs. Palmer/Mary McPherson; etcetera—and two later scenes require some extra boys and two couples out for a Sunday morning walk who can be easily recruited from the cast.

SUFFERING FOOLS
by Herman Goodden

BOB and RODNEY, already in character, are on stage talking together while the audience enters. Their conversation is too quiet for the audience to pick up but is easy and familiar with much gesticulating and pointing to the stage all around them. While talking, they can also set out the ring of chairs around the back of the stage where cast members will be sitting when they're not "on" and they can bring out the wooden bench, about five feet long, which is the play's only prop and set. BOB is more effusive than RODNEY but not overbearingly so. He pauses frequently to draw out the more reserved RODNEY, making sure they share some kind of consent or agreement about how things should be done. Though we never actually hear them, we should be able to tell that they're talking about the play which they're about to perform, going over some of the rustier bits, psyching each other up. When the house is in and the doors are closed, a stage hand announces that it's time to begin. They stiffen up noticeably with this bit of news but stand and make their way to the front of the stage, BOB leading the way and then making sure that RODNEY is standing right beside him in full view.

BOB Good evening everybody, and thanks for coming out. My name's Bob Palmer and I'm a gravedigger here in town. I'd give you the name of the cemetery but they told me they'd rather I didn't. Tonight we're going to be examining the life and times of this gentleman here and his name is Rodney Kincaid.

RODNEY averts his eyes from all and executes a stiff schoolboy bow; one arm tucked across his belly, the other behind his back.

He's a little nervous right now but he should loosen up as things go along. Right? *(pause)* Before we do anything else, I guess we'd better drop the big one and tell them you're retarded.

RODNEY *(quietly disagreeing)* Handicapped, Bob. Developmentally handicapped.

BOB Not that guff again. What's the difference? I can never keep them straight.

RODNEY Retards are... like mongoloids are retarded. They can't speak very good. And they got those droopy faces. I'm not like that. I look pretty good.

BOB That's the difference? Speech and face?

RODNEY That's what they told me.

BOB Do you believe them?

RODNEY Sure. Probably some other stuff. IQ's and stuff.

BOB Does it matter?

RODNEY Yeh. How'd you like getting lumped in with everybody and they can't tie their shoes or they're always shitting their pants?

BOB I wouldn't like it.

RODNEY Same here.

BOB Point taken. Now let me do the first bit.

RODNEY What's it going to matter if you do that first? That's later. Almost last. We should do the early stuff first.

BOB No. I'm sure about this. This comes first. Trust me. You want to tell it?

RODNEY No. *(pause)* Guess I will, though. *(dubious, almost blasé)* I jumped off a bridge.

BOB A railway overpass at four AM. He tried to jump into oncoming traffic on Wellington Road, missed the car but still managed to smash his pelvis when he hit the pavement. Had his ass in a sling for six whole months last winter and came this close *(holding fingers apart)* to becoming one of my clients. First I buried your father, then your mother and I almost buried you.

RODNEY *(stands up on the bench and holds his arms up overhead)* I had to wear this awful cast that made my bum itch and nobody wanted to sign it. I was "in traction" which means my legs were strung up and I couldn't move. Just lied there and watched TV and slept a lot.

BOB I went to see you in the hospital.

Rest of cast enters one by one, stage left and right, walking past RODNEY who's still "strung up" and shaking their heads "no" before taking their place in the ring of seats around the back stage area.

It wasn't even 24 hours after you jumped and nobody could believe it. Nobody wanted to believe it. I sat in a visitor's chair up against the radiator and watched them come and go for three hours – your aunt and your uncle, neighbours and social workers, the minister from your church. No one accused you. No one even really asked you. They hedged their way around those dangerous first minutes and practically begged you to lie. And you were such an accommodating fellow. The "accident" everybody called it.

RODNEY Then you came over and just stared at me for like two minutes. You didn't say nothing. You didn't even ask what happened.

BOB I knew that nobody goes for a stroll in the middle of the night on a railway bridge and then just sort of happens to fall off. *(lunges at RODNEY and spits)*

RODNEY Then you spit right in my face.

BOB It was the stupidest thing you've ever done. And there's been some lulus – but not in that league. Why didn't you at least come and see me first? Even a phone call?

RODNEY You woulda like that lots. Like four o'clock in the morning. Wouldn't you?

BOB Hey – we're supposed to be blood brothers. And what that means, among other things, is that you get to drag me out of bed and talk whenever you feel like offing yourself. I was so pissed off. And scared. And then to see everybody happily denying it the very next day… I mean, what was it all for? Call it occupational sensitivity. I dig the holes, we put people down and they don't come up again. And my God, you almost joined them. If that wasn't a warning, then I've never seen one. I'm fed up with being the only person who believes you. And that's when I started cooking up the idea of this show. Let's get one thing straight – he may be retarded but he can still feel things.

RODNEY Developmentally handicapped. Why'd you have to spit?

BOB You know why.

RODNEY You spit in my face because I felt like killing myself.

BOB No. Lots of people feel that way. Wouldn't be enough spit to go around.

RODNEY You spit in my face because I tried to kill myself.

BOB Bingo.

RODNEY Then I started crying.

BOB That's when you admitted what you'd done. And that's why I want to put this bit first. *(turning to house)* The story we're doing tonight is the story of a guy who started his life in your shoes and my shoes and everybody else's. Rodney wasn't diagnosed as anything at birth. Diagnosis came 12 years later and with it the gradual stripping away of every shred of dignity, freedom and hope. If what you see here tonight bothers you, don't go hiding behind some pleasant delusion that he's too stupid to feel that as sharply as you would in his situation – because that's bollocks.

RODNEY Here here.

BOB Do you know what I just said?

RODNEY *(points to audience)* I hurt as much as they do.

BOB Right. I often suspect you hurt more but for now we'll settle for emotional parity with the rest of the universe. Now – where do you want to start the show?

RODNEY At the beginning. Like I told you.

BOB Okay. Tell them what you remember about being born.

RODNEY Absolutely nothing. Can I tell about the appliances?

BOB It's your show.

RODNEY *(motor-mouthing.)* Our vacuum cleaner was a Hoover. No wheels on it. A big, long, tubular Hoover. The noise when it started up was like standing too close to jets. It whined and got louder and louder so I thought it might blow up. I'd get humming and wiggling my hands. Trying to shut it out. I'd be acting pretty weird and Mom couldn't stand it so she got so she only used it when I was out of the house. The kettle wasn't as loud but it was kind of worse because they must've used that sucker 20 times a day. It didn't have a whistle because I threw that part out. You know when the water's just starting to boil and it rolls around inside there or something? Like a loose burner maybe. And the handle was kind of loose and that rattled too. I used to dream about that kettle and the noise it made getting louder and louder all over the house. But it got to be all right on August 15th, 1958 and do you know why? Dad was painting the kitchen and a drop of paint got on the handle. Dad didn't see it until it dried and then it was okay.

BOB Why did that make it better?

RODNEY Couldn't have made it quieter. At least, not much. Could it?

BOB I wouldn't think so.

RODNEY I don't know why. It looked less fierce or something. Maybe it was… yeh… it was around then I met your Mixmaster.

BOB Ah – the King of the Household Beasts. Let's establish some personal history. You were born?

RODNEY *(fires out dates, very proud of his memory)* March 10th, 1951, at 4:12 in the morning.

BOB And you first met our Mixmaster?

RODNEY Thursday, September 26th, 1958. Just after school.

BOB Which made you?

RODNEY Seven and a half years old. In grade two with your brother, Gary.

RODNEY goes to the circle and selects GARY and MRS. PALMER to come upstage and join the action. The rest of the circle will supply the Mixmaster hum.

BOB You going to set this one up, Gary?

GARY Okay. So I talk about the…? All right. Well, first of all, I didn't invite him over, you know? He just followed me home. Came in the kitchen door – or at least I did. And Mom was making cookies or something.

RODNEY Welsh Miner's cookies.

BOB I was hanging around the kitchen hoping to get first crack at the bowl and the beaters *(machine starts humming)* when Gary showed up with this friend I'd never seen before.

GARY Mom had the machine up pretty loud and Rodney just stood frozen in the door. Wouldn't budge. Wouldn't come in at all. Then Mom turned it up a couple more notches *(the machine hums louder and higher)* until this guy…

RODNEY claps hands up over his ears and screams.

And then he ran for home.

RODNEY I'd come around again every couple weeks. Most days the Mixmaster wasn't going so I'd get to stay and we'd build forts in the basement or something. Sometimes Gary would get the machine out if he wanted to get rid of me.

GARY It never failed. I wouldn't even have time to plug it in before he left.

RODNEY He could be a real dink that way. Then it was March 12th, 1961. I'd just turned 10 years old. That's the first year when you get two digits. I figured I was ready.

BOB Mom wasn't even baking that day but Rodney went out into the backyard where she was raking out the garden and…

RODNEY *(earnestly)* Mrs. Palmer? I think you'd better come inside and make some cookies.

MRS. PALMER *(coming forward to address the house)* Well, Gary and Bob were always bringing fellows home from school. Some parents couldn't stand the noise but we liked to know what our kids were up to. Now everybody knew

Rodney was a little strange but… what child isn't? When they eventually decided that he was mentally retarded—and that was at least two years later—Mrs. Culbert across the way was almost gloating "I knew it," she said. "I knew that boy was touched." And I thought, Vera – of all the damned nerve. The Saturday before I'd watched her William supposedly raking the leaves, with his transistor radio out on the front lawn, playing his rake like a guitar. And she's going to tell me that's not retarded? I'm not retarded for watching it? She's not retarded for raising him?

RODNEY *(tapping her shoulder to bring her back to the situation)* Uh, Mrs. Palmer.

MRS. PALMER Just a minute. *(keeps RODNEY near to do motherly things with his hair and collar while addressing the house.)* I always liked Rodney. He was such a vigorous little guy. He could take the purest joy from the simplest things. And when my boys gave him a rough time—which was plenty often enough—he could look like the saddest little toad on earth. I knew what his request for cookies meant. He wanted a showdown with the Mixmaster. Good for you, I thought. Let's put this behind us.

BOB I was astonished. We never got cookies on demand but Mom seemed to know that this was an important moment. She finished up in the yard and came inside and got out all her stuff – Rodney standing stiff as a poker and watching every move like a gladiator sizing up his opponent.

MRS. PALMER All right, Rodney. Everything's in here. I'm going to start it up.

RODNEY *(gripping onto a chair for ballast)* You go right ahead, Mrs. Palmer.

MRS. PALMER *(The circle starts humming low and MRS. PALMER raises her voice to be heard.)* I have to start it low until the batter gets mixed together. Otherwise the syrup and molasses will splatter.

RODNEY I understand, Mrs. Palmer. That's perfectly all right with me.

MRS. PALMER There. I can go a little higher now. If you like?

RODNEY Please do. *(She does.)* What number you got there now?

MRS. PALMER *(checking the dial.)* Um... six. Do you want me to stop?

RODNEY No. Higher.

GARY He's shaking like a paint mixer. Look at that chair.

MRS. PALMER *(adjusting dial)* There. I'm up to 10. That's as high as I go.

RODNEY But there's a 12 on the dial. It goes up to 12.

MRS. PALMER Not for cookies. Ten's all you need. 12 is for icing and fudge.

RODNEY No, it isn't. We've got to have 12.

MRS. PALMER All right, but I won't be held responsible for the shape of these cookies. *(cranks it to max for about 10 seconds)*

GARY He's gonna explode! Run for cover!

MRS. PALMER snaps the machine off.

BOB He's done it.

GARY Pretty weird, Kincaid. Pretty weird.

MRS. PALMER Bravo, Rodney. Good for you.

BOB It was a really strange kind of victory if you thought about it but I don't think any of us did. All we knew or cared was that Rodney had slain the King of the Household Beasts and put one of his greatest fears to rest. But it had its downside too.

MRS. PALMER *(miming the pouring of the bowl)* Gary and Bob – you get one beater apiece. Rodney gets the bowl. *(Wiping off her hands, MRS. PALMER heads back to the circle.)*

BOB The next year Rodney went into grade five and that was the only year he failed. Including kindergarten, Gary was with him those first six years and I was with him the next three. What was he like at school, Gary?

GARY He was nuts. The year I remember him best was grade four with poor Mrs. Shipton...

RODNEY Mrs. Shitdog!

GARY ...and he put her right around the bend.

BOB He called her that to her face?

GARY He was fearless. She was the sweetest little white-haired lady. Got us all to join the Audubon Society and took us on bird-watching tours in the woods. We all had our binoculars and our guide-books and we were supposed to be looking for warblers or white-crested grebes. We'd just start to get close to a colony of them...

RODNEY stands on bench, shoulders hunched up, flapping wings and emitting a low and monstrous cawwing sound.

...when this grebe would start doing his vulture impersonation. About 10 years later he worked that up into his Richard Nixon impersonation.

RODNEY briefly does same impersonation flashing "V" signs instead of wings.

You were talking earlier about how long he lasted in the normal system. Well, I think this kind of stuff is why. He was always making so much trouble that I don't think his teachers had two seconds in which to consider that maybe he was simple.

BOB What other stuff did he do?

GARY Oh God, where do you begin?

RODNEY At the beginning.

GARY Fine. Very first day of kindergarten. I'll never forget it. You took that great big box of wooden beads and dumped them in the toilet.

RODNEY *(as if explaining the obvious)* It made the colours brighter.

GARY He had grudges going all the time with guys who picked on him. His real arch enemy in those early years was Wayne King and they'd wreck each other's notes and throw each other's clothes into the pool at the Y but Rodney did this one thing to King that I still think was brilliant.

RODNEY The soaker! *(RODNEY loves this tale and beams throughout the telling.)*

GARY This was grade four and every recess for about a week, Rodney would be a little late coming in. So he'd be all alone in the cloakroom. And what he was doing back there, twice a day, was peeing into King's galoshes. King didn't notice at first. When you're a kid in the wintertime, in and out of your boots, you've always got wet socks and you stretch your feet out under the desk and steam 'em dry. But King's socks weren't wet – they were sopping. By Friday, the stench was getting incredible. King noticed the smell of course, but didn't have a clue what was happening. Probably thought he had hoof and mouth disease. Kids were moving their desks further and further away as word got out what was happening. Finally on the Friday, Mrs. Shipton smelled a fish, gave Rodney a 30-second lead and followed him into the cloakroom. *(outraged biddy voice)* "Rodney Kincaid – you put that away!" King was ruined. They moved away about a year later. King said his father got a promotion but we knew that wasn't it. I mean, when someone's been peeing in your boots for a week, you've got no choice but to pull up stakes and move to another county.

RODNEY This is great.

BOB Did Rodney usually win?

GARY No. You know perfectly well he didn't. I mean, you remember the snakes?

RODNEY Aren't we going to tell about the heights, Bob?

BOB What about them?

RODNEY You know – just tell about them. I had hundreds of them. Thousands maybe. I still do.

BOB Yeh, all right. Rodney used to go around with a tape measure all the time and run it up your back when you weren't looking. He kept these measurements in a notebook; two listings – one for "shoes on" and one for "shoes off." And then he memorized them. In addition to people he knew he'd get measurements from the backs of album covers and movie magazines and he'd memorize them too. All totalled up he had at least a thousand different heights stored away up here. *(points to noggin)* You could test him too and he was always right 99 times out of a hundred.

GARY He knew everybody's height but his own. He always said he was five or six inches taller than he was. One day a bunch of us got him on the ground and measured him with his own tape and he wasn't even five feet tall yet.

RODNEY Yeh, well I'm five eight and a half now, Gary – shoes off.

GARY That's not what you said on my Christmas card last year. There you said you were six foot one.

RODNEY That was just a joke, Gary. Can't you take a joke?

BOB Could we get on to the snakes?

RODNEY Do we have to, Bob?

BOB Yeh, we do. Talk to us about it, Gary.

GARY Like what?

BOB How many times did you put him through it?

GARY It wasn't just me, you know? *(pause)* Three or four times, I think.

RODNEY *(pointedly)* Six.

GARY Six. And Bob, you came along…

BOB Once.

RODNEY The last time. The worst time.

GARY We built up to that one. It never went that far before. You better set this one up, Bob.

BOB Snake places, everybody. *(pause)* It was the summer after Rodney failed grade five. A stinking hot August afternoon by the creek behind the Baptist Church. There were seven or eight guys. I was the youngest and we'd all paid Gary a quarter to watch what was going to happen. Gary wasn't going to do anything. Rodney was. And we'd all heard it was great. We hung around for about 10 minutes and then Rodney appeared over the summit of the hill we called the Alamo. It wasn't often that normal kids invited him along so he was feeling pretty good. He walked up to Gary and greeted him by standing on his tiptoes, sliding his hand back and forth between their heads comparing heights. It looked like something a Hollywood Indian chief might do by way of saying hello.

GARY Ya ready?

RODNEY Yeh, I'm ready. I mean, I'm here. Come on away from the creek, you guys. Why don't we play hide and seek or flags or something?

BOY #1 No way, Kincaid. You know why we're here.

BOY #2 Come on Rodney – like you did yesterday.

GARY We might get into some games a little later, if you like. But these guys all came out because they want to see what you can do with the snakes. If you let them all down, they're not going to like you very much. I think we'd better go over to the creek and see what you can do.

RODNEY I don't know… I didn't like…

GARY It's an amazing talent you've got, ya know? Bruce was telling them it was like something out of "Tarzan." They really want to see it.

BOY #3 Or maybe we should just beat him up.

BOY #1 Hey, that would be pretty difficult.

BOY #4 You bet it would. Haven't you heard? He's just like Tarzan! *(beats fists on chest and gives the famous ape call)*

GARY You guys wanta shut up for a minute?

BOYS #1 & #3 *(sing-song unison)* Sor-ry Ga-ry.

GARY Come on, we'll just go over there and give it a few minutes and if that works out, then we'll go play flags or something.

The BOYS, GARY and RODNEY walk toward the creek which is set upstage. RODNEY gets on his knees in front of the bench, facing the house. Other kids kneel on bench behind him, or stand behind the bench, everyone peering forward to see into the creek. RODNEY leans out over the water, moving his hands over the surface in small circles, poised and ready to strike. In contrast, the kids behind him lack concentration, stumbling, pushing each other and giggling.

BOY #2 See any yet?

GARY Shhhh!

BOY #2 Whadya mean? Snakes don't have ears.

BOY #4 Snakes hear through their skin, ya dope.

BOY #2 Well, big deal – he's not going to hear me if he's underwater.

BOY #1 *(pushing #2)* Then, maybe you better join him.

BOY #4 *(whispering as he points upstream)* Is that one?

RODNEY shoots his hand into the water and they all instantly shut up, reacting with screams when he suddenly pulls his hand up until they see there's nothing in it. They're still recovering from RODNEY's little joke when he plunges his hand into the water again and pulls it out with a live one. The snake is invisible but the BOYS can make the audience see it as if they really see it.

BOY #4 *(admiringly)* He's got him.

BOY #1 *(aping RODNEY's clutch in the air)* Oh, he's a beauty.

BOY #3 *(repulsed)* Uhhhh – look at him flip.

We see RODNEY unwrapping the snake from his wrist and leading him from one hand to another, the boys watching every move.

GARY Come on, Rodney – like yesterday…. Get… get the tail and stretch him out… that's… that's it. Yeh.

With snake stretched, RODNEY runs his tongue along the entire length.

BOY #3 What's he…? He's tonguing him. Aw, make me barf.

RODNEY This is a very delicious snake.

The boys explode in laughter at this. Next RODNEY slides the snake through his mouth, his teeth gliding along the top and bottom. He pulls the snake away to smack his lips.

I think it's a T-bone snake.

They explode in laughter again and RODNEY howls in delight to be the centre of so much excitement and approval.

GARY Let's see you bite it…

BOY #4 Yeh, bite it!

BOY #1 Eat it!

BOY #3 Chew it all up!

RODNEY gives one last howl and grandiosely bites down into the snake, his eyes going wide, then spitting and throwing the thing away from his mouth. He freezes in that attitude of disgust, as do the boys all around him, recoiling and turning away. Only BOB still moves as he turns to address the house.

BOB The snake was mostly one big piece. It laid there shaking but couldn't move away. We came up from the creek and we didn't know what to do. Then Rodney looked up and smiled with this weak coloured blood all over his teeth.

The cast comes unfrozen, as each boy speaks his piece he heads back to his chair in the circle leaving just RODNEY, BOB and GARY at centre stage.

BOY #1 Oh, that is so ignorant.

GARY You killed it. You weren't supposed to kill it.

BOY #4 Way to go, Kincaid. I'm not going to be able to eat for a week.

BOY #3 See you later, Rodney.

BOY #2 Yeh, you can stay here and clean up your mess.

BOB We swore at him, kicked dirt at him and told him we never wanted to see him again. He didn't say a word and we left.

GARY You think you're telling the story of Rodney Kincaid. But instead you end up telling all kinds of rotten stuff about everybody else.

RODNEY What are people going to think, Bob? I hated that scene in rehearsal and I still hate it now.

BOB They're going to think that what happened actually happened.

RODNEY Well, I hate it.

BOB So do I. And it's time a few other people learned to hate it just as much.

GARY I'm not too nuts about it either, Rodney. I mean, I come out smelling like roses, don't I? I know you never really trusted me after that and I don't blame you. I'm sorry, if that's worth anything to you.

RODNEY I just wish we'd played flags or something, Gary.

GARY Yeh, well me too. But we didn't. Anyway, I got nothing more to do with your story so I'm outa here. Good luck with your show. *(heads back to the circle of chairs)*

RODNEY *(confidentially to BOB)* Is Gary mad at me?

BOB No. I don't think so. He's not very good at expressing himself.

GARY *(standing up)* What the hell do you expect me to say, Bob?

BOB I don't know. Do you think "I'm sorry" is adequate?

GARY It's all I got, Bob. I mean, the night he jumped off the bridge… you phoned me up next day… I was shocked to hear it but let me tell you something – I was *not* surprised. I sat there for a couple hours thinking about the kinds of things I used to put him through… and more than anything else in the world… I just wanted to cry. But I couldn't do it. I knew I didn't have the right. So I repeat it—and I do mean it, Rodney—I'm sorry. *(sits down)*

BOB *(to RODNEY)* Ready for the next bit? *(pause)* I was in Rodney's class for the next three years and tried to avoid him as much as I could. This gave me some distance. I started to see the pattern and how it worked. It was always Rodney stuck standing in the corner, being sent to the office, getting the strap – and it was always somebody else giggling into his hands because he'd just gotten away with blue murder. I admired his spunk, his resilience. This was a guy who'd do anything that came into his head. But he'd also do anything that other people put into his head. When me and Rodney were in grade seven, some of the guys in Gary's year were starting to get interested in cars and had learned how to let the air out of teachers' tires by pushing down that little pin in the valve with their thumbs. Everyone knew the office was wising up, so that was the day they tried to get Rodney to do it. It was morning recess and I saw Rodney all alone heading over to the principal's car. *(calling out loud)* Rodney. Hey, Rodney. *(runs over to him)*

RODNEY *(defensively)* What do you want?

BOB They're settin' you up. Don't do it.

RODNEY Oh, I bet you know all about it. Yeh, I sure do. Fat lot you know, Bob.

BOB *(pointing to a distant school window)* Rodney, these guys have been doing this for the last two days. Mr. Pringle is watching and when they catch you, they're going to pin the whole thing on you.

RODNEY *(looking at window and squinting his eyes)* How you so sure that's Pringle?

BOB I'm not sure but it's the office window. It's somebody… they're watching. And if you go through with this, you're going to get it.

RODNEY Let me see if I've got this right. *You* don't want *me* to get it?

BOB That's right.

RODNEY Hey – am I extra especially stupid today or what? I mean, why don't I believe you, Bob?

BOB I don't know. *(pause)* Is it the snakes?

RODNEY You just piss off about that!

BOB I will. But is that why you're still angry with me?

RODNEY I never done that on my own, you know? I picked them up sometimes and fooled around with them. But I sure never bit one until you guys made me.

BOB I know. That's what I'm saying. It was our fault and we were wrong to make you do it.

RODNEY And you didn't have to start calling me names when it was over, did you? If it was something you wanted? And Gary made more than two dollars off me chewing that thing and nobody called him anything.

BOB He was a first-rate turd, Rodney. We all were.

RODNEY He was worse than that.

BOB He was a third-rate turd, then.

RODNEY Eight million-rate'd be more like it.

BOB Okay. Eight million.

RODNEY And then he didn't have to go around telling everybody like it was something I did all the time.

BOB No, he didn't.

RODNEY How'd you like being called "snake-biter" by people who didn't even know the first thing about it?

BOB I wouldn't like it.

RODNEY Or finding a snake in your desk that somebody'd run through a lawn mower and everybody going, "Eat it, Rodney – it's your lunch?"

BOB The whole thing stunk. I'm sorry. Gary's sorry.

RODNEY No, he's not.

BOB I want to try and make it up to you. Don't let the air out of Pringle's tires. It's a set up. Trust me.

RODNEY I don't see why I should. *(looks around at the office, the group of boys and BOB, trying to decide)* I don't think you deserve it. *(drops to one knee, rolls up his pant leg and picks at some skin on his shin)* Got a scab on you?

BOB Don't pick at it... you're bleeding.

RODNEY You got a scab?

BOB Yeh, I think so. *(splays hands to examine his knuckles, finds one)* Yeh, I got one. Why?

RODNEY You have to pick it and rub the blood in with this one. That way, we'll be bloodbrothers. And if you're lying to me or you ever betray me, you'll get sick all through your guts and you'll die. This is for keeps, Bob. So don't do it if you don't mean it.

BOB *(stares at RODNEY in awe for a moment then rips the skin from his knuckle)* Yeh. I mean it.

RODNEY We'll have trust for the rest of our lives. *(BOB crouches down and presses his knuckle to RODNEY's shin.)* We'll have trust beyond the grave. *(BOB starts to pull his hand away.)* No. Give them time to mix or it won't work. Rub it in.

BOB *(still in transfusion position, addresses the house)* And that was how I made my peace with Rodney Kincaid. *(stands up)* I knew I'd crossed over a line and it was a little scary. *(flings an arm around RODNEY's shoulder)* I'd publicly thrown in my lot with this creep. *(indicates the boys behind)* And they weren't going to forget it. *(They both start to make their way upstage.)*

RODNEY But it wasn't so bad.

BOB No, it wasn't.

RODNEY We both liked rock & roll.

BOB I liked the music. I think you were more interested in the pop stars' heights.

RODNEY That's not fair. I liked the music too. The heights were something extra.

BOB And we were starting to get interested in girls. And that was good and bad, wasn't it?

RODNEY It started bad. There was a girl called Clare who lived behind us. I didn't really like her much but I watched her all the time. Just because she was a girl.

BOB What do you mean – all the time?

RODNEY *(His voice goes slow and spacey. If you want to isolate him in a cold blue light – go ahead.)* I mean for hours. I'd stand there at the top of the basement stairs. On the landing. I could see through our storm door right through the yard to their house. I'd have supper then try to go downstairs to play records… but I couldn't get past the back door. I'd just stand there and stare. It was like I couldn't help it. Even if the light in Clare's bedroom was off… I'd wait for her to finish supper and go up there. Most nights she'd see me and close her curtains shut. Some nights she wouldn't. A couple of times she told her dad and he told my mom and I'd get in trouble for just standing there and watching.

BOB If she closed her curtains, would you stop looking?

RODNEY No. I couldn't. Because some nights, she'd open them again. She was older than me. She went out with boys sometimes and didn't get in until real late. That one winter, I watched her a lot. It wasn't right but I couldn't stop. It wasn't good. It made my parents fight.

Lights up over MR. and MRS. KINCAID where they sit side by side in the circle.

MRS. KINCAID Mr. Pearson phoned again. With the usual complaint.

MR. KINCAID *(coming out from behind newspaper)* And I'm getting damned tired of it, too.

MRS. KINCAID He doesn't want his daughter being peeped at.

MR. KINCAID	All she has to do is close her curtains. Him too for that matter.
MRS. KINCAID	For pity sake, Andrew – isn't it time we admitted something?
MR. KINCAID	No. No, it's not. He's going for those tests. I think we should at least wait until those are over.
MRS. KINCAID	Those tests could go on for months. We're telling our neighbours to close their curtains and not mind Rodney. What do we do next? Tell them to lock up their daughters?
MR. KINCAID	Rodney wouldn't hurt anyone. There isn't a vicious bone in his body.
MRS. KINCAID	In case you hadn't noticed, he's becoming a man – a very strange young man.
MR. KINCAID	It's just puberty. It throws some boys for a loop but they grow out of it.
MRS. KINCAID	But Rodney stands there for hours. It's like he's hypnotized. I sometimes have to call his name half a dozen times so he'll hear me.
MR. KINCAID	So what do you expect me to do, Joan? Shall we call him in here now and tell him he's abnormal? Is that going to fix anything?
MRS. KINCAID	I don't know. I just want what's best for him.
MR. KINCAID	And I don't think we're going to know what that is until those tests are done. I intend to wait and not get the boy all worked up about something that might not even be true. And Mr. Pearson can go fly a kite. This is Rodney's house too. We live here. They live there. Everybody should just mind their own business.
MRS. KINCAID	But Rodney's watching *them*. Particularly Clare.
MR. KINCAID	And why do you suppose he does that? Do you think he's got this fascination with looking at the dark side of closed curtains? If she wasn't showing him something, he wouldn't watch.
MRS. KINCAID	What are you implying?

MR. KINCAID You heard me. *(picks up newspaper again)*

MRS. KINCAID I may have heard you but I certainly wish I hadn't. That's a horrible thing to say about a girl.

Lights out over MR. and MRS. KINCAID.

BOB Well, did she show you something? *(RODNEY nods head up and down.)* Everything? *(RODNEY nods head up and down.)* More than once?

RODNEY Eight times that winter. She even kind of waved me over.

BOB You didn't go?

RODNEY No. But that meant I wasn't just snooping. She knew I was there and she showed me stuff.

BOB I can see where that might make it pretty difficult to go downstairs and play records.

RODNEY Just about impossible. It was scary.

BOB How do you mean?

RODNEY I mean nobody else was doing that kind of stuff. It wasn't normal. I just wanted everything to be normal.

BOB Why? What was so great about normal?

RODNEY Normal was like everybody else and I was starting to see I wasn't like that. Do you know I once spent an entire evening looking through the Eaton's Catalogue for a thinking cap?

BOB How else were you starting to see that?

RODNEY Well, school. I failed grade five, right? Then I still wasn't working but I was passing all the time. It was really bad in grade seven. I didn't know any of it hardly but they were passing me anyway. And it was around then I started going to this office downtown. I went once a week for talks with a psychologist. He had me doing junk with coloured blocks and holes that were different shapes and I thought, "What is this shit? This is like I used to have to do in kindergarten. Is that where they're going to put me next?"

BOB So you figured some kind of change was coming?

RODNEY Yeh. And I didn't want to go. It was strange. It was like I started missing things at our school even before I left. I was noticing what I'd miss. I grew up with you guys. I didn't want to lose all that. *(pause)* And the girls.

BOB Which girls?

RODNEY Mary McPherson. What were we doing in arithmetic that year? Decimals or something? I didn't get it. At all. So instead of doing that, I looked at the girls. Every day I'd choose a different girl from the class. You know – went up and down the rows and chose each one. Just in my head, like.

BOB *(incredulous)* Sylvia Blair?

RODNEY No. I skipped her. Too bossy.

BOB Tank?

RODNEY She was fat but she was all right. I chose her for a day. Sure. I like 'em better too big than too little.

BOB And what would you do when you chose these girls?

RODNEY Nothing. Just thought about them. What it would be like to be married to them. Eating dinner, smoking cigarettes, watching TV, hugging… you know – like we were married all the time. And the one I kept coming back to was Mary McPherson. Do you know she never hit me once? I looked forward to Sylvia Blair's day because I knew I wouldn't think about her and then I got to pull Mary in instead. I didn't do Cynthia Smeethers either because she always smelled like over-cooked potatoes if you got too close. It took about a month to get through them all—including repeats—but by the time I was done I was sure that Mary was the one.

BOB Okay. So Mary was the one. What did you do about it?

RODNEY *(sadly)* Nothing. I was going to but there wasn't time. I mean, Mary was a popular girl. All kinds of guys were after her and I knew she'd choose them first so I had to come up with a truly long-term plan. I mean, someone like you or Gillis could just move in and get her. Right?

BOB *(ironic)* Yeh. Me and Gillis pretty well had our pick of the crop, Rodney.

RODNEY Well then, let's say you were more immediately appealing. You guys didn't memorize bus routes or heights and then talk about them all the time. You didn't spend the whole summer of 1968 watching the guys from the city paint all the red fire hydrants yellow. There's a hydrant across the road from your parents' house. Want to know when it got painted? Just ask me 'cuz I can tell you. It was 2:30, Thursday afternoon August the seventh, 1968. They replaced a part on that hydrant too. Remember the short hydrants—the old ones—and they used to have that chain attached to the end of the plug that hooked up to the base of the hydrant? That was the year they got rid of the chains. Look around, Bob. They're all gone. Nobody else saw 'em leave.

BOB Let's get back to your truly long-term plan that you never put into action. What was it?

RODNEY *(embarrassed)* It wouldn't have worked. It didn't work.

BOB I know. I know.... What was it?

RODNEY *(resignedly)* I was going to mow her grass and shovel her snow. I was going to do it all the time – for years. Guys like you and Gillis would come and go but I'd always be there doing this nice thing for her for free. Eventually she'd realize that I meant business. That I was sincere.

BOB I think I know where you got this idea.

RODNEY The grade seven health textbook.

BOB Excuse me. *(turns from RODNEY to the house)* I'll keep this brief but we've got to say something about the stuff that this guy reads. There's *David Copperfield* by Charles Dickens which he's read at least six times in the last few years.

RODNEY More like 10.

BOB Particularly since the death of his parents, this story of the poor lost orphan trying to make his way through the madhouse of adult society... it strikes a lot of chords.

RODNEY *Great Expectations* too.

BOB He's also read the entire *Hardy Boys* series, has collected more than 2,000 *Archie* comics and was so enamoured of the health textbooks that he swiped a full set from grades four to eight. Now those textbooks were published in the '40s so by the time we came to read them, the social values being promoted had turned themselves inside out. Chapters on healthy socializing came with lots of pictures and cartoon style balloons, clearly broken into sections marked DO THIS and DON'T DO THIS. The fellow most frequently pictured in the DO THIS section looked remarkably like Rodney – not very tall, a little scrawny, short hair and decked out in clothes that only a mother would choose. The fellow in the DON'T DO THIS section usually looked like Keith Richards of The Rolling Stones—ragged hair, scruffy clothes, appalling posture, miserable attitude—the very personification of cool. The health textbooks depicted a totally fair, totally hokey society in which a guy like Rodney—provided he stopped chewing snakes and peeing in his arch enemy's boots—just might stand a chance at finding real happiness in life. So, of course, he believed them.

RODNEY Are we doing my scene now?

BOB You got it.

RODNEY All *right. (picks up an imaginary snow shovel and starts to clear a small area of the stage)*

BOB Way down deep in the silliest portion of your heart, you know the way that world works. There he is, friends – digging that snow like he's been digging that snow and mowing that grass for 12 long years and hark: the ice is finally starting to melt and here comes Mary now.

MARY *(With a sweater wrapped loosely around her shoulders, Mary gingerly steps up to RODNEY.)* Rodney. Oh, Rodney. Do you mind if I have a word with you?

RODNEY *(standing up from his task and holding his shovel like a staff)* Not at all, Mary. I've often hoped you might come out one day and "have a word" with me as you say. It has been an inspiring hope; my sole reason for working, perhaps even for living. By all means, speak to me.

Even if it is but just one word, what might that one word be?

MARY *(holding a hand to her heaving bosom)* Pray, don't think me too bold, but I believe that word is "love."

RODNEY Oh Mary, do I dare to hope that we might get married?

MARY I defy the world to try to keep us apart. I look at your immaculate walks, your neatly trimmed borders, and I know it was meant to be.

RODNEY But how will we live, Mary? For in honesty, my prospects are not good and I begin to suspect that I'm not as intellectually endowed as other fellows you might meet.

MARY These are trifling and insubstantial fears. You have a head and a brain, that brain has two lobes; a perfectly adequate endowment. And when one works with the vigorous application I've watched you bestow on these tasks for 12 long years, he needn't worry about prospects. Besides, my parents just died and there's a million dollars in the house.

RODNEY Then there are no obstacles in our way.

MARY None.

RODNEY Oh Mary.

MARY Oh Rodney.

They embrace, RODNEY still holding the shovel in one hand.

RODNEY *(grinning like a gorp)* Tell me this, Mary. When we are married as man and wife, will we be able to take off our clothes and go to bed and rub our bodies each against the other?

MARY If we're married, I don't then see what could possibly prevent us.

RODNEY Oh Mary, this is surest, sweetest bliss.

MARY *(turns to BOB with a strained expression)* What is it with this dialogue?

BOB *(pointing to RODNEY)* He thinks it sounds like Charles Dickens.

RODNEY And it does too – in spots.

BOB That's all there is for now, Mary. Thanks very much.

MARY *(heading back to circle)* Charles Dickens – my ass.

BOB Don't give him any more ideas, Mary. *(turns to RODNEY)* Okay, so that's how it was supposed to work but everybody knows it didn't. Did you even mow her grass once? Or shovel her snow?

RODNEY No. I didn't have time. I mean I only got the idea that fall. On Halloween. And the grass wasn't growing. I was waiting for the snow to get started. Setting my clock for six in the morning and getting up to see if it was here yet. But it didn't come in time. Then, that second week in December, everything changed.

BOB The workshop. How'd you first find out about that?

RODNEY This stuff is awful. Can't we stop now?

BOB No.

RODNEY *(sits down on bench, is lying down on it by end of speech)* I got up at six on Monday morning, December 8th, 1963. There wasn't any snow so I went back to bed. It was about 7:30 my Mom came through and that was half an hour earlier than usual. I knew something was wrong. I thought maybe another President's been shot.

MRS. KINCAID *(The lights grow dim and MRS. KINCAID in her housecoat moves up to RODNEY's bedside. Her voice is soft and halting throughout. She finds this speech murderously difficult.)* Could you wake up, dear? That's a boy. It's time to get up. *(RODNEY looks around apprehensively.)* Yes, it's early isn't it? See – it isn't even starting to get light out. There's something I have to discuss.... Can you sit up? I don't know... it seems the school you've been going to... well, they say it wasn't the right one. We made a mistake. All of us... it's not your fault. I don't know why... it's taken them this long to decide that school was wrong... but they have. So what that means is starting this morning... that's why I'm waking you up now... you're going to be going to a new school. It'll be hard at first—I know that—but you'll make new friends. And the work will be easier. More suited for you. And you'll do better. Won't fall behind so much. And that'll be nice, won't it? *(She looks at him briefly, then quickly turns away.)*

RODNEY *(sitting up further and trying to make his mother face him)* I don't want to go to a new school. They can't make me. Not if you tell them I don't…

MRS. KINCAID *(She turns and hugs him in a flood of tears, paralyzing RODNEY, blurting her words.)* We didn't want to do it. I'm so sorry. Please don't blame us.

MR. KINCAID *(appears at bedroom door, daubing his neck with a towel)* All right, you two – that's enough of that. *(pause)* We'll be going in 15 minutes, Rodney. You'd better get ready.

RODNEY exits, MRS. KINCAID stands up as MR. KINCAID kicks the cot/bench out of the playing area and drags in two chairs for the car scene.

She rehearsed that speech for a week. I'd been up two hours with her the night before trying to help her find the best way to say it.

MRS. KINCAID We couldn't believe what the authorities seemed to be telling us. And why had it taken them so long? And was I somehow responsible? I'd had a few beers on the New Year's Eve two and a half months before Rodney was born. A few weeks before that, I slipped on the ice while Christmas shopping. Could either of those things… somehow… have hurt my child?

MR. KINCAID Rodney was a worrier, just like his mom. So we didn't say anything about the workshop until his first morning. Joan wanted to be the first to tell him. She didn't want Rodney to be frightened. She didn't want to cry. *(pause)* I guess we blew that one.

MRS. KINCAID I know you believe it was right to wait, Andrew. But it wasn't. We should've been preparing him for the change. It was appalling to just spring it on him like that.

MR. KINCAID Joan stayed in our bedroom crying while I set out breakfast. *(MRS. KINCAID exits to chair.)* But Rodney couldn't eat and neither could I. Our Shreddies were turning to mush in our bowls and I was thinking "Who are these authorities that they know so much about your child? That you believe them?" It just seemed so unfair… to let a child go along that far thinking one thing… and then turn on him and say, "no – we had it all wrong – you belong over here now." What a thing to do to a child. This wasn't just failing a year and holding him back. This was taking a big red "F" and stamping it all over his life… writing him off… so he'd never be able to try again. Part of me just wanted to pack him into the car and drive away – just the two of us on a never-ending holiday. *(pause)* But instead I drove him out to the workshop.

RODNEY and MR. KINCAID get into the car he's created with two chairs, RODNEY miserable and silent, MR. KINCAID yammering like a maniac about things he doesn't believe.

A big change like this can be a real challenge, eh Rodney? To say to yourself, if this is the way things are, then I'm not going to let it get me down. I'm just going to make the very best of it. That's the trick. To take what looks like a… well, a setback… and turn it into an advantage.

RODNEY *(so worried and worked up he's about to snap)* Is it like a reform school? Because I was bad at the other school?

MR. KINCAID Good heavens, no. It's a school. A place where you learn things but more at your own level.

RODNEY What kind of level?

MR. KINCAID Your level. Slower you could say. You know how much trouble you were having with your subjects.

RODNEY *(looking all around)* Which school is it? There's nothing but factories out here. I hate it out here.

MR. KINCAID It's a school where you actually do things. They have these programs where you get to do a job. And they pay you for it.

RODNEY How much? How much do they pay me for it?

MR. KINCAID I don't know. *(starting to crumble)* Not much. I don't know.

RODNEY What's the name of the school? I've never heard of any so-called school where work's easier and they pay you for it. What's the name of it? Can't you even just tell me what it's called?

MR. KINCAID Lookit Rodney, I'm getting angry and I don't want to do that. We're almost there. I can't answer all your questions because I don't know. Let's just go there, you spend your first day and we'll talk about it tonight when you know a little more. All right?

RODNEY shifts back to his side of the car, more stiff and aloof than ever. MR. KINCAID makes turning motions with his steering wheel.

This is the place here.

RODNEY *(sitting up and forward in his seat, reading a sign as they move up the laneway)* What the... Dad, this isn't... it's a workshop for the mentally retarded. I'm not going... What are we doing here? You're not stopping here.

MR. KINCAID This is the place. This is the workshop.

RODNEY Dad, this place is for retards. It says on the sign. No. Just take me back to school. I'll be a little late. Or I'll go tomorrow and we'll say I had a cold. You can give me a note or something. Please Dad.

MR. KINCAID gets out of the car and indicates RODNEY should do the same.

Dad, listen to me.

MR. KINCAID Rodney, I have to go to work. Please get out of the car. They're expecting you inside. Let's go. Now.

RODNEY No.

RODNEY locks his door, throws himself across the seat to lock his father's door. MR. KINCAID reaches in and grabs RODNEY by the collar of his coat and drags him across the seat and out the driver's door, RODNEY falling into the parking lot below, MR. KINCAID shutting his door when it's clear.

MR. KINCAID Damn it all Rodney. Please get up.

RODNEY *(pulling himself into a ball that'll be hard for MR. KINCAID to get a grip on)* No. No, I won't. I don't belong here.

MR. KINCAID turns and looks away in fatigue and dread, summoning strength for the big push ahead. RODNEY assumes his dad isn't listening and repeats himself.

I don't belong here.

MR. KINCAID *(almost to himself)* I know that. *(turning to RODNEY and scooping him up)* I'll drag you in there by the feet if I have to. Now get up.

RODNEY I don't care. I'm not going.

MR. KINCAID Oh yes you are. And you're coming now.

These two fight and thrash their way across to the workshop area of the stage while MRS. WINTERS walks up to the front of the stage to address the house.

MRS. WINTERS My name is Bertha Winters and I've been director of the Sheltered Workshop for the Mentally Retarded since 1959. In 1975 our mandate changed and our facility was renamed the Special School for Developmentally Delayed Adults…

RODNEY *(has stopped fighting with his father and walks up to MRS. WINTERS to see what she's blathering about)* What changed in 1975?

MRS. WINTERS Our mandate changed and we discarded the earlier name in favour…

RODNEY What the hell's a mandate? Nothing changed. You kept doing the same stuff.

MRS. WINTERS The nature of my job was the same but I had to make reports to different funding and government bodies. The changes didn't impact so much on you, Rodney, but I had much more paperwork as a result, hired a special secretary to keep a whole range of new files in order and received…

RODNEY *(sarcastic)* Woah! Really big change, Mrs. Winters. We're all really impressed. My job's the very same. I'm still sortin' screws 23 years after I first showed up and you're still…

MRS. WINTERS If you don't mind, Rodney, I consider this very inappropriate behaviour. My understanding was that we were supposed to be examining what happened on the first day you came to our facility...

RODNEY Yeh, you like that day, don't you? I was scared shitless and you made my dad look like a goof.

MRS. WINTERS I did no such thing, Rodney. It was a stressful day for all of us. Your father perhaps wasn't seen in his best light that day. We understand the kind of pressures he was under.

RODNEY You lying shitbag!

MRS. WINTERS *(looking away and calling out)* Bob! Bob Palmer!

BOB *(rushing onto stage and looking a bit sheepish)* Yes, Mrs. Winters.

MRS. WINTERS I don't see how you expect me to continue under these conditions. This isn't constructive. This is just abusive and I have no intention of continuing if you can't find some way...

BOB *(holds up hands in peace-making gesture)* All right. Okay, it won't happen again. *(walks RODNEY back to his father speaking confidentially)* Lookit, Rodney, we can't go on if you don't stick to the original order and script. Mrs. Winters isn't going to take that guff and neither are the rest of us.

RODNEY So what?

BOB In case you forgot, we promised each other something. We booked this theatre, we got all these people to come out, we wrote up scripts. And we did all that so we could tell the story of your life and people would see what it was like. They'd believe you for a change. They'd take you seriously. That's what you wanted and I want it too. Right?

RODNEY *(pauses while this sinks in)* Yep. You're right. Okay, Bob – I'm ready.

BOB Good. Now remember that. *(breaks away from huddle with RODNEY to address the group)* Okay everybody. We're still on page 34 and it's the first day of the workshop scene. These two are still coming in from the parking lot and you, Mrs. Winters, are in your office doing whatever it is you do in there until you hear the noise of these two out in the hallway. Everybody got that? *(holds arm up in the air for a second, then decisively brings it down)* Take it away.

MR. KINCAID *(back to full throttle tussle with RODNEY, coming through the workshop door and dragging RODNEY in with him, looking about to see where MRS. WINTERS will enter from)* Mrs. Winters! Mrs. Winters!

While flailing in resistance, RODNEY inadvertently smacks MR. KINCAID hard across the face. MR. KINCAID backs off for a second then runs at RODNEY and lines him up against a wall or table.

Just knock it off right now or I swear I'll belt you into the middle of next week!

MRS. WINTERS *(emerges into hall and stares aghast at this scene)* Mr. Kincaid! This can't be your…

MR. KINCAID *(still speaking at RODNEY in a barely controlled fury)* You don't like it. I don't like it. But everybody says you belong here. Now what the hell am I supposed to do with that? It's rough shakes, Sunny Jim, but you're here. And that's the way it's gonna be.

Backs away, tentatively, hands held ready in case RODNEY makes a break for it. RODNEY stands still, swallowing hard and starting to cry.

MRS. WINTERS Mr. Kincaid, this hardly seems like a suitable introduction for the boy.

MR. KINCAID *(swerves and aims his rage at her instead)* Then maybe you should've come over this morning with your god damn nets and picked him up yourself! *(turns and heads back to door, not even looking at RODNEY)* I'll be back at 4:30 to take you home. Don't make any trouble. *(exits back to circle)*

MRS. WINTERS *(very gingerly approaching RODNEY who's still blubbering right where his father left him)* Hello, Rodney. My name's Mrs. Winters. Perhaps we'll start by showing you around the place. Let you meet some of your new friends.

RODNEY *(wipes tears from his eyes then faces her, speaking in the coldest, most composed voice possible)* Why don't you just fuck right off?!

MRS. WINTERS All right. I tried. *(turning away)* Bob! Bob Palmer!

BOB *(comes storming up to RODNEY)* Show me where that's written in the script, Rodney? *(pause)* What? You mean, it isn't? Mrs. Winters isn't going to stay if you keep insulting her every chance you get.

RODNEY Good. I don't want her here.

BOB Hey look – I thought we were supposed to be doing the story of your life.

RODNEY Yeah. And she's got nothing to do with it. She's the story of my death. I hate her guts. Get her outa here.

BOB But how are we going to tell about the workshop if she's not here?

RODNEY We don't have to. There's nothin' to tell.

BOB You've been there how long?

RODNEY Twenty-three years and there's nothin' to tell. I hated it when I got there and I still hate it today. The place stinks, the people are morons and she's a bitch. They've had me sortin' screws for 23 fuckin' years and it's boring. *(so agitated, he's on the brink of tears)* You wanna know about it? Every morning I go to my table and there's a new box of screws there. Their threads are all messed up – ya know what I mean? You can't screw them into the nuts. At least, not most of them. I gotta try 'em all out. Some days I find about 10 of 'em that aren't messed up. So they aren't rejects after all. I put those ones in a different box and once a month we pack those up and send 'em back to the factory. Okay? It's bad enough livin' through stuff five days a week. I'm not going to have it in my show.

BOB *(pause)* There's nothin' else you want to say about the workshop?

RODNEY One lunch a day and two breaks.

MRS. WINTERS That's hardly a fair representation of the workshop programme.

BOB Please, Mrs. Winters – don't push it just now. *(confidentially to RODNEY)* Okay then, I guess that's it for the workshop. We've got some changes to make here and you're in a bit of a state. Why don't you go get a coffee and cool out for a bit?

RODNEY Okay. Come back in five minutes?

BOB Sure. *(RODNEY exits, BOB addresses the group.)* Okay everybody, pages 36 through 44 are out. We'll be picking up the story 14 years later with Rodney's visit to his Aunt Bea and that means Rodney will need the special pants so make sure he's wearing those. *(pause)* Is he gone? *(pause)* We thought he might pull something like this but we have a contingency plan. Mrs. Winters went to a lot of trouble to keep this evening free and it's only fair that she get a full hearing. Mrs. Winters?

MRS. WINTERS *(coming forward to address the house, clearly rattled)* Thank you, Bob. I'm not as prepared for this as I'd like to be. I was not unimpressed... *(takes a deep breath)* I knew Rodney was less than happy at the facility... at the workshop. *(pause)* Bear with me. I want to be frank with you and that's not easy after more than 30 years in social work. *(pause)* A strong case could be made claiming that Rodney's initial instincts were right: he should never have been placed in the workshop. His skills in language, mathematics, his memory – are phenomenal for someone of his IQ. Rodney's eight years in the normal school system challenged and stretched him in a very fruitful way. Until the post-war era, there were no sheltered workshops for someone in Rodney's situation. They were simply thrown into the public school system and once they reached their ceiling of development... then you'd pull them out of school and call it a day; find some task in the community or the home they could adequately perform. There's no question that Rodney would've been much happier under that kind of system.

I should point out that it's been Rodney's choice to sort screws for 23 years. We've tried again and again to introduce him to other more interesting jobs and he refuses to co-operate. He smashes equipment and supplies. He swears at the other trainees and superintendents. He gives us no choice in the matter.

There's been a big push the last few years to streamline our clients back into the normal system. But I'll believe it when I see it. You'd be amazed at the number of kids who are stuck in group homes and are lucky if their parents agree to see them once a year at Christmas. Or the number of adults who never get to talk to anyone who isn't paid to listen to them. The homes and the schools all seem to run much smoother if you round up these pests into one big government run ghetto and forget them. I sometimes wonder if it wouldn't be more humane in the long run to cut the pretence that we care at all and just strangle them at birth.

All of which is my way of saying – I will not be the villain in this piece. I personally have tried harder to help Rodney Kincaid than anyone else in this room. And he's only one of more than 200 clients entrusted to our over-crowded and under-financed facility. We've let him down. We've insulted his intelligence. We've just about killed him. But we've done a hell of a lot more for him than you. Thank you and goodnight. *(turns and heads for a backstage exit, suddenly freezes)*

RODNEY *(dressed in special polyester pants, bellows from backstage)* Is she still here?

MRS. WINTERS turns and heads for auditorium exit, pursued by RODNEY with sploshing coffee cup in hand.

Get outa here! I already told you, ya got no place in this show so just get out and stay out!

MRS. WINTERS exits, RODNEY looks down at his trousers.

Oh great! Now I've spilled coffee all over my pants. *(calling out)* Jesus H. Christ, Bob – what'd ya let her back in for?

BOB *(ambling over to RODNEY)* Rodney, we've been over this and over this. If we're going to do the story right, then we had to have Mrs. Winters.

RODNEY Well maybe I don't want to do the story right. Maybe the only reason I agreed to go along with this whole stupid thing was because I was hoping we could fix a few things and make it better than it was. *(pause)* I mean, it's been a pretty embarrassing evening for me so far and some of this stuff really hurts. It drove me nuts having to go through that thing with my dad again. There was something there I never saw before. Jesus – I hate my life the way that we're doing it. I just hate it. *(RODNEY starts to break down.)*

BOB Yeh, well whose fault is that? Mrs. Winters mentioned how you don't do any jobs but the screws. How you *won't* do any jobs but the screws. And I was remembering that time you didn't show up for the interview at the graveyard about that groundskeeping job. Now that's kind of strange, isn't it?

RODNEY What?

BOB Well, it all gets so awful that you'll throw yourself off a railway bridge. But you won't do anything that might improve your situation.

RODNEY Yes I will.

BOB Like what?

RODNEY Well – I'm doing this show aren't I?

BOB No. Not really. You keep trying to rewrite what already happened. And that stuff's done. That's not going to fix anything. But what you could actually fix up is what happens when this show's over and we walk out of here. But I think you're too chicken to fix that.

RODNEY Up your's Bob.

BOB Don't try and duck this, Rodney. We know you hate your life the way it's been. We all get the message. Now, what're you going to do about it? It's your move, pal. You do something or I give up.

RODNEY You can't do that, Bob. We're bloodbrothers.

BOB Not if it all goes one way. Then what you've got is one guy and a leech.

RODNEY I'm no leech, Bob.

BOB Glad to hear it. Now show me. *(pushes RODNEY)* Show everybody. *(pushes again)*

RODNEY *(pushes back)* I'll show you. *(pushes again)* I'll show you for sure.

BOB You're going to have to push harder than that… *(BOB sustains a major body blow, then struggles to keep RODNEY at bay.)* Okay. Okay, that's good. That's what we're after. Now what're you gonna do when we walk out of here?

RODNEY What? You mean do other jobs than just sorting screws?

BOB I mean get out of the workshop. Forget that place. Even Mrs. Winters thinks you're too smart to be in there.

RODNEY Damn right.

BOB She thinks you never should've been put there in the first place.

RODNEY *(incredulous)* Come on, tell me another one.

BOB All right, I will. I think she likes you.

RODNEY *(laughs nervously)* That's… that's pretty weird, Bob. *(pause)* I think maybe you're ready for the workshop.

BOB Maybe I am. But you're not. *(points to coffee stain)* Even if it does look like you peed yourself.

RODNEY *(gazing down at pants with concern)* Do you think it'll come out?

BOB We'll get 'em cleaned. Now are you going to talk about these wonderful pants?

RODNEY I don't know. I mean, I listen to you when you talk about them and it all makes some kind of sense. But I can't talk about them as much as you do.

BOB Okay. We'll just have to do the pants in parts, then. Whose were they?

RODNEY My dad's.

BOB When did you first wear them?

RODNEY Saturday, March 22nd, 1979.

BOB And why did you wear them?

RODNEY It was mom's idea. My other good pants were in the wash. I was going over to Aunt Bea's for dinner. I used to do that every Saturday night until she died and Mom used to say the least I could do was make an effort. I didn't see why because Bea never noticed. All we ever used to do is eat pork chops, peas and potatoes and go through to her living room and watch the same three shows on TV until Bea feel asleep on the couch with her mouth hanging open. I hated that. It looked like somebody punched her.

BOB And you liked the pants?

RODNEY Definitely. They were really light. Not like my corduroys. It almost felt like I wasn't wearing any pants at all. There was a really warm thaw that night. It was exciting just to be outside and moving around. You know that kind of weather? I got the fidgets. Usually I'd have to shut off Bea's TV at nine and she'd sit up and say, "Oh – I must've dozed off." Then I'd tell her I was going home and thanks very much for the dinner. I just couldn't do it that night. It was so hot and boring in there. I just waited until she fell asleep and snuck out a whole hour early. Just left her TV running. I had this whole extra hour so I wasn't going to ride home on any stupid old bus. I was going to walk clear across town in these pants that felt like wings. And I'd just headed out when it happened. *(points to far end of stage)* They were the only other people on the street. She cut her hair and must have been like twice as old but I knew it was her.

The couple, arm in arm, are about to pass by.

Mary McPherson. *(they stop)* It is you. I knew it. Hello.

MARY *(She looks at RODNEY, puzzled and trying to remember.)* I'm terribly sorry…

RODNEY Come on, Mary. It's me. Rodney Kincaid from public school. Do you remember me?

MARY *(stalling for time until the memory kicks in)* Well yes… I think so… *(Then her eyes widen and she covers her mouth and she really does remember.)* Oh, Rodney Kincaid. You were the one who… that's right… of course. You did a lot of… well, I won't mention it.

RODNEY *(sees that MARY can't stop laughing)* What are you thinking of?

MARY I was just remembering Wayne King's boots. *(starts laughing again)*

RODNEY Yeh, that was just kid stuff. I straightened out.

MARY Did you? I'm sorry to hear that. *(seeing that RODNEY doesn't enjoy all this laughing, she pulls her composure together)* You left school around grade seven, didn't you?

RODNEY Well, I didn't leave exactly. I mean my parents moved down to Wisconsin for a couple of years so I went with them and went to school down there. Like I finished and then a little later I graduated down there, with honours, and then I came back up here because my parents liked it better up here and I did too so I came with them. We came together, like. *(still staring at MARY, he nods at her partner)* Who's he?

MARY Oh, I'm sorry. Rodney Kincaid, this is my husband, Dennis Muller.

DENNIS *(totally smooth, confident and oblivious)* Pleased to meet you, Rodney. We just got back to town ourselves. I'm in systems analysis with Thorndike-Thomas. What do you do?

RODNEY Oh, I'm just… I'm working in this screw factory. Just part time.

DENNIS Yep. I know all about that. Putting in time until something better comes along. I put in five of the hardest summers of my life working for the Brewer's Retail. And the pay wasn't bad, you know, but that sure wasn't where I wanted to be. *(could easily go on in this vein for 20 more minutes but notices RODNEY is ignoring him and staring with frightening intensity at MARY)* Excuse me, but are you hearing any of this?

RODNEY Could I come and see you, Mary? Where you live? Tell me where you live.

MARY I don't…. No. No, Rodney – I don't think you should. Are you ready, Dennis?

DENNIS Sure. *(starts to lead them away)*

MARY It's been nice seeing you again, Rodney. I hope everything works out for you.

BOB *(comes wandering out onto stage)* My God, Rodney, you were practically climbing right into her eyeballs there.

RODNEY *(still staring after MARY, too distracted to enter into a conversation with BOB)* Six doors north of Aunt Bea's. Mary McPherson lives six doors north of Aunt Bea's.

BOB Lot of good that's going to do you. You just scared her half to death and totally snubbed her husband. You're lucky he didn't haul off and deck you.

RODNEY I'll bet she never gets all bare naked and rubs up against *him*. I mean, I've known Mary a lot longer than he has. That's got to stand for something. *(in a mincing na-na voice)* "Really pleased to meet you, Rodney. I'm a systems analyst. What do you do?" God, what a loser. Did you see the way she asked me when I left school? And Dennis said they just came back to town. I'll bet she never found out about the workshop. I mean, we've known each other since we were five. What's Dennis compared with that? It'll be easy enough to work my way around him. *(In his daze of delusion RODNEY walks his way right off stage and leaves BOB alone.)*

BOB You've seen quite a bit of Rodney tonight and if you're like me, there've been times when you've said to yourself, "Retarded? Hell, I've seen people stupider than him reading the weather on TV." It wasn't because of Rodney's IQ that they pitch-forked him into that workshop. I'm convinced that for the most part, it was because of stuff like this. Rodney woke up the next morning to find a foot of fresh snow on the ground. He took this as a good sign and decided the time had come to put his truly long-term plan into practice.

He caught the first Sunday morning bus back to Aunt Bea's. He wore his special pants and he brought his snow shovel. *(We see RODNEY enter and commence shovelling.)* Dennis had already been out to clear the walk but he'd made a pretty sketchy job of it so Rodney set about doing his efforts one better. A group of adults, gussied up for church, made their way along the path he was clearing and Rodney couldn't help imagining their conversation.

Two ladies closely followed by two men move across the stage, exchanging "good mornings" with RODNEY. The men fall a little further behind.

MAN #1 That must be Mary McPherson's husband.

MAN #2 Yes. Seemed a friendly enough chap, didn't he?

MAN #1 For sure. Say, but isn't his wife a good looker?

MAN #2 She certainly is. A regular stunner. I'll bet she takes her clothes off for him when he finishes up out here.

MAN #1 And well she should, too. He's doing a wonderful job of it.

RODNEY sees these four back to their seats in the circle and resumes shovelling, looking up when MARY makes her entrance down the half-shovelled walk. In every possible particular, her entrance should echo the previous Charles Dickens fantasy sequence.

MARY Rodney. Rodney, could I have a word with you? *(pause)* I'm sorry, Rodney, but we really don't need anyone to shovel our snow. It may not have looked like much but Dennis already did it.

RODNEY *(resumes shovelling and speaks under his breath)* It sure didn't. It was a lousy job.

MARY *(becoming more firm)* Well, yes. It was all we wanted. This late in the season it all just melts by noon. *(pause)* Rodney, please stop. We don't want this. And we won't pay you for it.

RODNEY I don't want money.

MARY Then why are you doing it?

RODNEY Why do I need a reason to do something? Why can't you just let me do it?

MARY Because then I'd feel like I owe you something and I wouldn't like that feeling. It would put me in a false situation. I hardly know you, Rodney. I don't want to owe you anything. Is that clear? *(reaches out to stop his arms)* Is that clear? Look at me, Rodney. If there's something you want, just come out and ask me.

RODNEY only stares at MARY, incapable of saying anything which will only shatter his final hope.

Why do you always look at me that way? *(She places a hand on one of his shoulders.)* Please, can't you just tell me?

RODNEY turns away from her, shoulders heaving and starts to quietly cry.

Oh my God, why are you…? Please, Rodney, I can't handle this. I don't know who you think I am or why you can just…

DENNIS *(moving up from behind)* What is it, Honey – won't he leave?

MARY turns around to DENNIS and though we don't hear anything, she gestures to him to "go easy," then heads back into the house. DENNIS approaches RODNEY who's now paralyzed in shame, still crying, eyes cast down.

Hey, Rodney. I'm sorry about the snow but we just don't need it shovelled. Are they laying you off at the screw factory? I could let you have a few bucks if things are really tight. *(pulls out his wallet, starts leafing through the bills)* Pay me back when you can. Is that it?

RODNEY *(speaks evenly but in a voice drenched in tears)* You're the crappiest snow shoveller I've ever seen. *(RODNEY takes up his shovel and exits.)*

DENNIS *(putting his wallet away and heading back into the house)* Well, good morning to you, Creep-oh.

BOB *(comes strolling back out to address the house)* Rodney didn't think any less kindly of Mary in the wake of that little incident. In fact, he paid her a strange sort of homage by rechristening the pants.

Technically, they were still his father's but he usually got permission to wear them for any special occasion. Aunt Bea died and he started having weekly dinners at our place. Our oldest daughter would meet him at the door and say, "Whose pants ya wearin'?" and he'd answer, "The Mary McPherson Pants." Another thing he started doing for the first time was attending dances at the workshop. He didn't dance at all, wouldn't even consider a romance with one of the woman trainees – he'd just stand around for three hours and listen to the records. I had to talk Rodney into the idea of starting our show with his jump from the bridge. In exchange for that, Rodney wants to close with a scene that involves his dad. It's a June evening three years after the shovelling of Mary McPherson's walk. Rodney is sneaking into his parents' darkened bedroom where Mr. Kincaid lies alone and asleep in the wake of a stroke from which he never will recover. Rodney pulls out the lowest dresser drawer and rummages through it in search of a special pair of trousers which he can recognize by feel alone. Gently extracting them from the carefully folded pile, he closes the drawer and heads back to the door.

MR. KINCAID *(a hollow whisper)* Joan? Is that you, Joan?

RODNEY *(standing still, facing the door)* No, Dad. It's me.

MR. KINCAID After those pants, I'll bet.

RODNEY Yes sir. I need them for a dance at the workshop.

MR. KINCAID Why do you suppose you like those pants so much?

RODNEY They remind me of someone.

MR. KINCAID Thank you, Rodney. That's very sweet of you.

RODNEY You're welcome, Dad.

MR. KINCAID I want you to have them, Rodney. They're yours. But you keep them for special.

RODNEY I will, Dad. *(RODNEY continues to stand frozen, prompting MR. KINCAID to start feeding him his final line.)*

MR. KINCAID Goodnight. *(pause)* You're supposed to say goodnight. *(pause)* You say goodnight, you go out the door, the lights come…

RODNEY *(interrupting, turning around)* I don't want to go out that door. I know what happens. It just gets worse and worse. You die and Mom dies and I start living alone and the only time anyone ever talks to me is at the workshop.

MR. KINCAID What about Bob?

RODNEY He gives me supper once a week. We do this show. But nothing changes.

MR. KINCAID You don't know that. At least you're alive Rodney. Something *could* change.

RODNEY Dad, don't make me go out that door.

MR. KINCAID You've got to eventually. You know that.

RODNEY No… I can't go back to the same old stuff.

MR. KINCAID Whoever said you had to?

RODNEY But… you mean…? Everybody's been telling me that.

MR. KINCAID Not anymore, they're not.

RODNEY Please, Dad. Can we just talk a little?

MR. KINCAID *(beckons him over, RODNEY sits with him on the cot)* We'll end it here and then we'll have our talk. All right? *(RODNEY nods his assent, MR. KINCAID looks out to some invisible technician.)* Okay – if you could bring down the lights, this is how we're going to end the show.

MR. KINCAID takes RODNEY into his arms as the light slowly fades to black.

The end.

Buttonholes In Silk

by
Gail Fricker

Born in England, **Gail Fricker** trained in theatre at Warwick University with a degree in Dramatic Arts. She worked briefly as a drama teacher before becoming a professional actor and director. In 1980 she founded Apple Theatre, specializing in theatre for young audiences, and wrote their award winning plays *Happy Hunting Ground* and *Lifescanner*.

In 1990 she began touring Ontario with Apple Theatre, and soon made Canada her home. Her career began to branch out into storytelling, and took a leap when she completed her Masters in Story Arts in Tennessee. In recent years she has travelled extensively and has been invited to tell stories at festivals in Kenya, Japan, Denmark and throughout Canada. She is the author of *Dynamic Ideas For Drama and Dance* and has released two story audio cassettes *To Catch A Tale* and *To Tell A Tale*. She is the recipient of several Ontario Arts Council and Canada Council grants, and a respected speaker at many international conferences.

She is now settled in Stratford, Ontario and has returned to teaching drama part time while she and her artist husband raise a family.

INTRODUCTION TO *BUTTONHOLES IN SILK*

Have you ever been bored or detained in a conversation against your will? If so, you will understand what it's like to be buttonholed. In Gail Fricker's *Buttonholes In Silk* the concept of the reluctant listener is used to explore the complex issues of self-definition, family relationship and reconciliation as experienced by three women of differing generations. The result is a touching conversation or trio – a composition for three voices.

In Fricker's play the voices belong to three mature women, consisting of Mother, Daughter and Grandmother. This triangle we discover, in three separate conversations, is unified by more than family experience.

Initially Daughter comes home to England in hopes of discovering and asserting her own identity, and to break her estrangement with her mother. The two have not spoken since her emigration to Canada, so she enlists the support of her Grandmother and pushes for a joint holiday and reconciliation. Until recently, it had been a long-time family tradition for the three women to travel to the seaside and Daughter hopes her initiative to recreate the custom will permit them "to change things... to break the cycle before it's too late."

Structured as three one to one conversations, each scene is permeated by the personality of the absent woman, permitting us to glimpse the relationships existing between each generation. Their dialogue reflects each character's tenacious nature and their tendency towards preoccupation. This permits us to see the threads of sameness that weave together the history and experiences of the three generations of women.

To punctuate their shared family history the play opens and closes with a series of four slides reflecting different generations of women at the seaside. The set consists of a surface defined by stones and beach pebbles, with folding, low slung deck chairs being carried on and off stage by the actors; there is ample opportunity to experiment with lighting and sound effects.

This minimal staging effectively reflects the unchanging nature of the seashore and permits us to focus on the dynamic roles the script affords females. Fricker has crafted a thought-provoking play whose very fabric challenges its audience, and characters alike, to recognize that in order to converse we must learn not only to speak but also to listen.

Marian Doucette

Buttonholes In Silk was first produced as part of Alumnae Theatre's New Idea Festival in March 1997, with the following cast:

GRAN	Razie Brownstone
MOTHER	Lindsay Empringham
DAUGHTER	Shelly Cass

Directed by Derek Dorey

Characters

GRAN	Working class Englishwoman. 90 years of age
MOTHER	Lower Middle Class Englishwoman. 60 years of age
DAUGHTER	British Citizen now living in Canada working as theatre professional. 30 years of age.

Setting

Brighton, England. On the beach. Late Summer. Today.

About the Set

An area centre stage defined by a surface of stones and beach pebbles ranging from large rocks the size of a human head to almost sand. Folding, low slung deck chairs, first three, then two.
A surface for slide projection.
Lighting to suggest outdoors, various weather states.

This play is dedicated to my Nan, Daisy, to keep her memories alive and to my Brother, Graham.

BUTTONHOLES IN SILK
by Gail Fricker

<u>Scene One</u>

Four slides are projected, one after the other: Slide 1 – five women aged 30 to 50 on the beach. Year 1935. Slide 2 – three women aged 45 to 55 walking along the pier in summer. Year 1955. Slide 3 – three women aged 45 to 55 walking along the pier in the rain. Year 1960. Slide 4 – Mother and two young daughters playing on the beach. Year 1965.

Soundscape of the beach.

DAUGHTER enters with bags, blanket etc. Places them down CS. *Exits. Returns with three fold-up deck chairs and sets them up. Exits. Returns with GRAN, pushing her wheelchair or helping her on her sticks.*

DAUGHTER It's a little chilly but it feels good.

GRAN It's chilly.

DAUGHTER Here, sit down here Nan. *(sits her down in the chair)* Okay?

GRAN This isn't right.

DAUGHTER Put the blanket around you Nan, it's chilly. *(She puts it around GRAN's knees.)*

GRAN It's chilly.

DAUGHTER I'll never hear the end of it if you catch a cold.

GRAN It's my knees.

DAUGHTER You'll be warm enough, don't worry. *(She looks out to sea.)* There's quite a wind, the waves are high. *(GRAN kicks off the blanket while DAUGHTER isn't looking. DAUGHTER turns to see it laying on the floor.)* Nan, it's too chilly out. You need the blanket.

DAUGHTER picks it up and brushes the sand off, while her back is turned, GRAN takes a quick sip from the hip flask.

GRAN I'm not worried.

DAUGHTER No, but we don't won't you catching pneumonia on us. *(tucking her up in the blanket)* There now, keep it on Nan or you'll get me in trouble.

GRAN It's chilly.

DAUGHTER Yes Nan, it is chilly. *(She goes to put on an extra sweater. As she does this, GRAN kicks off the blanket again.)*

GRAN It's fallen off.

DAUGHTER *(in disbelief)* I can see that. *(She bends down to pick it up. GRAN goes to take another sip from the flask.)*

DAUGHTER What do you have there?

GRAN Nothing.

DAUGHTER What is it?

GRAN Warms the cockles.

DAUGHTER What is it?

GRAN *(drinks)* It's not chilly anymore.

DAUGHTER Nan!

GRAN Want some?

DAUGHTER No! *(puts blanket back on)* Keep it on Nan – then you'll keep warm! *(sits down next to GRAN)*

GRAN Where's your mother?

DAUGHTER Back at the car, flapping.

GRAN She's coming though?

DAUGHTER Eventually! If she doesn't forget anything. Do you remember when she forgot the blanket?

GRAN The blanket.

DAUGHTER Yes. We were on our way to Brighton.

GRAN Today?

DAUGHTER No, when I was still little. You remember.

GRAN No.

DAUGHTER It was a really nice day and we wanted to get to the beach early, but we had to spend half the day packing the car. Mum wouldn't leave anything behind. She'd always take so much. You'd think we were going for a year, not a day!

GRAN I don't remember.

DAUGHTER And when we were half way there, Mum suddenly realized she had left the blanket behind. We had to turn the car around. We couldn't go and buy another one—oh no—we had to turn the car around and drive all the way back. Dad was fuming, but Mum was so uptight, there was no changing her mind. Do you remember that?

GRAN There was no blanket.

DAUGHTER That's right… the three of us sat in the back in silence, not daring to speak, staring from one to the other… I don't think you were there, were you?

GRAN You could hear them flying over.

DAUGHTER What?

GRAN Sometimes they wouldn't even warn you.

DAUGHTER Who Nan? Warn you about what?

GRAN There's a whistling sound.

DAUGHTER Where?

GRAN A sharp piercing whistling…. Then it all went quiet. Everybody held their breath and waited to see where it had landed.

DAUGHTER What are you talking about?

GRAN *(leans forward and whispers)* Doodlebugs! *(She drinks from the hip flask.)*

DAUGHTER Doodlebugs?

GRAN Had one land in the back passage. George and Mr. Selec put it out. The children were so frightened. Crying. Huddled together under the stairs.

DAUGHTER In the bunks that grandpa had made?

GRAN Every night when she went to the bunk she'd take her teddy bear, her blanket – tatty old thing it was, never forgot her blanket.

DAUGHTER Who?

GRAN And she wore her favourite dress to bed. The blue one. *(pause)*

DAUGHTER Mum?

GRAN She was so frightened that the house would burn down. Frightened she'd lose everything. She'd cry herself to sleep most nights. I can remember her crying. So worried.

DAUGHTER But you survived didn't you… you managed.

GRAN Yes, I s'pose we did.

DAUGHTER And here we are now back at sunny Brighton. *(standing and looking out to sea)* Nothing's changed! The ceaseless ebb and flow of the tide.

GRAN takes a drink from the hip flask.

It is a bit nippy. I forgot how much more damp it is here.

GRAN Isn't it cold in Canada?

DAUGHTER Well yes…

GRAN I thought you got a lot of snow.

DAUGHTER Yes Nan, and "we all wear parkas and live in igloos." She won't come out there you know.

GRAN It's a long way.

DAUGHTER And too much foreign food, she says! Where's her sense of adventure? Routine and habit. Can't have anything different. Routine and habit! She doesn't want to see anything or go anywhere, but she wants to know what's in the neighbours' shopping bags, and always knows exactly what car is parked in the neighbours drive, peeping out from behind the curtain!

GRAN Whose car?

DAUGHTER I thought she'd soften. Change her mind, but nothing's changed. Routine and habit! After sixteen years she still doesn't speak to… I don't know why I expect a miracle.

GRAN BINGO!

DAUGHTER What?

GRAN I always went to Bingo on a Friday.

DAUGHTER I'm not talking about Bingo Nan.

GRAN I'd catch the number nine bus at the corner and get off just at the bottom of Kilburn High Road.

DAUGHTER And you'd have the same pen and sit in the same chair for luck.

GRAN And win too.

DAUGHTER I know you did. I came with you once or twice.

GRAN All the girls at the table together. If anyone won we'd all shout out…

DAUGHTER & GRAN BINGO! *(They laugh.)*

GRAN drinks from the flask and passes it to DAUGHTER who drinks for the first time.

GRAN Every Friday, rain or shine.

DAUGHTER Just like the annual trip to Brighton. Do you remember when we came down and it rained so hard that the beach had turned into one big puddle?

GRAN I had my new Mac on.

DAUGHTER And you were so determined to sit on the beach in your new Mac and eat your fish and chips. You wouldn't move.

GRAN We always sit here.

DAUGHTER Mum and me and, I think, Aunt Alice. We all had to huddle under a plastic bag we found in the garbage. We got soaked to the bone while you ate your last mouthful.

GRAN You should have worn a Mac!

DAUGHTER We should have gone home!

GRAN That's what your mother said.

DAUGHTER *(turning away)* I've got a new job Nan.

GRAN Yes.

DAUGHTER I start rehearsals in the spring for a festival of new works. I'm really excited about it. The Arts Council gave us a grant to workshop it and we got great reviews.

GRAN Yes.

DAUGHTER They gave us a four-star rating Nan.

GRAN What?

DAUGHTER Four stars.

GRAN Where?

DAUGHTER The newspaper Nan.

GRAN Yes dear.

DAUGHTER But Mum is still waiting for me to get a "proper" job.

GRAN Buttonholes.

DAUGHTER No rehearsals Nan… acting.

GRAN Buttonholes in silk. Beautiful silk it was. The material kept sliding everywhere. I made a proper mess of it.

DAUGHTER How old were you Nan?

GRAN And covered buttons. She told me to cut a piece of material and put it under the button head and put it on the pad and pull down the handle.

DAUGHTER Was this your first job?

GRAN I was just fourteen. I didn't know how to do it. I made a right proper mess of it.

DAUGHTER What did she say?

GRAN I went off to the park at lunch time and I was too frightened to go back, so I never did.

DAUGHTER You just stayed in the park?

GRAN I couldn't say anything to my Mother though. The next day I paid the two 'n six tram fare but didn't go to work – I spent the whole day in the park instead – till it rained...

DAUGHTER What did your mum say?

GRAN You have to sit there rain or shine.

DAUGHTER Did you go home?

GRAN I had to go home to face the music.

DAUGHTER And?

GRAN *(looking straight at DAUGHTER)* Talk to her, love .

DAUGHTER Do you like my hair Nan?

GRAN Very nice.

DAUGHTER Thank you.

GRAN I had my hair done special.

DAUGHTER When?

GRAN For the dance.

DAUGHTER Who'd you go with Nan?

GRAN Oh, with your grandpa, I think. I was married by then. I had a new dress for it.

DAUGHTER What was it like?

GRAN A beautiful green.

DAUGHTER Your favourite colour.

GRAN I had white gloves up to my elbows.

DAUGHTER Silk ones?

GRAN Oh no, they were lace ones. They matched the lace on my dress. It had a bit of lace on the end of the sleeves – short sleeves, and lace around the bodice. I can't remember if it had lace around the hem as well. Yer grandpa said I was the belle of the ball.

DAUGHTER I bet you were as well.

GRAN I did look good in that dress. She'd done me proud.

DAUGHTER Who?

GRAN She made it for me.

DAUGHTER Mum did?

GRAN Yes.

DAUGHTER She wouldn't do that for me. All she ever makes is wedding dresses… and I'm not about to have one of those.

GRAN Talk to her love.

DAUGHTER She doesn't want to talk to me. She doesn't want to know anything about what I'm doing. I have a new boyfriend, and I can't even bring him home because he doesn't fit the frame. None of them do. They might be divorced, or too old, or too young, or black, or Chinese or even a bloody Catholic – none of them fit what she expects. She doesn't want to know anything that doesn't fit the frame of the little box she's put me in. I think she still believes there is a Prince Charming, and we all live happy ever after.

GRAN I had lots of boyfriends.

DAUGHTER *(uninterested)* Really?

GRAN We used to meet them on the beach at Aldburgh. Bert kissed me under the pier.

DAUGHTER Nan!

GRAN And Frank always cuddled on the blanket. *(She fondles the blanket on her knees.)* Cold hands, I remember his cold hands.

DAUGHTER You lay on the beach blanket?

GRAN Then there was one, I think his name was Jerry, he was really keen on me and kept sending me flowers and love letters.

DAUGHTER What did he say?

GRAN I got one postcard from him asking to meet me at the Ritz Hotel – but I'd met George the day before on the beach and I much preferred him.

DAUGHTER What did you do?

GRAN Well I couldn't phone him or nothing, we didn't have a phone. I sent a message on a postcard to him that I wouldn't be able to see him until the following day. But I didn't go. I was having too much fun with George.

DAUGHTER Nan, you stood him up. *(both laughing)*

GRAN I don't suppose he's still waiting. *(laughing)*

They take a drink from the hip flask.

Yes I did play the field… or the beach. Always bring a blanket to the beach my love.

DAUGHTER You see – you understand Nan. You're just like me. Will you tell her? She'll listen to you.

GRAN No she won't.

DAUGHTER Why not?

GRAN I'm her mother.

DAUGHTER But it's different with you. You're older…

GRAN I don't think things change really. We still come to Brighton.

DAUGHTER No – that's just it – things never change because we're not allowed to change them! The three of us here in Brighton.

GRAN It's not raining though.

DAUGHTER And we're all supposed to pretend that nothing is wrong. I'm tired of pretending. We have to change things Nan. I've read books about it. Someone has to break the cycle before it's too late.

GRAN drinks from flask.

DAUGHTER *(looks at watch)* It's time to get the fish and chips. I'll go. *(exits)*

Scene Two

Five minutes after scene one. MOTHER enters with bags and a blanket.

MOTHER Are you on your own?

GRAN Hello.

MOTHER Where is she?

GRAN Fish and Chips.

MOTHER I've got a picnic. I said I'd bring one. *(fusses around GRAN, tucking in blanket etc.)* It's nippy. Aren't you cold? I brought you an extra blanket in case you get cold.

GRAN No. *(taking a sip of the flask)*

MOTHER *(looking through bag and producing a picnic)* She shouldn't have left you alone. I told her not to leave you. She doesn't listen.

GRAN I found them in your room.

MOTHER Anything could have happened. Are you all right Mum?

GRAN I told you not to take them to your room.

MOTHER What?

GRAN You know you can't play with your toys in the bedroom. Just in the back room. That's where the toys belong.

MOTHER What are you talking about Mum?

GRAN The dolls.

MOTHER What dolls? Are you all right?

GRAN You liked that one with the black hair. You took it everywhere with you. Always took it to church on Sundays. You wouldn't put it down. You cried and cried when your brother took it from you. Always knew how to make you cry.

MOTHER Um.

GRAN And you had me make a Sunday Best outfit for it. It was blue. We used a bit of that dress you had. That one you'd never take off and wore to all the parties.

MOTHER Oh yes.

GRAN Didn't we make a rag doll out of that?

MOTHER I don't remember.

GRAN I told you not to take them in your bedroom. You didn't listen.

MOTHER *(ignoring the comment, busy with the sandwiches)* Do you want egg or cheese and pickle?

GRAN Egg.

MOTHER I've got your favourite cheese. The one you like.

GRAN Egg.

MOTHER There now, I made them special for you. *(passes a sandwich to GRAN)*

GRAN Four stars! *(She takes a bite of a cheese sandwich.)*

MOTHER Where?

GRAN I said egg.

MOTHER Oh, I'm sorry. *(fishing through bag)* I must have got them mixed up. That's egg I think. *(passes the sandwich and they eat in silence for a while)*

GRAN It's a new job.

MOTHER Who's got a new job Mum?

GRAN She said she has a new job?

MOTHER Oh, she been talking about that again. It's not a real job Mum, just something she's doing.

GRAN Dad was always doing things.

MOTHER Um.

GRAN Always busy. Never had a real job.

MOTHER *(defensive)* But he was always working. He was always busy in the shed out back.

GRAN Never went in there. Never knew what he did in there.

MOTHER He made that swing for us. I remember Dad putting that up in the passage. The girls had fun on that… so did we when we were kids. I remember playing in the passage.

GRAN He did all sorts of things. Never complained. Always made ends meet.

MOTHER He liked his work.

GRAN Same as you. Lucky you got that training at Harrods. You were so pleased when you came home. You were dancing with your sister round the back room.

MOTHER I wasn't.

GRAN You always wanted to be a dressmaker – don't know why. Don't know where you got it from.

MOTHER I just did.

GRAN I didn't want you to work in the business.

MOTHER You never said anything.

GRAN "Just let her do it" Dad said. "She'll soon find out if it's right."

MOTHER laughs.

Just let Her do it. She'll soon find out.

MOTHER Another sandwich?

GRAN Egg.

MOTHER I've got some tea somewhere. *(gets out flask)* Tea?

GRAN I don't want sugar.

MOTHER I know Mother. There's no sugar in it.

MOTHER pours GRAN some tea and while she is busy pouring her own, GRAN adds a sip from the hip flask to the tea.

GRAN It's nippy.

MOTHER Are you cold Mum? Do you want the blanket.

GRAN *(shouting)* No!

MOTHER ignores the rebuff. Gets some sewing out of the bag and begins to sew.

Bottom!

MOTHER What's wrong Mother?

GRAN Bottom.

MOTHER Do you want a cushion. I can get you a cushion from the car if you want.

GRAN That's who I played. I couldn't remember.

MOTHER Are you sure you're okay?

GRAN We had paper dresses that we made. Lilly and Madge helped me. We weren't very old. We practised in the bedroom. I had to play Bottom and Madge was the fairy 'cause she had ballet shoes.

MOTHER You weren't in a play Mother.

GRAN I was! *Midsummer Night's Dream.*

MOTHER I didn't know that.

GRAN Mum didn't know what we were doing, until after we had invited everyone in the street. She couldn't say no then.

MOTHER You sound just like Her.

GRAN But my Mum was so proud of us when she knew it was for the war. She even collected the shilling at the door. They all crammed into the front room. Standing room only there was. *(pause)* I liked doing that, I did. I liked acting.

MOTHER It's turning grey. I think it might rain. We'll have to get going if it rains. Did she say where she'd gone to get fish and chips?

GRAN It doesn't snow all the time.

MOTHER No, I don't think it will snow Mum.

GRAN Over there.

MOTHER Where?

GRAN In the cold place.

MOTHER Where?

GRAN Where she lives. It doesn't snow all the time.

MOTHER Oh, that foreign place. I don't know why she doesn't come home.

GRAN You liked it there.

MOTHER I haven't been there Mum.

GRAN Aldborough. You liked it there.

MOTHER It's not the same Mother.

GRAN When we went there in the war. You didn't want to stay. You cried and cried.

MOTHER I thought we were just going for a holiday, not staying for two years.

GRAN But then you made new friends. You used to run in the fields and play on the beach. I had to go out and call you when it was dinner time. When it was time to go back to London, you didn't want to go. You said it was better down there. You wanted to live there.

MOTHER *(smiles)* It was good there.

GRAN What are you making?

MOTHER Oh, just doing some mending. Fixing some buttons on George's shirt.

GRAN Do you remember that red jumper you made?

MOTHER When I was in junior school.

GRAN You were so proud of it.

MOTHER I had to stand up in front of the whole school in assembly. I remember that.

GRAN You kept practising again and again at home.

MOTHER I had to stand up and I said: "I done it all myself."

They laugh together. MOTHER is softening. They look at each other in a gentle silence. GRAN breaks the silence.

GRAN Talk to her love.

MOTHER looks away, sad and teary-eyed.

When's George coming?

MOTHER We brought the car with us remember?

GRAN He always picked you up. Very polite. Always said "Hello Mr. and Mrs. Taylor."

MOTHER *(smiles)* Yes.

GRAN You was just 14.

MOTHER 15. I met him when I was 15.

GRAN I don't remember.

MOTHER At Joan's party. He walked me home the first night I met him.

GRAN You were very young. Should have played the field more.

MOTHER Mum!

GRAN We didn't know it was serious.

MOTHER You never said anything.

GRAN You never told us. "Trust her" Dad said, "She'll make up her own mind."

MOTHER And I did.

GRAN Yes. *(They both smile at each other.)* "Trust her love!" *(pause)* I miss it.

MOTHER What?

GRAN London.

MOTHER It's so dirty there now. You're better down here with the sea breeze.

GRAN It's nippy.

MOTHER Are you cold? I've got that extra blanket. *(She gets up to put blanket around GRAN. Standing behind her.)*

GRAN That's what you said.

MOTHER What?

GRAN It's dirty here.

MOTHER Where?

GRAN London. That's what you said when you left. I didn't want you to move. Too far away from home.

MOTHER Oh don't upset yourself Mum. *(comforting GRAN)*

GRAN You said it was better in the country.

MOTHER It was.

GRAN I didn't want you to go. I didn't know when I'd see you next.

MOTHER I came back to visit.

GRAN *(holding onto MOTHER, almost crying)* Yes, I let you go and you came back.

MOTHER gently kisses GRAN on the forehead.

MOTHER I think we should get you home. The tide's coming in.

GRAN But she…

MOTHER We'll meet her back at the car. Come on now. *(helping GRAN onto her feet)*

GRAN Yes. It's nippy.

MOTHER Yes it's nippy. Lean on me Mum.

They exit. MOTHER carries the blanket and the bags. MOTHER returns for two of the chairs and leaves a note on the third – "meet us at the car." Exit. Slow blackout.

Scene Three

One Year Later. October. MOTHER enters with three fold-up deck chairs and begins to set them up beside each other. Enter DAUGHTER carrying picnic basket, bag and blanket.

MOTHER Is this the spot?

DAUGHTER What?

MOTHER It's been a year… I don't remember. *(putting up third chair)*

DAUGHTER Why do you have three chairs? We don't need three.

MOTHER I'd packed three.

DAUGHTER But you knew she wasn't coming.

MOTHER I packed the car last night.

DAUGHTER Routine and habit.

MOTHER I always pack three.

DAUGHTER And you always pack so thoroughly.

MOTHER Do you have the blanket?

DAUGHTER Yes I have the blanket.

DAUGHTER puts down bags. MOTHER fussily arranges the bags around her, sits on end chair and begins to crochet. DAUGHTER unfolds the blanket and gently lays it on the middle chair.

DAUGHTER Are you sure this is the right spot?

MOTHER Um.

DAUGHTER It's not the same without her.

MOTHER Um. Yes.

DAUGHTER It's different.

MOTHER I thought you liked changes.

Silence. DAUGHTER stares coldly at MOTHER.

DAUGHTER Why didn't you tell me ?

MOTHER What?

DAUGHTER That she was ill.

MOTHER She's not ill.

DAUGHTER She never goes out anymore.

MOTHER She hasn't done that for a year.

DAUGHTER And she's had a fall.

MOTHER Three.

DAUGHTER You never said anything.

MOTHER You were away.

DAUGHTER You can still call. I am on the phone you know.

MOTHER Each time I ring you're not home.

DAUGHTER I have rehearsals most nights.

MOTHER All I ever get is that machine.

DAUGHTER Leave a message.

MOTHER You're always working. Never home to talk to.

DAUGHTER You never talk to me anyway.

MOTHER You never listen.

DAUGHTER I tried to call you the week before I left.

MOTHER I wasn't there.

DAUGHTER I know.

MOTHER We went away.

DAUGHTER I guessed that.

MOTHER I told you that we'd be at your sisters.

DAUGHTER You never said.

MOTHER I thought I did.

DAUGHTER No.

MOTHER I don't remember.

DAUGHTER Convenient.

Silence. DAUGHTER stares out to sea. Speaks without facing MOTHER.

It's a low tide. It's getting nippy.

MOTHER Do you want the blanket ?

DAUGHTER No, I'm fine.

MOTHER stands and reaches out to DAUGHTER.

MOTHER That button's nearly off.

DAUGHTER Stop it.

MOTHER I'll fix it for you.

DAUGHTER I can do it Mum.

MOTHER I know you can, but you don't do you?

Silence. They stare at each other. DAUGHTER removes the jacket and hands it to MOTHER. MOTHER sits and begins to sew on button. DAUGHTER looks at MOTHER's crocheting.

DAUGHTER What are you making?

MOTHER I'm crocheting a bonnet for Laura's little girl.

DAUGHTER Who?

MOTHER She lives at the corner at number 10. You remember, they got married three years ago. I made the bridesmaid dresses.

DAUGHTER Oh.

MOTHER She's just had a baby girl.

DAUGHTER *(uninterested)* Nice. Are you finished, I'm getting chilly.

MOTHER Finished.

MOTHER hands DAUGHTER the jacket. Their hands touch as the DAUGHTER takes the jacket.

DAUGHTER Thanks Mum. *(smiles, then silence)* I'm hungry. Shall I go and get the fish and chips.

MOTHER No, I've packed us a lunch.

DAUGHTER But we always have fish and chips.

MOTHER I thought you might like a change. Something different. Pass me that bag. Can you get the plates out? *(unwrapping food, plates etc.)*

DAUGHTER In here?

MOTHER Yes. Your Father and I went to a new restaurant last week. It's just opened up in town. We thought of you – you'd like it.

DAUGHTER Mum, these are samosas.

MOTHER Yes they had all sorts – some with meat, some vegetable. I know you can't eat beef, so I got you some vegetable ones.

DAUGHTER You went to a curry house?

MOTHER I don't know what you call it. It wasn't all that hot stuff though. It was quite nice.

DAUGHTER You ate foreign food?

MOTHER You can't eat fish and chips every day! *(laughs, then silence)*

They begin to eat. In amongst the packages that MOTHER has taken from the bag, she has pulled out a magazine and a newspaper – The Globe And Mail. *The DAUGHTER notices.*

DAUGHTER Mum, this is *The Globe and Mail.*

MOTHER I know.

DAUGHTER It's a Toronto newspaper.

MOTHER Yes.

DAUGHTER Where did you get it?

MOTHER It's delivered every Friday.

DAUGHTER You have it delivered?

MOTHER You live there don't you.

DAUGHTER You read *The Globe and Mail*?

MOTHER It's your home.

DAUGHTER Maybe. *(silence)* Yes you're right, it is my home.

A sad smile of acknowledgement and acceptance between them. They continue to eat in silence. The DAUGHTER begins to hunt through bag.

MOTHER What are you looking for?

DAUGHTER Did you pack a drink?

MOTHER Yes. I think it's in this bag. I packed all the food that Nan likes in here.

DAUGHTER But you knew she wasn't coming.

MOTHER This morning. *(taking out packages)* I got some of that cheese she really likes.

DAUGHTER It stinks.

MOTHER I don't think she notices. And some of those figs. Good for her bowels she says.

DAUGHTER Is that what it is?

MOTHER Oh no, I've got her pills in here as well. We'll have to be back by supper; she has to take two before she eats. I have to make sure she doesn't miss them.

DAUGHTER You do look after her don't you Mum.

MOTHER She's my Mother.

Silence.

DAUGHTER Have you spoken to your son? I called him. He's doing well, so are the grandchildren. The oldest is ten now. He wants to talk to you Mum.

MOTHER Um.

DAUGHTER It's been seventeen years Mum. Will you speak to him? Will you talk to him? At least listen to him. *(silence)* Talk to him Mum.

DAUGHTER looks at MOTHER. Cold silence. DAUGHTER stands.

What's the point of this?

MOTHER You wanted to come here.

DAUGHTER You're not going to change. I don't know why we bother to come here.

MOTHER Your Nan likes it.

DAUGHTER But she's not here is she? *(silence)* It's a depressing place, Brighton. It's always grey here; even the pebbles are grey. It was bad enough when we came in the summer. I don't know why we come now; no-one else is here. *(turns to look at MOTHER)*

MOTHER We came for a picnic.

DAUGHTER No. We came to talk. *(Mother avoids eye contact.)* There's no point to this if you're not going to talk. Mum? Will you speak to him? *(no response)* Don't ignore me Mum! You can't put the phone down on me now. *(no response)* Oh I give in. I'm going.

DAUGHTER packs up the bags and folds up two of the deck chairs. MOTHER stares out to sea.

It's freezing here. Thank God I'm leaving tomorrow. *(stares at MOTHER)* Well? Don't give me the cold shoulder treatment just because I mentioned my brother. It doesn't work with me anymore Mum. *(MOTHER looks at her but does not speak.)* Oh Shit!

DAUGHTER exits taking two chairs. Returns and MOTHER is staring out at sea still seated.

Are you coming ? Give me the car keys, I'll drive.

MOTHER I miss him too you know.

DAUGHTER What?

MOTHER Do you think I don't think about him? You don't carry and nurture a child and then forget about him. Yes I think about him. Yes I miss him. I'm his mother, of course I miss him.

DAUGHTER Then talk to him.

MOTHER What's the use of talking when no-one listens. I miss you, but I can't talk to you anymore. You don't listen to me. You just run away.

DAUGHTER And where did I learn that from? It's a family trait, remember?

MOTHER You chose to leave.

DAUGHTER I had to.

MOTHER You just want to change everything. There's some things you can't change.

DAUGHTER moves away to look to sea. Silence.

MOTHER Do you want to leave?

DAUGHTER I want to talk.

Silence. They stare at each other. DAUGHTER breaks away and skims pebbles on the water. MOTHER breaks the silence.

MOTHER How's Tom?

DAUGHTER *(surprised at her MOTHER's interest)* It's over. It didn't work out.

MOTHER I'm sorry.

DAUGHTER He just didn't think the same way as me.

MOTHER He's a man!

DAUGHTER *(laughing)* True!

MOTHER When I was a little girl your Nan locked out your Grandpa.

DAUGHTER What? Why?

MOTHER He'd come home from the pub and he'd had "talking beer" yer Nan said. She locked the door and she said she wouldn't let him in until he'd sobered up. Aunt Alice and I were watching everything from the top of the stairs. Then she turns and looks at us and says "Men, they're just a different breed, and never forget that!" and walks off down the passage.

MOTHER and DAUGHTER both laugh.

They are just a different breed. Don't forget that!

MOTHER and DAUGHTER smile at each other.

DAUGHTER I did try to call you Mum. I wanted to talk about Tom.

MOTHER I'm always here to listen.

DAUGHTER Are you?

MOTHER As yer Nan says "I might not understand, but I'll always listen."

DAUGHTER *(smiles)* Thanks Mum. *(DAUGHTER goes to hug MOTHER.)*

MOTHER *(pulling away quickly)* It's getting chilly. Pass me the blanket.

DAUGHTER Yes. *(puts the blanket around MOTHER's knees)*

MOTHER I think I have some hot tea in here somewhere. *(looking through the bag)* I must have left the flask on the counter. I can't find it. I have Nan's. *(She holds out the hip flask to DAUGHTER.)*

DAUGHTER You packed it?

MOTHER Who do you think always packed it?

DAUGHTER What do you have in there? *(MOTHER drinks from flask.)* Mum!

MOTHER Warms the cockles.

DAUGHTER What is it?

MOTHER Keeps the cold out. *(holds it out to DAUGHTER)*

DAUGHTER Thank you.

DAUGHTER drinks. Hands it back. They both hold the flask together for a second and almost touch.

Thank you Mum.

MOTHER *(pulling away)* It's getting chilly.

DAUGHTER We could leave.

MOTHER We've just arrived.

DAUGHTER We don't need to stay anymore.

MOTHER *(They connect with eye contact.)* No. I s'pose not.

DAUGHTER Let's go home.

MOTHER Yes.

They begin to pack up the bags, fold up the chair. It is a long process, done in silence, but the DAUGHTER carefully watches her MOTHER. The mood has softened.

DAUGHTER I'll take this to the car. *(takes out chair)*

MOTHER folds up blanket then stands and looks out to sea with the blanket over her arm. DAUGHTER returns. Comes up beside her MOTHER.

MOTHER It's a nice spot.

DAUGHTER Yes it is.

Silence. DAUGHTER goes to speak to MOTHER but changes her mind.

The tide is changing.

MOTHER Yes.

DAUGHTER It's bloody cold. Let's go.

DAUGHTER picks up the bags and exits leaving MOTHER looking out to sea.

MOTHER It's a nice spot.

DAUGHTER *(calling from offstage)* Mum?

MOTHER I'm coming, dear.

MOTHER picks up a pebble and throws it into the sea. Exits. Fade up soundscape of the beach.

Four slides projected one after the other as in the beginning. Fade out lights.

The end.

THE TERRIBLE FALSE DECEPTION

A FOUR ACT PLAY IN FORTY MINUTES (OR FORTY-TWO WITH LAUGHS)

by
Rafe Macpherson

Rafe Macpherson wrote the so-called first "act" of *The Terrible False Deception* in a letter, as a joke for an actress friend. She was so delighted that he sent her the second "act" which delighted her even more. Emboldened by all this delight, he sent her the third "act" and didn't hear from her for several months. When asked about the third installment, she replied with some distaste that she preferred the first two and changed the subject. This seemed to be the general opinion of others to whom he showed the script.

Fortunately, the director, Lin Joyce, didn't feel the same way and, against his wishes, submitted the play to the 1988 Rhubarb Festival, Toronto, where to his surprise, it was very well received.

Suffering from massive writer's block, he has written nothing of consequence since. However, he has now begun work on two more one-act plays to be performed with *The Terrible False Deception* to make a full evening of theatre.

Rafe has been a dresser in Toronto since 1976. He is also Wardrobe Assistant for the Canadian Opera Company.

INTRODUCTION TO *THE TERRIBLE FALSE DECEPTION*

Rafe Macpherson's satiric farce *The Terrible False Deception,* is not a script for most high school situations, nor, probably, for some adult community theatres. But its metatheatrical playfulness is so skilled, its wit so exuberant, and its technical acting demands so delightfully challenging, that we could not resist its inclusion. For some groups, it may well be the hit of the season.

There is a deliberately manipulative self-contradiction in the title, *The Terrible False Deception.* A false deception cancels itself out, is not a deception at all. Or is it? Factor in the extravagance of "Terrible," and you have in a nutshell the playful quality of this clever piece of entertainment. The daily work of theatre and its worlds of illusion are visited and revisited in four very short "acts" which employ identical blocking and inflection to tell four distinct, though interrelated, stories. The scene is a conventional Victorian drawing-room, including, if possible, a staircase. Costumes can provide general suggestions of 19th-century Russia, but the playwright's advice is to make them "more theatrically showy than authentically "period."

Like all good farces, *The Terrible False Deception* requires great actorly discipline and yet provides plentiful opportunity for very broad character strokes. In the first act ("Theatre of the Self-Aware"), the actors play actors, running through the technical conditions of their performances, commenting as they go:

Woman 2 enters carrying a vase of flowers….

Woman 2 I bustle in trying not to look too self-conscious…. I do too much business, *(crossing to pedestal table)* like smelling these flowers as I put them on this table *(crossing to credenza)* and straightening this mirror and running my finger along here *(the credenza)* to check for dust and touching my face….

Man 1 *(off)* I have to shout my first line from off-stage.

Then, in the second act ("Theatre of the Unaware"), we have the satiric pseudo-Chekhovian drawing-room piece to which act one is the physical key. (One might, in fact, imagine this play on a double-bill with one of Chekhov's short pieces.) The third act ("Theatre of the Underwear") is a rather rude deconstruction – same acting frame on which to hang a play, but now that play, rather than being fake Chekhov, has mutated into an exuberantly bawdy and verbally graphic game of sexual misidentification and comic transgression. And then, in the finale ("A Brief Explanation"), we meet the "real" actors onstage after what turns out to have been a run through – same technical picture one last time, but now it reaches back into the previous material to comment on what has gone before, even to acknowledge act three's questionable taste. At the same time, the last act is yet another new small play, following the repeated blocking and voicing through a fourth story, this time about the tensions among the four performers who have donated their services to this show. (Well in fact, the tension springs from the revelation that not all of them are actually working for free!)

So *The Terrible False Deception* is a four-act play about a three-act play which it contains within itself. And it is a play which heaps deception upon deception. Deftly performed, with simultaneous flair and control, it has the potential to be both highly entertaining and theatrically intriguing.

Skip Shand

l to r: David Keeley, Kate Hurman, Robin Craig, Lorne Cossette

The Terrible False Deception was first produced at Buddies in Bad Times Theatre's Rhubarb! Festival, Toronto, in 1988, Annex Theatre, Toronto, with the following cast:

WOMAN 1	Robin Craig
WOMAN 2	Kate Hurman
MAN 1	David Keeley
MAN 2	Lorne Cossette

Directed by Lin Joyce
Designed by E.K. Ayotte

Characters

WOMAN 1	a pretty young ingenue (38 if she's a day)
WOMAN 2	an older woman
MAN 1	a handsome young man
MAN 2	an older gentleman

Production Notes

Blocking for each "act" must be identical and vocal inflections for correspon-ding lines, from scene to scene, should also sound as similar as possible so that the effect would be, for a non-English speaking audience, of seeing *and* hearing the same play four times.

Costumes should be more theatrically showy than authentically "period." In the original production, E.K. Ayotte duplicated the ante-bellum ball gown worn by Bette Davis in "All About Eve" for WOMAN 1. As well as some in-joke value, its hoop skirt provided maximum opportunity for "dress acting."

The stage can be reset for each scene by having MAN 1 return his glass to the liquor cabinet and then striking (removing) the vase during the black outs.

And finally, despite WOMAN 1's startling third act revelation, please resist the bright idea to cast a man to play her.

THE TERRIBLE FALSE DECEPTION

A Four Act Play in Forty Minutes (or Forty-Two With Laughs)

by Rafe Macpherson

ACT ONE – Theatre of the Self Aware

A Victorian drawing room with at least two doorways. If possible, one should be a stairway descending to the stage to provide WOMAN 1 with grand entrances. Upstage centre is a credenza on which is a pile of letters and above which hangs a large mirror. On one side of the stage is a settee (referred to as a "sofa") on which the "cushion" should be a small bolster. At the upstage end of the settee is a pedestal table on which to put the vase. On the other side of the stage is a liquor cabinet or small table on which is a full brandy decanter and a large snifter.

WOMAN 2 enters carrying a vase of flowers. She is wearing a dress suitable for a housekeeper and cut low enough to put a letter down the front.

WOMAN 2 I bustle in trying not to look too self-conscious. I hate being the first one on stage, especially if I have dialogue. I always feel so uncomfortable talking to no one. Some actors can do it but I just feel so false. I do too much business, *(crossing to pedestal table)* like smelling these flowers as I put them on this table *(crossing to credenza)* and straightening this mirror and running my finger along here *(the credenza)* to check for dust and touching my face. *(crossing to liquor cabinet and playing with decanter)* I'm a good actress, really, but I just don't know what to do with these small parts. I should be playing leads. I sigh. Suddenly, I look around furtively and then cross to this credenza and search through this pile of letters until my look of triumph shows that I've found the one I want. *(crossing down centre, brandishing letter)* I know I'm indicating but I need a lot of direction and, on this one, I didn't get any. What can I do? Well, at least, I'm working.

MAN 1 *(off)* I have to shout my first line from off-stage.

WOMAN 2 I look startled and shove this letter down the front of my dress. Then I rush to this sofa and pretend to be plumping this cushion. I couldn't think of anything else and the director said he liked it.

MAN 1 bounds heroically onstage, crossing quickly down centre. He is young and handsome and wearing some sort of flattering military uniform.

MAN 1 I enter and pause for a moment, in case there's applause. *(if there is, he smirks; if there isn't, he looks annoyed)* I look around, catching sight of her for the first time, although I could have seen her from the door.

WOMAN 2 I cross down to him from behind the sofa, being careful not to upstage him, after what happened in rehearsal the other day and… uh… I…um, almost forget my, uh, line.

MAN 1 I look irritated. I think it's so unfair to other actors not to know your lines. I ask her a question.

WOMAN 2 I nod and point to the credenza.

MAN 1 I cross to the credenza.

WOMAN 2 *(aside)* While I turn away looking worried.

MAN 1 And I look through these letters. I look puzzled and then, giving a small shrug, I cross to the liquor cabinet and pour myself a drink. God I wish this were real brandy and not this awful cold tea.

WOMAN 1 enters. She is wearing an extremely ornate white ball gown.

WOMAN 1 Suddenly, I burst into the room, throwing out my arms to show happiness, vitality and youth. Okay, I'm a little too old for this role but I can still get away with it. That's why I made them put me in white and not that ghastly green thing they wanted. Any designer with half a brain knows that ingenues don't wear green. Especially pale green.

I make a completely unnecessary eight-point tour of the stage to show off the dress and then, turning dramatically, I stretch my arms forward *(to MAN 1)* and run to him, taking his hands in mine to show innocence and adoration.

MAN 1 I speak in a voice that I hope sounds choked with love and bury my face in her hands…

WOMAN 1 *(sotto voce to WOMAN 2)* …so that he can't see the worried look I'm giving her.

WOMAN 2 *(sotto voce to WOMAN 1)* I pat the front of my dress and nod conspiratorially.

WOMAN 1 *(to MAN 1)* Relieved, I turn back to him…

MAN 1 …as I raise my head…

MAN 1 & WOMAN 1 *(in unison)* …and we kiss and, then, stare adoringly at each other until the fourth actor shouts his line from offstage… *(long pause)*

He doesn't… the smiles freeze on our faces. How long do we have to hold this?

Pause.

MAN 2 *(off)* Finally, I deliver my line.

MAN 1 I look puzzled.

WOMAN 1 I show fear.

WOMAN 2 Apprehensively, I cross to the doorway.

MAN 2 enters. He is wearing "period gentleman" clothes, carrying a top hat.

MAN 2 I stride in pompously, trying not to look embarrassed for having missed my cue and *(to WOMAN 2)* give my hat to her.

WOMAN 2 I take it, shrinking back and rolling my eyes in terror.

MAN 1 & MAN 2 Which we don't seem to notice. Ha, ha, ha.

WOMAN 1 *(crossing to WOMAN 2)* Although I do. God, she's a lousy actress.

MAN 1 *(to MAN 2)* I greet him pleasantly.

Overlapping.

We move toward each other while speaking this overlapping…………

MAN 2 We move toward each other while………………
……lapping dialogue,

MAN 1 ....we shake hands.

MAN 2 which is difficult and we shake hands.

MAN 1 *(He takes WOMAN 1's hand. She circles around him so that she is downstage of him.)* I take her by the hand and introduce her very proudly *(to MAN 2)* to him.

WOMAN 1 I curtsy demurely and, at the same time, indicate panic. I haven't quite got this one yet and it's such an awful translation anyway. How'm I supposed to act this? *(She crosses to settee and sits.)*

WOMAN 2 I fuss with this hat too much. Look, believe me, I got *no* direction.

MAN 1 *(to MAN 2)* I address him respectfully, bowing slightly from the waist and then, point to the liquor cabinet.

MAN 2 I shake my hands in refusal, hoping it won't get a laugh because, offstage, I'm a well-known lush. I hear them talk. I know what they say about me. I never mean to but I have to have something to get me through these things… ha ha… especially *this* thing.

MAN 1 *(to WOMEN)* I give them both an ironic look. So, I'm out of character, so what? *(to MAN 2)* Then, I turn back to him and make an inquiring gesture.

WOMAN 1 *(rising from settee)* I move to this table and, with a studied lack of concern, I casually arrange these flowers.

WOMAN 2 I still play with the hat.

MAN 2 I take centre and, in a voice more resonant than any of these amateurs could ever hope to achieve, I deliver this speech with more technique and more… sheer talent than the lot of them, with their theatre school twitching and their artsy-fartsy warm-ups and "What's my motivation?" and, "Oh dear, he's been drinking. How unprofessional."

WOMAN 2 I interrupt this speech with an hysterical aside to the audience.

MAN 2 Well, who wouldn't drink, if, after all my years of experience, you ended up in trash like this opposite trash like them? But there's one thing that cannot be taken away from me. I have never missed a performance and I have never once dried on my lines.

MAN 1 I wish… I had a long speech like his.

MAN 2 And another thing. Drunk or sober, I can act rings around the bunch of them. *(pointing at WOMAN 1)* Especially *this*, tenth-rate, over-the-hill prima donna and… *(pointing at WOMAN 2) this* neurotic, no-talent cow.

WOMAN 2 *(crossing to WOMAN 1)* I rush over to her, which is hard to do in this dress.

WOMAN 1 A look of pain and sorrow mingled with resignation plays brilliantly on my face.

MAN 1 I look stunned, at first, and then, it turns to outrage *(to WOMAN 1)* I stare at her in disbelief. This is a very real moment for me.

WOMAN 1 Wearily, starting with my back to the audience, but slowly turning to face out front, I begin this long monologue, almost inaudibly, at first. If I take it way down, then I've got somewhere to go. I begin to build in volume and intensity, using every vocal trick I know – pitching my voice high… and then, suddenly, dropping it into my lower register, making my voice quaver… and then, speaking in a monotone stressing certain words that play against *the* text, all the time, increasing the volume, st-st-stammering occasionally, making… arbitrary pauses, making my voice catch in my throat, playing my voice like an instrument, hoping that no one will see that I'm not crying real tears. Building, building, more emotional, more intense. This is good stuff. I'm really on a roll here. I start to run my hands through my hair until I remember it's a wig and wring my hands in anguish instead. Crying out, in despair, I drop to my knees. Oh, this is fantastic! I'm really feeling this.

WOMAN 2 *(to WOMAN 1)* I move to comfort her, think better of it and, sadly, take this letter from my dress and *(to MAN 2)* hand it to him.

MAN 2 *(to WOMAN 2)* I take it, looking scornfully at her and, with my other hand, I start to lead her offstage…

Overlapping.

But we get confused because I try to get her to exit first.

WOMAN 2 But we get confused because………………………………

MAN 2 ....so we get into this awkward position.

WOMAN 2 but I can't because I still have a line to say, so we get into this awkward position. *(angrily gives MAN 2 his hat)*

(to WOMAN 1) I give her a tragic look as I'm being led offstage.

They exit.

MAN 1 I stand here, looking betrayed, stoical and severe, wishing that I had more than this one line to say, hoping that the lights on this drink will distract the audience, if I jiggle it a little. I think I've saved myself. I've come out of this thing looking good. I know it.

WOMAN 1 I kneel here, wishing I could cry real tears so that they'd shine on my face. I'm looking right out into the house. Maybe I shouldn't be on my knees at the end of this play. I dunno about the sight lines in this theatre. Maybe I can't be seen. I raise my head so that, for a second, my face is totally illuminated, just before the lights dim.

The lights dim.

ACT TWO – Theatre of the Unaware

A drawing room. WOMAN 2 enters, carrying a vase of flowers.

WOMAN 2 Larks-o'-Mercy, how pretty these flowers are. How they brighten this house upon which, I fear, darkness will soon descend. Lovely they are but how quickly they'll fade. Thus does the natural bloom of youth give way to this discolored parchment which I myself display.

(crossing to table) As these cheery petals are to what they will be, scant days hence, *(puts vase on table)* is my mistress, Irena Irenevnaya, to me. *(crossing to credenza, straightening mirror and checking for dust)* For I was once a beauty too. I know it. *(touching face, crossing to liquor cabinet and playing with decanter)* Grunienko, the cobbler's son, told me so, that summer in Mirminsk, *(sighing)* just before he drowned.

(looking around furtively) But come now, Katja Katrinovna, no more on that subject. You have a terrible duty to discharge.

(crossing to credenza and rifling through letters) Oh, this frightens me so. Ah, here it is. *(brandishing letter and crossing down centre)* It is wicked to deceive my master but what greater evil awaits my mistress and me if I do not. Something terrible will come of this. I feel it.

MAN 1 *(off)* I'll be in the drawing room, my dearest angel.

WOMAN 2 My master! …and he's coming here! He mustn't find this. *(stuffs letter down front of dress)* Oh, my ribs will not contain my fear. *(rushes to settee and plumps bolster)* My heart is pounding so. Oh, let it not betray me.

MAN 1 *(bounding on and crossing quickly down centre)* Ah. *(pause for applause; smirk or annoyance – turning to her)* There you are, Katja Katrinovna. How are your preparations for the Duke's ball coming along? I am sure, with your excellent ministrations that your mistress will outshine any woman there.

WOMAN 2 *(crossing down to him from the settee)* Thank you, sir. Yes, she looks ever so becoming in her new, white organza that we bought in… um… Schettledorf, last, uh, Thursday week, afternoon.

MAN 1 *(irritated)* Excellent…. By the way, has the mail arrived yet? I am expecting something.

WOMAN 2 *(pointing to credenza)* Yes sir, it's on the credenza.

MAN 1 *(crossing to credenza)* Good, good, I hope it's come.

WOMAN 2 *(aside)* How can he not hear the pounding of my heart?

MAN 1 *(rifles letters)* Hm. Not yet. Strange that it's so late. Ah well, perhaps tomorrow. *(crossing to liquor cabinet)* Now, a small glass of something won't hurt me. Not a bit of it. *(pouring drink)* A brandy's just the ticket and excellent stuff, too. Next year, I'll buy a case of it.

WOMAN 1 *(enters, throwing out arms)* Here I am my dearest angel. I've kept you waiting, haven't I? You must blame Katja Katrinovna. She's such a cross old thing. Why, I should have been ready hours ago if she hadn't clucked so, like a dear old mother hen. I wanted to wear the pale green peau-de-soie that you love so but, no, she wouldn't hear of it *(making eight-point tour)* and, finally, the old tyrant forced me into this silly, white organza. *(stretching arms forward, running to him and taking his hands)* Am I pretty enough for you? Will I do?

MAN 1 My own, little Irinka. My heart near bursts for love of you. *(buries face in her hands)*

WOMAN 1 *(sotto voce to WOMAN 2)* Katja? Do you have it?

WOMAN 2 *(sotto voce, patting front of dress)* It is here, next to my pounding heart.

WOMAN 1 *(relieved, to MAN 1)* Flatterer. Prove it then, with a kiss.

MAN 1 *(raising head)* Gladly, gladly.

They kiss.

Overlapping.

MAN 1 Oh, my dear one............You are my most cherished possession.

WOMAN 1 ....All that I am............all that I am is yours.

Long pause.

MAN 2 *(off)* I say, hello. Is anyone at home?

MAN 1 Who can that be?

WOMAN 1 Are we expecting someone?

WOMAN 2 *(crossing to door)* Unannounced is unwelcome, I say.

MAN 2 *(enters)* Good evening, Illya Illinoiivitch. Pardon this intrusion. I know you must be busy. My own house is topsy-turvy over this infernal ball, tonight. *(gives hat to WOMAN 2)*

WOMAN 2 *(shrinking back in terror)* Thank you. Thank you. *(aside)* Why do I fear this man?

MAN 1 & MAN 2 *(in unison)* ...this, this infernal ball.... Ha ha ha.

WOMAN 1 *(crossing to WOMAN 2)* I beg you, Katja, do not betray us.

MAN 1 I am pleased to see you, Andrei Yuseff Yuseffkanova.

The men move toward each other and shake hands, words overlapping:

............No, no not a bit of it............Nonsense.

MAN 2 If I am interrupting...........I, myself, dislike these,

MAN 1 We are pleased to see you.

MAN 2 ...uh, these impromptu visits.

MAN 1 *(He takes WOMAN 1's hand. She circles downstage of him.)* Andrei, let me introduce you to my wife and bride of less than two weeks. Here she is, my Irena Irenevnaya Illinoiivitch, my dearest possession.

WOMAN 1 *(curtsying)* How do you do, Andrei Yuseff Yuseffkanova. You are most welcome here and do us significant honour. *(She crosses to settee and sits.)*

WOMAN 2 *(fussing with hat)* Oh, how my heart beats. This man knows something. His visit brings us ruin. I feel it.

MAN 1 *(to MAN 2, bowing slightly and pointing to liquor cabinet)* I know you have come for a reason, Andrei, but first, let me offer you a glass of rather excellent brandy.

MAN 2 *(shaking hands in refusal)* No, no thank you, Illya Illinoiivitch, I do not drink nor, I trust, ever shall I. The quest for truth and justice is my only vice... that... ha ha... and an occasional good cigar.

MAN 1 *(aside to WOMEN)* Pompous old owl, is he not? *(to MAN 2)* Then, if I cannot offer hospitality, I'll be direct and inquire as to the nature of this fortunate visit.

WOMAN 1 *(rising from settee and crossing to table to arrange flowers)* I will be calm. I think I know why he has come but I've not lost yet.

WOMAN 2 *(playing with hat)* Ruin is hard upon our heels! I feel it.

MAN 2 *(taking centre)* Illya Illinoiivitch, since you were a young lad, visiting our dasha, on the lake, I have known you, so, you know me to be a man of few words and much principle. If a duty is distasteful to me, it is, nevertheless, a duty, so I will be direct and tell you something that cannot but be painful to you.

WOMAN 2 *(hysterical aside)* With every word he utters, the hooves of the stallions of hell pound closer, ever closer.

MAN 2 This afternoon, I had reason to speak with old father Pretskevskin, the Post Master. He told me a curious thing...

that the return half of your yearly trip to Moscow had been cancelled and redeemed for cash and that the name on the ticket had been changed to another. The poor simpleton didn't like the look of it... couldn't understand why you'd want to miss the Baron de Clichy's annual Borzoi Festival. The order apparently came from you but I saw the truth of it at once and came here to warn you.

MAN 1 What... are you saying?

MAN 2 I am saying that the ticket was changed to your wife's name and that this fraud was carried out by her maidservant. They meant to keep the money from the return half and stay in Moscow. I've done some digging, Illya Illinoiivitch, and I've learned that *(pointing at WOMAN 1)* your *wife* is really an actress and *(pointing at WOMAN 2)* *this* woman is her personal dresser.

WOMAN 2 *(Crossing to WOMAN 1)* Oh, Miss Irena, we are unmasked!

WOMAN 1 It's alright, Katja. We gambled and we lost.

MAN 1 *(stunned)* Irinka, my dearest possession, is it true? What does this mean? *(outraged, staring at her in disbelief)* No. I know what it means. You were leaving me. Two weeks married and I am played the fool.

WOMAN 1 *(Back to audience, slowly turning to face out – almost inaudibly)* No, Illya, I am the fool. I thought I wanted this. I thought I wanted you. What I want is my freedom. *(increasing the volume)* Ah, "freedom." Both a promise and a threat. Oh, I'm so confused. *(upper register)* You see, an actress's life is all past and present, *(lower register)* never future. I thought you could give me my future. *(quavering)* On stage, the world is glittering – but, off it, what am I?

(monotone) A rootless creature taking work where she can – a comedy in Minsk, an operetta *in* Omsk. The Duke of Somewhere smiles at me and-and-and-and all of Moscow pays me court. The Duke of Somewhere... Else ignores me, *(catch in throat)* and it's three rubles a week doing a melodrama in Irkunsk.

(voice like an instrument) You have been clever, Andrei Yuseff Yuseffkanova but there is something about me that you do *not* know. I am not the young girl you thought me to be. I am almost twenty-three. More and more, the Duke of Somewhere was *not* smiling at me and it was two rubles a

week in Brabomsk. And then, I met you Illya. You offered me a future. You will never know what I was, I decided. This will be my greatest and final performance. I will be your "dearest possession" but, Illya, no one can possess another, or so I believe.

(starting to run hands through hair) I know that a woman should submit to a man, *(wringing hands instead)* and shape herself into that which he most desires. But you see, I've been spoiled; spoiled by solitary train rides to theatres in little towns where fellow actors looked to *me* for guidance; spoiled by a lifetime of making my own decisions. *(sinking to knees)* Oh, Illya, please try to understand. The theatre made me an independent creature, selfish and reliant on no man. The theatre ruined me.

WOMAN 2 *(starting to move to WOMAN 1)* Oh, Miss Irena, there never was a finer actress. *(stops, takes letter from dress, hands it to MAN 2)* Here it is, sir, the cause of our undoing.

MAN 2 *(taking letter)* Misrepresenting a first class railway ticket *and* intercepting the Czar's mail! *(takes WOMAN 2's hand, leads her to door)* You are under arrest, old woman.

Overlapping.

You'll get forty lashes of the knout...........yes, forty lashes.

WOMAN 2 ....Oh please, sir...........please be kind...........

MAN 2 That is...........if you are lucky.

WOMAN 2 ....We are theatrical people. *(angrily gives MAN 2 his hat)*

(to WOMAN 1) What will become of us now, Miss Irena? Oh, Moscow, Moscow.

They exit.

MAN 1 Irinka. No. You are Irena Irenevnaya to me now, a stranger. Are all women like you, repaying your benefactors with lies and betrayal? I gave you everything a wife could need from a husband, *(jiggling brandy snifter)* even love, and I'll do you one more kindness – you'll have your trip to Moscow... and I will never leave this house again.

WOMAN 1 Moscow. Do I want it now? My destiny is there... and my freedom. *(checking sightlines)* But if I cannot please a man, then

I am not a woman. What need has Moscow of me? *(raising head)* Moscow. Moscow. Now I'll have to go to Moscow.

The lights dim.

ACT THREE – Theatre of the Underwear

A drawing room. WOMAN 2 enters, carrying a vase of flowers.

WOMAN 2 Christ, I'm horny. It's all I can think about. Night and day, I can't think about anything but sex. And this dress makes it even worse. Period clothes really turn me on. Oh, I need to get laid. I need it bad. *(crossing to table)* Everything I smell, *(puts vase on table)* everything I touch makes me think of S-E-X.

(crossing to credenza, straightening mirror and checking for dust) Can I stroke myself with it? Can I ram myself with it? Can I cram myself with it? *(touching face, crossing to liquor cabinet and playing with decanter)* I wanna be rammed. I wanna be crammed. I wanna scream and roll around *(sighing)* and go crazy.

(looking around, furtively) Oh, I really gotta do something about it, *now*. I can't wait 'til my afternoon nap. *(crossing to credenza and rifling through letters)* Yeah, maybe this'll work. *(crossing down centre, brandishing letter)* I saw this video once, where this woman got herself off with ordinary household objects. First, she took a letter and she…

MAN 1 *(off)* Are you there, Mother? I got a bone to pick with you.

WOMAN 2 Hell, you can't be alone for a minute in this dump. *(puts letter down front of dress)* Ooh, that feels nice. *(rushes to settee and plumps bolster)* Then, she took a small cushion, about this big and she…

MAN 1 *(bounding on and crossing quickly down centre)* Ah. *(pause for applause, smirk or annoyance – turning to WOMAN 2)* Real funny, Mother. That plastic vomit thing was just real funny… to find on the bed, like that, first thing in the morning. And whad'ya think Miss Cristal thinks, finding a vomit thing like that. You promised no more jokes when we got married. They're not funny.

WOMAN 2 *(crossing down to him from behind settee)* They are, too, funny. They're a scream. Everybody thinks they're goddam hilarious except you and that… uh, little, uh, twit you married.

MAN 1 *(irritated)* Nice talk, Mother. I could have you put away, in a flash. You know that, don't you?

WOMAN 2 *(nodding and pointing to credenza)* Try it, sonny. I go, my furniture goes with me.

MAN 1 *(crossing to credenza)* Not this side table. This side table is mine.

WOMAN 2 *(aside)* It's a credenza… and I thought it was mine. Christ, I swear my mind is going.

MAN 1 *(rifles through letters)* What *is* this? Bills, bills, "to occupant," "to occupant." Nobody writes anymore. *(crosses to liquor cabinet)* And this liquor cabinet, this is mine, too. *(pouring drink)* And don't you go drinking this stuff. I'll know. I marked the decanter.

WOMAN 1 *(enters, throwing out arms)* Hey ho, everybody. Please, no applause for the gown. Mary, was this rag a bitch to get into. No mammy to pull mah corset strings and crinolines for days. I vow a girl just isn't a girl unless she's trussed like a chicken and her boobs are gonna pop. *(making eight-point tour)* I'm so glad we rented these costumes for the whole week-end and not just for tonight. I could wear this drag forever. Too bad that pale green number wasn't my size. It was divoon. *(stretching arms forward, running to MAN 1 and taking his hands)* Oh, baby, do you look hot. Lick my hands, stud.

MAN 1 Oh baby, oh baby. *(buries face in her hands)*

WOMAN 1 *(sotto voce to WOMAN 2)* You look kinda sick, honey. You okay?

WOMAN 2 *(sotto voce, patting front of dress)* Yeah, yeah. This dress just fits funny. That's all.

WOMAN 1 *(relieved, to MAN 1)* Oh baby, you're getting me all wet.

MAN 1 Oh baby. Oh baby.

They kiss.

MAN 1 & WOMAN 1 *(in unison)* Oh baby. Oh baby. Oh baby.

Long pause.

MAN 2 *(off)* Hey, knock, knock, where's the party?

MAN 1 Aw heck. Just when you got me goin'.

WOMAN 1 I don't mind. I like an audience.

WOMAN 2 *(crossing to door)* It's probably the old broad upstairs. You pass gas in here and she complains about the noise.

MAN 2 *(entering)* Look, I am not going to this Klondike thing tonight, and that's final. I feel stupid in these clothes. I hate dressing up, so here, you can have your hat back. *(gives hat to WOMAN 2)*

WOMAN 2 *(shrinking back in terror)* My hat? This isn't my hat. What would I be doing with a man's hat?

MAN 1 & MAN 2 *(in unison)* What's with her? It's only a hat. Ha ha ha.

WOMAN 1 *(crossing to WOMAN 2)* You blow this one, for me, old lady, and you're dead meat. I'm warning you.

MAN 1 *(to MAN 2)* Aw jeez, Uncle Ted, you gotta come. It's gonna be great.

The men move toward each other and shake hands, words overlapping.

I mean, really..............aw, it'll be great................Hey, that's great.

MAN 2 ....No, no, I don't think so...........okay, okay, but just for a while though.

MAN 1 *(He takes WOMAN 1's hand. She circles downstage of him.)* Hey introductions. Uncle Ted, this is her. The little lady I been tellin' you about. The little wifey. This is Miss Cristal.

WOMAN 1 *(curtsying)* It's Cris*tale*. Cris*tale*. Like the French say, Cris*tale*. *(She moves to settee and sits.)*

WOMAN 2 I fuss with this hat too much. Look, believe me, I got *no* direction... oh, shit, I'm in the wrong act.

MAN 1 *(to MAN 2, bowing slightly and pointing to liquor cabinet)* Uncle Ted, you'll be interested in this. See the liquor cabinet? I finished it myself. It's great, eh?

MAN 2 *(shaking hands in refusal)* No, no. I like Deco. Now that's what I call furniture. Like, I'm not saying you did a bad job. It looks real nice. It's just the whole piece is not my style. Now what's *in* the liquor cabinet... ha ha... now that's my style, eh?

MAN 1 *(to WOMEN)* He gets a drink over my dead body. *(to MAN 2)* Okay, Uncle Ted, I'm gonna lay somethin' on the line here. How come you never come to our wedding?

WOMAN 1 *(rising and crossing to table to arrange flowers)* Plastic. They're plastic. I hate that. Those silk ones can be nice. But these are tragic.

WOMAN 2 *(playing with hat)* Oh, hell, she's found the flowers.

MAN 2 *(taking centre)* Alright, I never wanted to mention this but, like, you're the one who brought it up, eh? I woulda let the whole thing go 'cause I don't wanna interfere in people's happiness, eh. I say, if people are happy, then that's great and, if I know somethin' about people that would make 'em unhappy, well, like I just won't say nothing, 'cause I'm an honest person and I just can't stand by and watch someone being dishonest with someone and not say nothing, so, that's why I didn't come to your wedding 'cause, like, I woulda felt like I hadda say something.

WOMAN 2 *(hysterical aside)* Felt he had to say something! This asshole hasn't said one damn thing worth hearing since he came in here.

MAN 2 I hate to say this but, Miss Cristal here, haven't you noticed that she's different from other women? More "feminine?" She gets horny real fast?

MAN 1 Yeah... but I like that.

MAN 2 Oh, you're making this so hard for me. Look, she's a man, eh? Aw, for cryin' out loud, she's my own brother. *(pointing at WOMAN 1) She's* got a schlong bigger than *I* have and *(pointing at WOMAN 2) you* knew. You're our sister!

WOMAN 2 *(crossing to WOMAN 1)* Well, I never saw your schlongs.

WOMAN 1 You're all boring me rigid. You know that?

MAN 1 *(stunned)* I can't believe this. You're a guy? I mean, you're really a guy?

(outraged) You look like that and you're a guy? I mean, all this time... and you're a guy?

WOMAN 1 *(Back to audience, slowly turning to face out – almost inaudibly)* Oh, give it a rest, will yuh, pull-eeze. So what's wrong with tryna' grab the brass ring? *(increasing the volume)* If a girl wants a little romance in her life, where's the harm? So I like to look pretty. So I don the occasional frock.

(upper register) So I falsify a touch. *(lower register)* Big crime.

(quavering) I had this bet, see, with some girlfriends, that I could pass for real because, baby, I *am* real *(monotone)* but they said, "Cris*tale*, you are *not* real". And I said, "Up yours dears, *(louder)* any man'd think I'm real." And they said, "Pr-pr-pr-prove it." And I said, "Okay, I'll get me a real man and make him marry... me and like it." *(catch in throat)* So, I found a retard, so what? I won the bet and I got me a real man because I am a real woman.

(voice like an instrument) I just wanna be happy and Air Head here, thought I was a real woman and that made me happy. Look, I'm not into whips or water sports or anything. I'm not decadent – I just wanna be loved... by a man. Is that so terrible? *(starts to run hands through hair)* I wanna do my hair *(wrings hands instead)* and do my nails and get schtupped, three or four times a day.

(sinking to knees) I had a dream. Girls do a lot of dreaming. I just tried to make my dream come true. That's all. What have I done that's so wrong? Oh Mary, I hope you all choke to death on your own puke.

WOMAN 2 *(starting to move toward WOMAN 1)* Well, you sort of cheered the place up and I didn't like to say anything. *(stops, takes letter from dress and hands it to MAN 2)* I was trying to get myself off with this but now I don't feel like it.

MAN 2 *(taking letter)* Well, that's ridiculous. Paper's no good, eh. You gotta use clamps or something. *(takes WOMAN 2's hand, leads her to door)* C'mon back to my place, Sis. I'll show you mine.

Overlapping.

...........Oops, sorry. I'm left-handed. Ol' southpaw, here.

WOMAN 2 Ow. Jeez, you're clumsy...........Let go...........Leggo my hand.

Angrily gives MAN 2 his hat.

WOMAN 2 *(to WOMAN 1)* You're sick, you know that? I'm cuttin' you outa the will.

They exit.

MAN 1 I can't believe this. I mean, really, I can't believe this. *(jiggling brandy snifter)* You were the best lay I ever had. In the dark, I was never sure what that thing was… and I didn't like to ask.

WOMAN 1 Oh, Mary, I dunno. Maybe I made a mistake. The other queens say I got an attitude problem and maybe they're right. *(checking sightlines)* How did I get this way? When did I start turning into what I've become? You know, if I could do my life over again, I woulda' done things different. Girl, I sure wouldn't have married my own nephew *(raising head)* and I think I would've worn that green dress.

The lights dim.

ACT FOUR – A Brief Explanation

A drawing room. Same business as before only very *fast. WOMAN 2 enters carrying a vase of flowers.*

WOMAN 2 *(vase, table, mirror, dust, face, liquor cabinet, decanter, furtive look, credenza, letters, brandish, down centre. It can be done.)* Well, I think that went very, very well, considering. A little rough but, really, it's very tricky having to repeat the same blocking with the same intentions but with a different character each time. A few runs with an audience and we'll be fine. I just wish we could do something about this set. I was sort of hoping for a real Victorian drawing room but what can you do with these young designers and no money.

MAN 1 *(off)* Are you on stage, Margo?

WOMAN 2 *(shoves letter down front of dress and rushes to settee and plumps bolster)* Yes I am, love. I'm just giving the set a little perking up.

MAN 1 *(bounding down centre,* very *quickly)* Good luck. *(No pause for applause – turning to her)* Look, I was just wondering if we're going to do another run through or can I get out of my costume?

WOMAN 2 *(crossing to him from settee)* Uh, no, I don't think we'll be doing another run, just problem areas. Do you have any… uh… problem areas?

MAN 1 *(irritated)* Yeah, I do. For example, you know when I go through the letters?

WOMAN 2 *(pointing to credenza)* Yes.

MAN 1 *(crossing to credenza)* Well, I feel like I'm repeating myself.

WOMAN 2 *(aside)* It's the point of the play.

MAN 1 *(rifling through letters)* Yeah, but what if we're compelled to do it? *(crosses to liquor cabinet and pours drink)* Look what I'm doing now. Maybe I can't stop myself. I hate this stuff.

WOMAN 1 *(enters, throwing out arms)* This dress is too much. It really is. It's so over the top but I love it. *(making eight-point tour)* You don't think it'll turn green under the lights, do you? Some fabrics do. *(stretching arms forward, running to MAN 1 and taking his hands)* And you, mister, look fantastic.

MAN 1 *(kissing her hands)* Thanks.

WOMAN 1 *(sotto voce to WOMAN 2)* Don't you think so?

WOMAN 2 *(sotto voce, patting front of dress)* I wanted him in tails.

WOMAN 1 *(relieved, to MAN 1)* Well, I love a man in uniform.

MAN 1 *(raising head)* Yeah, I think it works, doesn't it?

No overlapping dialogue. They kiss. There's a short pause.

MAN 2 *(off)* Damn it. Where the hell is everybody?

MAN 1 What's wrong with him, now?

WOMAN 1 Oh God, who knows?

WOMAN 2 *(crossing to door)* We're onstage, love.

MAN 2 *(entering)* Well, Margo, love, I'm afraid this little masterpiece of yours is not going to open. *(gives hat to WOMAN 2)*

WOMAN 2 *(shrinking back in terror)* What do you mean?

MAN 1 & MAN 2 *(in unison)* Ha ha ha.

WOMAN 1 *(crossing to WOMAN 2)* It's just nerves. He'll be okay.

MAN 1 *(to MAN 2)* Do you feel like we're all moving parts in some elaborate machine?

The men move toward each other and shake hands, words overlapping.

See? Now, I have to come over here...........and I have to shake your hand.

MAN 2 ....what the hell are you on about?...........what are you doing?

MAN 1 *(He takes WOMAN 1's hand. She circles downstage of him.)* Look, I bet she's going to curtsy.

WOMAN 1 *(curtsying)* Why shouldn't I curtsy if I want to? *(she crosses to settee and sits)*

WOMAN 2 *(fussing with hat)* What do you mean, we're not going to open?

MAN 1 *(to MAN 2, pointing to liquor cabinet)* What's the matter? Don'cha like the set?

MAN 2 *(shaking hands in refusal)* No, no, you don't understand dear boy, I don't like this play. Alright, the first two scenes are amusing enough but that last one... ha ha... it's just filth.

MAN 1 *(to WOMEN)* That's nothing. I've seen far worse. *(to MAN 2)* So what's your problem?

WOMAN 1 *(rising and crossing to table to arrange flowers)* Seen far worse? I've been in far worse.

WOMAN 2 *(playing with hat)* The third scene is as dramatically valid as the first two. That's the joke.

MAN 2 *(taking centre)* Well, I thought it would be good for me to do something modern and experimental. Redgrave did it. Gielgud did it. But if I'm going to waive my salary in the interests of the avant garde... if this *is* the avant garde... I will not be embarrassed by it. I have to call myself a "well-known lush," in the first scene and my audience might think it's true.

WOMAN 2 *(hysterical)* But I'm referred to as a "lousy actress" and there isn't one person sitting out there who'll believe that.

MAN 2 As I said, the first two scenes are actually quite clever but the third one absolutely ruins the whole thing. Vomit jokes and bad language and transvestites. It's sophomoric vulgarity for its own sake and I won't be a party to that kind of theatre.

MAN 1 Maybe... we're all dead.

MAN 2 But I'm not going to argue the relative merits of this thing because we're not doing it. I just found out that, while you and I, sonny, were persuaded to work for the love of our art, these two bitches are being paid. *(pointing at WOMAN 1) She's* signed a standard Equity minimum contract and, *(pointing at WOMAN 2)* and *she* arranged it.

WOMAN 2 *(crossing to WOMAN 1)* Oh, no.

WOMAN 1 Well... there just wasn't enough money for everybody.

MAN 1 *(stunned)* You're getting paid? For this? *(outraged)* Maybe we're all trapped together in some kind of existential hell.

WOMAN 1 *(Back to audience, slowly turning – almost inaudibly)* I just wanted to do this play and this is the only way we could get it done. *(increasing the volume)* It's such a good role for me. I mean, where else am I going to get to play *(upper register)* a Chekhovian heroine and *(lower register)* a drag queen *(quavering)* at the same time. *(monotone)* I've been in this business a long time, you know, and I've done *A* lot of good work but who gets to see... it in Timmins? I'm-I'm-I'm-I'm queen of the *(catch in throat)* regional theatres *(voice like an instrument)* and I can't get arrested in my own home town. *(starts to run hands through hair)* So, when I found this play, *(wrings hands instead)* I thought it'd be a perfect showcase for me *(kneeling)* and why should I work for free? If you two agreed to, that's your problem.

WOMAN 2 *(moving to WOMAN 1)* I'm sure it's because I'm a woman. He wouldn't treat a male director like this. *(stops, takes letter from dress and hands it to MAN 2)* Here's the contract. I don't know how it got into those letters.

MAN 2 takes letter, takes WOMAN 2's hand, and leads her to doorway.

Overlapping.

MAN 2 We're calling Equity, right now. They'll put a stop to this.

WOMAN 2 ....Oh, great...........That's all I need...........
Wonderful. *(angrily gives MAN 2 his hat)*

(to WOMAN 1) I'm really sorry, honey, I hear that agents were coming tonight and everything.

They exit.

MAN 1 Or maybe we're just four characters being manipulated by an author's whim. *(jiggling brandy snifter)* I feel real but what if I'm just a dramaturgic device?

WOMAN 1 You give me the creeps when you talk like that, you know? Hell, I would've been so good in this play. *(checking sightlines)* I think it was a mistake being on my knees for this part. *(raising head)* What's wrong with the lights?

The lights dim.

The end.